D1387669

Windsor and Maidenhead

95800000149856

ARIANNA HUFFINGTON

Media Visionary and Wellness Evangelist

Leah McGrath Goodman

WEIDENFELD & NICOLSON

First published in Great Britain in 2020 by Weidenfeld & Nicolson
an imprint of The Orion Publishing Group Ltd
Carmelite House, 50 Victoria Embankment
London EC4Y 0DZ

An Hachette UK Company

10 9 8 7 6 5 4 3 2 1

A CIP catalogue record for this book is
available from the British Library.

ISBN (Hardback) 978 1 4746 1071 1
ISBN (eBook) 978 1 4746 1072 8

Typeset by Input Data Services Ltd, Somerset
Printed and bound in Great Britain by Clays Ltd, Elcograf S.p.A.

www.weidenfeldandnicolson.co.uk
www.orionbooks.co.uk

CONTENTS

To my mother,
Kathleen Hill McGrath

'Life is a dance between making things happen and letting them happen.'

Arianna Huffington

'Arriving there is what you're destined for.
But don't hurry the journey at all.
Better if it lasts for years,
so you're old by the time you reach the island,
wealthy with all you've gained on the way . . .'

Excerpt from 'Ithaka', by C. P. Cavafy,
a favourite poem of Arianna Huffington

AUTHOR'S NOTE

This book is based on exhaustive research and interviews delving into Arianna Huffington's extraordinary life and career. The reporting covers thousands of pages of documents, articles and emails and, in many cases, draws from Huffington's own words from her writings and dozens of hours of audio. It also traces back to Huffington's roots in Athens, Greece, starting in the 1950s. As a result, some of the information in the book stretches back more than seven decades and leans heavily on historical accounts, documents and even photographs where they corroborate the facts.

Much about Huffington's early life and circumstances is extremely difficult to verify – a reality made even more challenging by varying accounts given by Huffington herself. Wherever possible, recollections from friends, colleagues and acquaintances, both current and former, have helped to confirm or resolve conflicting stories.

For purposes of understanding the details of this book, the reader should not assume that the individual whose dialogue or specific emotion is recorded is necessarily the person who provided the information, although, in most instances, that is the case. At every opportunity, individuals are identified to preserve transparency and information has been double-checked with witnesses wherever possible – especially those being quoted – then vetted by secondary and tertiary sources where applicable. It should be stressed that some sources close to Huffington did not wish to comment or were unresponsive to earnest inquiries. Others were happy to speak, but not to be named. These wishes were respected.

During the writing of this book, Huffington herself, as well as her representatives, were, at times, not always open to answering certain questions, but frequently stepped up to provide details about Huffington's activities, interests and business ventures. In addition, some of the more recent events covered in this book have yet to reach their final conclusions and, though the latest information has been provided, it is clearly subject to change.

While it is true groups of people will often diverge in the retelling of their versions of the facts, when enough people have weighed in, certain facts will prevail over others. In my writings, prevailing facts have been favored over outliers. It should also be noted that many details of Huffington's colorful life have been downplayed, or even omitted, on the grounds that they were too personal, to sensitive, or too plain bizarre. The focus of this book was primarily to show how Huffington rose from truly challenging beginnings to become one of the most prominent and powerful women in media.

The fact that a detailed biography has yet to be written about Huffington – even as she approaches her 70th birthday at the helm of one of her most successful ventures yet – is a testament to how far we still have to come as a society in acknowledging the role of women in business.

This book seeks to rectify that.

PART 1

GREECE

'I had no fear of failure. Perseverance is everything.
I don't give up.'

Arianna Huffington has been called many things through-out her improbable rise to fame and power, from 'start-up diva' to 'zeitgeist artist' to 'the most upwardly mobile Greek since Icarus'. Spanning five decades, her meteoric journey has brought her wealth and influence as a million-aire media mogul, political pundit, one-time California gubernatorial candidate – and, most recently, self-anointed wellness evangelist.

But, above all, Arianna Huffington is the master of the metamorphosis.

It was not until the age of fifty-four, when she launched the online news site *The Huffington Post,* that Huffington became a household name. Born in Athens, Greece, on 15 July 1950, her life has carried with it not only the strong influence of her Greek family and heritage, but a wealth of wisdom she has drawn from spiritual teachers, politicians, celebrity friends, business associates and leaders across the globe, all of whom have proven foundational to her books and entrepreneurial ventures.

Huffington has written fifteen books, which follow her incarnations as biographer, political thinker and wellness guru, but it was through her launch of *The Huffington Post* in 2005 – during her reign, the most popular online news site since the dawn of the internet – and, in 2016, her formation of New York-based wellness company Thrive Global, that she amassed an estimated net worth of $150 million. While undoubtedly *The Huffington Post* is what she is known for, there can be no real understanding of Huffington without knowing the story of her upbringing and her earnest search, traversing Athens, London, New York, Washington and California to find her place in the world.

Greece – and Athens in particular – played a dominant role in Huffington's life until she moved to London in her late teens. Since the 1920s, Greece lurched from monarchy to dictatorship to civil war, plagued by fraud, vote-rigging and the erosion of the nation's electoral system by some of its highest-ranking leaders. As a child, Huffington witnessed the economy of the countryside falling apart, prompting a mass migration to Greece's larger towns and cities.[1]

Greece was moving away from its quasi-feudal existence of past centuries to embrace a sort of rough-hewn, cobbled-together democracy, but Greece's rulers throughout the mid-1960s were not above supporting dictatorships and directly undermining the country's parliamentary system. Greece's King Constantine II went so far as to even ban elections. It was not until 1974, nearly a decade after Huffington left her homeland for the UK, that Greece would vote to give its waning and antiquated monarchy the boot, becoming a full republic.[2] All of this, the young Arianna observed first hand, with much of it shaping her early conservatism and political views.

At the time of Huffington's birth, Greece was mired in the chaotic aftermath of the Second World War and women were still treated as an underclass. Women were not allowed to vote. They did not win that privilege until the mid-1950s, more than thirty years after women in the US and UK. To this day, Huffington speaks very candidly about the sexism she and other women of her family encountered in Greece while she was growing up.

Huffington's mother, Elli Georgiadi, in her late teens joined the resistance movement against the Nazis, who occupied Greece from 1941 to 1944. Elli's family had fled Russia during the Revolution. She was self-taught and multilingual and could speak German. Throughout the war, she proved exceedingly clever at circumnavigating the Nazi threats. In Greece, the resistance movement was one of the most impressively virulent of all of Nazi-occupied Europe, with both armed and unarmed groups filling the power vacuum left behind by the Greek monarchy and established political classes fleeing Greece for British-controlled areas of the Middle East to escape war.[3] Elli, unwed at the time and largely uneducated, stayed in Greece and worked for the Red Cross.

It is unclear whether Huffington's mother had any association with Greece's *andartes*, or guerrilla groups, who took refuge in the mountains during the war, but stories Huffington tells of her mother's bravery protecting the Greek Jews and wounded soldiers during the occupation make it plain that Elli, at the very least, was not afraid to face Nazis bearing guns. When her mother was ambushed by a phalanx of German soldiers at the age of nineteen while hiding two Jewish girls in a mountain cabin, Huffington says her mother stood firm, even as the soldiers grew more menacing:

> [They] started to shoot, threatening to kill everyone if the group did not surrender the Jews the Germans suspected, rightly, they were hiding. My mother, who spoke fluent German, stood up and told them categorically to put down their guns, that there were no Jews in their midst. And then she watched the German soldiers lower their guns and walk away.[4]

When the Germans headed out, Elli stopped one of them and scolded the soldier for snatching a hair comb from her long tresses. 'Can I have my comb back?' she demanded. 'I need it more than you!' Huffington says her mother told this story to her and her sister when she was just nine years old.[5]

These tales of a fiercely resolute mother left a lasting

impression on the young Arianna. 'She took risks for what she believed in,' Huffington says.[6] The guidance of her mother played a major role in Huffington's life and career trajectory, informing many of the themes Huffington would revisit in her talks and appearances – and especially in her books. More than any other, Huffington's relationship with her mother seems to have been one of the most pivotal of her life and her success, characterized by acts of love, heroism and humble beginnings writ large. Throughout much of Huffington's life, Elli lived with her, and continued to do so until her death in 2000. 'Really, I feel that nothing would have happened in my life without my mother,' Huffington has said. 'She was fearless.'[7]

In the 1950s, the Greek Orthodox Church mandated that no child could be baptized without bearing the name of a saint. To meet this requirement, Huffington's mother had added the hyphenated 'Anna' to the end of the name 'Ariadne,' paying homage to St Anne.[8] In Greek mythology, Ariadne was a Cretan princess who fell in love with Theseus, the mythical king and founder of the city of Athens. She delivered him from the deadly labyrinth guarded by the Minotaur. Ariadne was also scion of Queen Pasiphaë, daughter of Helios the sun god, and Minos, the king of Crete and the son of the god Zeus.

Huffington's favourite Greek heroine, however, is not Ariadne, but Cassandra, a female prophet who in Greek mythology tries to warn others of impending doom but is often disregarded until it's too late.[9] Over the years, Huffington's many political writings and books have frequently embraced the role of Cassandra, lampooning corporate greed, government corruption and the onset of the worst financial crisis since the Great Depression (warnings that, in the tradition of Cassandra, sometimes precede the events, but often too late to stop them).

By the end of the war, an estimated 10 per cent of Greece's 80,000 Jews had survived, the lowest percentage of any nation. Of the roughly 1,200 Jews in Greece who voluntarily registered with the Germans as Jewish, around half were immediately sent to the gas chambers. The rest, around 650 men and women, were cherry-picked by Josef Mengele, the Nazi's 'Angel of Death,' for horrific genetic experiments.[10] The bulk of the survivors, many of whom spoke Greek, came from Athens, where they were sheltered by fellow Athenians deeply sympathetic to their cause, or joined up with the *andartes* in the mountains, where members of the resistance, like Elli, protected them.

The risks Huffington's mother faced were steep. From the early 1940s on, the corpses of young warriors and children littered the streets of Athens. Thousands more, suffering from malnutrition and tumours, staggered through the capital, one of the hardest-hit areas of the war. The wealthy and middle classes, at least for a time, were able to feed themselves. In the countryside, many hoarded provisions rather than send them to the city. But in Athens, the impoverished could not keep up with soaring prices and were left to starve. Between October 1940, when Greece entered the war, and October 1944, when the Germans pulled out, the value of a single loaf of bread leapt from 10 drachmas to 34 million drachmas on the black market. The cost of cheese rose by a factor of 2 million. Once the Greeks were unable to pay for food, they were forced to barter.[11] 'Apart from the occasional German vehicle or patrol, the streets were eerily silent, as no one had the energy to do anything except struggle to keep alive,' says historian Robin Waterfield.

In the final months leading up to the liberation, there was near-complete anarchy in Athens, where hundreds of guerrillas and civilians were slaughtered. 'Assassinations, hostage-taking, torture, summary executions and street battles [reigned],' Waterfield writes. The end of the war was punctuated by the regular round-up of left-wing suspects by the Greek authorities – primarily the guerrillas of the resistance movement, who were associated with the communists, despite the fact many had nothing to do with communists or communism. Civil war erupted between the anti-communist and guerrilla groups.

Injected into this was the outsize influence of the British prime minister Winston Churchill, who was insistent on eliminating any trace of communism inside Greece, supporting the right-wing Greeks' grip on power. The new government also was backed by the Americans, though it included some Nazi collaborators.[12] Yet even with discord and violence continually at Athens's doorstep, Waterfield writes, 'The Greeks' spirit was never broken ... They fought back with bullets, demonstrations and strikes with vivid graffiti and with legendary gestures.' It was amid this unbreakable spirit that Elli survived the war and Arianna – christened Ariadne-Anna Stassinopoulos – was born.

It was also how Elli came to meet Huffington's father, Konstantinos Stassinopoulos. Both members of the resistance movement, Huffington's parents met in a sanatorium in Kifissia, Greece, after the war, where they were recuperating – Elli from tuberculosis, Konstantinos from time spent at a German concentration camp.[13] Elli was told that she could never have children.[14] The couple fell in love quickly. At their wedding, Elli was conspicuously pregnant.[15] 'I was conceived before they were married,' Huffington says.[16]

Konstantinos, a struggling journalist, had published an underground newspaper called *Paron* ('The Present')[17] during the Second World War, but was arrested and spent the rest of the war in prison.[18] He barely survived. For the rest of his life, he suffered from what Huffington's younger sister, Agapi, calls, 'melancholia'.[19] Huffington notes, 'What he experienced in a German concentration camp forever marked his life.'[20] According to Waterfield, the atrocities of the war 'and the unbelievable experience of seeing neighbours starve to death radicalized and politicized many Greeks'. Between 1940 and 1949, just before Huffington was born, Greece was roiled by continuous warfare that cost 600,000 people their lives.[21]

It was Konstantinos who first introduced Arianna to journalism. He also enjoyed some success as a businessman and management consultant, publishing an economics journal called *Chronos*.[22] Her mother instilled in her a passion for education and learning. Huffington says that during periods of political upheaval in Greece, there were times she had to choose between pursuing her studies and obeying the law. In 1967, during a coup of Greek generals, Huffington, then a teenager, faced soldiers on every street corner on the way to her economics class. Arianna would often traverse the sloping, cobblestoned streets of Plaka, the old part of the city, on her way to school.[23] At the time, Greece was under the dictatorial rule of a military regime that had imposed a curfew. 'Torn between the fear that paralyzed me and the desire to ignore the curfew,'[24] Huffington says she decided to evade the soldiers and head to class, explaining that her mother 'didn't believe in excuses'.[25] But she didn't make it to class. In fact, she barely made it a block before a soldier armed with a machine gun stopped her and marched Arianna back home.[26]

After the war, Huffington's father, Konstantinos, frequently found himself stymied by a lack of funds and mounting debt as a publisher. 'Most of what he made he would lose in launching another magazine or his latest newspaper,' Huffington recalls.[27] He was also a gambler.[28] After years of raising money and spending it, he was forced to declare bankruptcy.[29] While Huffington credits her father's enthusiasm for journalism as an inspiration for the launch of *The Huffington Post* in 2005, it was his financial woes in print media that convinced her that publishing news online was the future. When she launched *The Huffington Post* in Greece in 2014, she announced, notably, 'It's no accident *HuffPost* is not in print!'[30] In many ways, however, she treated *The Huffington Post* as a print publication. 'We call *The Huffington Post* a newspaper,' she told

Inc. magazine in 2010. 'I don't think that newspapers are dying. I think there will be fewer of them, but there will always be newspapers.'[31]

In her early years, Huffington lived in Kifissia, where her parents met and one of the most affluent northern suburbs of Athens, traditionally home to wealthy and politically connected Greek families. When she was still in grade school, Huffington's parents separated.[32] While they were still very much in love, Konstantinos engaged in a number of affairs – something to which he felt entitled and to which his wife took grave exception. 'He basically told her one day to stop interfering in his private life,' Huffington says. 'He was a serial philanderer.'[33]

Once it became clear Konstantinos's behaviour was not going to change, Elli decided to leave him. 'The very sort of European idea that you have your private life and you have your married life did not go down well with my mother,' Huffington recalls.[34] Her parents' marriage and break-up brought hardships and the family continued to struggle with money. In 2012, Huffington spoke of this period of her life in *The New York Times*:

When I was growing up, my family was a tiny microcosm of the current Greek economy. We were heavily in debt; my father's repeated attempts to own a newspaper ended in failure and bankruptcy. Eventually my mother took my sister and me and left him. We all lived in Athens and we continued to see my father, though we had our own one-bedroom apartment. It wasn't the bankruptcy that got to my mom in the end, but the philandering.'[35]

The loss of her father's presence in the home and his infidelity was something Huffington would examine many times throughout her life. In her 2006 book *On Becoming Fearless ... In Love, Work and Life*, Huffington revisits how her mother, despite her own financial fears, decided to put the emotional well-being of herself and her daughters first: 'With her innate fearlessness, she did not let financial concerns stop her from leaving [my father] when I was 11 years old. For my father, as for many Greek men of his generation, there was nothing wrong with extramarital affairs ... His marriage was part of his public life, his affairs part of his private life. But that was not okay for her, and even though she had no job and no obvious way to earn money, she took her two children and left, trusting that, somehow, she would make ends meet. And somehow, she did.'[36]

Elli sold off many personal items to support herself and her daughters, including treasured family possessions, her own jewellery and an heirloom carpet from the Caucasus. She took out loans from her family, friends – and even her landlord on one occasion. 'She constantly had to borrow money or sell whatever few things she had left,' says Huffington.[37] By the time they had uprooted themselves and resettled in their new home, Huffington was twelve years old and Agapi ten.[38] Though they did not have very much to live on as Huffington describes it, this period of their lives paved the way for a strengthened unity among the three women, cementing bonds that would last a lifetime:

> My mother was clear about one thing: she would cut back on everything except our education and good, healthy food. She owned two dresses and never spent anything on herself. I remember her selling her last pair of little gold earrings. She borrowed from anyone she could, so that her two daughters could fulfill their dreams of a good education ... At the time, Greek girls still offered dowries to be married. My mother used to tell me, 'Your education is your dowry.'[39]

Arianna became the dutiful, studious daughter, while Agapi grew into an extroverted free spirit. They lived in an apartment with their mother on Mourouzi Street across from the Athens fire station, nestled among the museums and galleries near the National Garden. Money remained tight, according to Huffington, but it was not so scant that she did not have private tutors, after-school activities and ballet classes, along with her sister. Huffington was well cared for, attending a traditional Greek private school.[40] She and her sister would pass the time play-acting and choreographing dances where Huffington would direct and Agapi would perform. Despite the siblings' close quarters, both Arianna and Agapi have said that their plight did not feel as dire as it might have been, because of their mother's insistence on putting them first. 'It was packed, but sweet,' Agapi says. 'I never had a sense that we lacked anything, because my mother was always very generous.'[41] Elli would engage in what Huffington calls 'marathon midnight cooking sessions' of Greek and Russian dishes, 'culinary binges that ranged from Russian piroshki to Greek stuffed grape leaves'.[42]

When launching *The Huffington Post* in Greece, Huffington remembered how her mother brought the world to life through cooking and conversation. 'She would preside over long sessions in our small kitchen, guiding us through our daily problems by discussing Greek philosophy. And of course, she was always cooking, clearly believing that if you didn't eat something every twenty minutes, something terrible would happen to you.'[43] When she was able to do so, Elli borrowed money from her five brothers to move herself and her daughters to London once they were teenagers to pursue better opportunities.

In Huffington's speeches and writings, her mother is consistently portrayed as a devoted, heroine-like figure, while Huffington's feelings for her father can seem more complex. 'My father was a serial journalism entrepreneur who launched a succession of small newspaper ventures, all of which failed,' she says.[44] Even so, witnessing her father's repeated struggles may have been instrumental to Huffington's own success. Each time Konstantinos erred, the precocious Arianna was attentively watching – and learning. In the 2012 *New York Times* article, she spoke of her father as a man who acted 'irresponsibly in his private and professional life',[45] and in an interview in 2014, she stated, 'he had the sense he could write his own rules'.[46] This is a trait many would ascribe to Huffington herself.

Other times, her descriptions of her father were more romanticized. In her 1994 book *The Fourth Instinct: The Call of the Soul*, she characterizes her father as a 'passionate dreamer' who 'oscillated between the world of business, to make a living for his family, and the world of ideas and publishing that made our living precarious'. (Her father later transitioned from newspaperman to economist, becoming president of Alpha-Omega, an Athens-based financial consultancy.)[47] In the book, she recalls many overheard conversations from her childhood in which her father fretted over whether he would be able to scrape together enough money to save the latest newspaper or magazine he'd launched that was foundering. Huffington would lie awake at night, worried, wishing she could help. 'I never thought my father was irresponsible,' she says, contradicting herself, 'whatever hardships involved for our family and however painful his separation from my mother when I was 10, I idealized both him and the world of writing and ideas he loved so much that sometimes, secretly, I felt a flash of burning jealousy over a pile of his manuscripts.' Throughout her life, Huffington's views on her father would veer from forgiving to condemning. The relationship, even after his death, would remain layered, opaque, impenetrable.

Her mother and father never divorced. While her parents' break-up took a heavy toll on Huffington and her sister, the family dynamics improved dramatically after the separation. Konstantinos remained a key fixture in Huffington's life, taking her and Agapi with him on holidays to the Greek islands and abroad. He brought them to his office and on junkets where they would sometimes meet his business associates, enjoy the nightlife, stay at upscale hotels and immerse in adult conversations. 'We swam young in a big ocean,' Agapi says.[48] The sisters were even included in gambling jaunts to Corfu, where Konstantinos would give Arianna and Agapi chips to cash in so they could play the lottery machines.[49]

In a black-and-white photo of Huffington and her sister, taken in what appears to be their early adolescence, they're standing and smiling, their father between them, at the Eiffel Tower in Paris. Konstantinos is in suit and tie, balding and bespectacled. Huffington, almost as tall as him, is dressed in a long suede coat, hair tied in a flowing scarf, eyes nonchalantly averted, already looking preternaturally glamorous.

Even so, Huffington speaks of her teen years as a time of feeling shy, withdrawn and insular. She preferred to bury herself in her books and her studies to socializing with friends. Much of her bookishness seems to have stemmed from her need to escape her parents' less-than-harmonious marriage. 'I was a reclusive child,' she says, 'I never felt I needed friends. I actively preferred being alone in a room reading.'[50] Despite her introverted tendencies, she could still be assertive, however. At one of her childhood birthday parties she remembers shooing away the neighbourhood children because they were impeding her reading time and splendid solace.[51] By thirteen, she says, she was 'awkwardly tall', towering above most of her fellow students. Arianna also wore glasses, like her father, which she had needed since the age of seven. In *On Becoming Fearless*, she recalls at length how difficult those years were:

> I still cringe at how self-conscious I was as a teenager. Let's start with the fact I was freakishly tall for a Greek girl, standing five-ten at 13, when my classmates were five-nothing. I remember the trauma of being excluded from the school parade, which included all the tallest girls at the school, because I was, yes, too tall. Add to that unruly curly hair, heavy acne and thick glasses and, well, you get the not-so-pretty picture. I was only happy when I was lost in my books.[52]

In her early teens, Huffington visited the United States for the first time, participating in a Vermont-based summer programme called 'The Experiment in International Living', which allows high school students to live abroad while learning about other languages and cultures. During this time, she stayed with four different families in York, Pennsylvania, a manufacturing town known for producing hydro-power turbines, dental equipment and false teeth. Living in an area not far from America's Rust Belt with agricultural and industrial roots, Huffington witnessed for the first time the struggles of the American working class, as well as the ideals of the American dream. This experience later informed her 2010 book *Third World America: How Our Politicians Are Abandoning the Middle Class, and Betraying the American Dream*, released during the aftermath of the global economic crisis. 'Everyone in Greece knew someone who'd left to find a better life in America,' Huffington says. 'That was the phrase everyone associated with America – a better life.'[53]

It was an idea that would stay with her long after she'd left the US and begun seeking a better life herself.

Encouraged by her mother, Huffington devoted herself to her education and began looking at other opportunities abroad. When she was fifteen, she saw a photo of Cambridge University in the UK on the cover of a magazine. 'I brought it home, threw it on the kitchen table, and said to my mother, "I want to go there",' she says. 'Most people I mentioned it to told me that I was crazy.' But from then on, Arianna had no other goal but to attend.

> I saw this picture of Cambridge . . . And it was like the ugly duckling and the beautiful swan. My mother said, 'OK, let's see how we can get you there.' And she basically investigated how I could go to the British consulate in Athens and take my [tests] for England and all the steps you had to take . . . And she said, 'We must go and see Cambridge!'[55]

Almost no one, with the exception of her mother, believed Huffington could go to Cambridge, one of the world's most elite universities. 'Everybody else laughed,' Huffington says. She did not even speak English.

Undaunted, Elli borrowed money so she could fly with

her daughter from Athens to London to visit the university.[56] Huffington says she vividly remembers how they bought 'the cheap tickets with the seats that didn't go back', and how, when they arrived, it was raining, and they took a northbound train to Cambridge. They strolled the lanes and the riverbank, agog at the centuries-old stone buildings and sweeping lawns. They did not meet any of the professors or the academic staff at the time. 'She and I just walked around Cambridge and it kind of made it real for us, that I could actually go there,' Huffington says. 'The idea of visualization, that was my mother.'[57]

At the time in Greece, Huffington says, 'no one was considered educated until you'd also gone to a foreign school'. Most students would spend five years in Greece finishing their undergraduate degrees, then matriculate overseas for their postgraduate work. Not wanting to wait, Huffington decided to take a different route. 'I thought, why not go straight to Cambridge? Skip those five years in Athens,'[58] she says.

Huffington's mother helped the young Arianna to navigate the entrance exams and admissions process, working with the British consulate in Athens to line up the standardized tests Huffington would need to take to apply to an English university. Once her younger sister, Agapi, reached her early teens, Huffington's mother, in a bold move, relocated her children to London permanently. This was how both of her daughters were able to learn English in their early years and eventually attend English universities. How this move was achieved on the shoestring budget Huffington describes of her early years is not clear, but taking big, calculated risks would increasingly become a central part of her life.

Huffington told the *New Yorker* in 2008 that if she were to write about her own life, she would open it in the spring of 1969, when she and her mother moved to a rented flat in London to prepare for her Cambridge entrance exams. They lived in Manchester Square, which lies north of Oxford Street in the Marylebone district of London, known for its magnificent garden squares and Georgian terraces. While Huffington has often spoken of her impoverished upbringing, it is clear from a number of interviews earlier in her life that her family not only had sufficient funds to afford international travel, but also provide Huffington with the kind of privileged education that would bring her opportunities far beyond Greece. In 1987, she told the *Washington Post* that while her family wasn't exactly wealthy, 'I never lacked anything.'[59] Throughout her life, she credited her mother for many of her early advantages: 'My mother instilled in me that failure was not something to be afraid of, that it was not the opposite of success. It was a stepping stone to success. So, I had no fear of failure. Perseverance is everything. I don't give up. Everybody has failures, but successful people keep on going . . . She was my life mentor.'[60]

Huffington's mother was not accidentally enlightened. She was an avid reader of books on child psychology, self-realization, yoga and meditation, and she loved the Greek classics, as did her daughters. She 'was in a constant state of wonder at the world around her', Huffington says, and did not hesitate to remind her children, family and friends to enjoy life as much as she did. When confronted with the workaday stresses of others, Huffington says her mother could be merciless:

> I still remember, when I was 12 years old, a very successful Greek businessman coming over to our home for dinner. He looked rundown and exhausted. But when we sat down to dinner, he told us how well things were going for him. He was thrilled about a contract he had just won to build a new museum. My mother was not impressed. 'I don't care how well your business is doing,' she told him bluntly, 'you're not taking care of you. Your business might have a great bottom line, but you are your most important capital. There are only so many withdrawals you can make from your health bank account, but you just keep on withdrawing. You could go bankrupt if you don't make some deposits soon.' And indeed, not long after that, the man had to be rushed to the hospital for an emergency angioplasty.[61]

Huffington recounts, 'Whenever I'd complain or was upset about something in my own life, my mother had the same advice, "Darling, just change the channel. You are in control of the clicker. Don't replay the bad, scary movie."' Agapi says when she and Arianna were adolescents, her mother introduced them to a book called *Autobiography of a Yogi*, by Paramahansa Yogananda.[62] Yogananda was an Indian guru who introduced millions of Westerners and Indians alike to the teachings of meditation and established churches throughout southern California. Published in 1946, the book became one of the most popular spiritual books of the twentieth century. Many celebrities and business leaders have praised its virtues, including the Beatles' George Harrison and Apple's founder Steve Jobs, who ordered copies of the book to be distributed to mourners at his funeral in 2011.[63]

Huffington says she believed in God from an early age and felt drawn to a wide variety of spiritual teachings. She studied Hinduism and also fasted on the name day of the Virgin Mary.[64] When she was seventeen, she travelled to India to study comparative religion at the Visva-Bharati University in Shantiniketan, a small town in the Birbhum district of West Bengal. The school was founded by Nobel Prize-winning writer Rabindranath Tagore, a novelist, essayist, poet and mystic. At thirteen, Huffington says, her mother had already introduced her and her sister to calming themselves through regular meditation: 'When I was growing up, meditation was seen as a cure for just about everything. My mother convinced us that if we meditated, we would be able to do our homework faster and improve our grades. We knew that meditation made us more peaceful and less upset when things didn't go our way, but we also realized that it made us happier.'[65]

After taking the batteries of exams for Cambridge, Huffington still had to get through the final in-person interview. 'I definitely had a big wave of self-doubt,' she says. 'I was the underdog.' When she arrived, Huffington met the other students she would be competing against for a spot and felt intimidated. There were twelve of them in all. 'One English girl turned to all of us, but I remember she was looking directly at me for some reason, and she said, "One of us is going to get in. That one is going to be *me*." I remember feeling scared at first when she said that,' Huffington recalls. '[I thought] yes, of course, she is going to get in, why did you ever think you were going to get in?' She went into the interview filled with trepidation. In those early years, it was only the words of her mother, 'who made me feel always that I could aim for the stars and, if I failed, she wouldn't love me any less', that allowed her to steel herself, feel the fear and take the chance anyway.[66]

When the day finally came that Huffington would hear the results of her Cambridge application, not even meditation could soothe her. 'I was so nervous,' Huffington recalls. 'My mother said, "OK! Let's go to the movies all day." So, we would go from one movie to another, literally all day, and we got home and there was a telegram.'[67] It said: 'AWARDED. GIRTON. EXHIBITION.' Huffington was thrilled, but she didn't know what it meant. Only after speaking with her tutor did she learn that she had been accepted by Cambridge University's Girton College on a partial scholarship.

With the help of their mother, Arianna and Agapi would both attend prestigious schools in Britain. 'She sold everything along the way to pay for the schools and the private lessons that prepared me for the Cambridge entrance exams and my sister for the Royal Academy of Dramatic Arts,' Huffington says. 'She made it clear if I failed, if I didn't get into Cambridge, it was not a big deal. But I got in.'[68]

PART 2

LONDON AND CAMBRIDGE

'I never thought of being a writer. That was an accident.'

Huffington attended Cambridge University alongside an impressive list of global luminaries and future world leaders, including Charles, Prince of Wales, a fellow student. The grandiosity of her new environs, with its tightly clipped lawns, soaring Gothic architecture and sequestered gardens, represented a dramatic shift from the meagre family existence she had led with her mother and sister back in Athens.

Cambridge is where Sir Isaac Newton, in the seventeenth century, laid the groundwork for modern physics and where, less than two decades before Huffington graduated from Cambridge, James Watson and Francis Crick announced in 1953 they had discovered the structure of DNA. Among the countless writers and scientists who, at one time or another, have called Cambridge home are Darwin, Tennyson,

Marlowe and Byron. To this day, the town's centre remains a medieval marvel, its high streets and winding alleys crammed with cafés, theatres and shops. The city now also boasts 4,500 science and technology firms, including Amazon and Apple.

Arriving in London at the height of the 'Swinging Sixties', Huffington was part of the first generation to enjoy the true freedom of movement and expression that parents of her era – who had mostly spent the Second World War trying to survive – had not. The 1960s also marked the coming of age of the first Britons free of conscription, bringing a renewed sense of hope for sweeping change. Against this backdrop, Cambridge opened Huffington's eyes to new modes of thought and fresh possibilities, just as England was emerging from the pall of the post-war era and stepping into a decade of Technicolor exuberance. Huffington later in life would often be asked how her views could veer so seamlessly from highly conservative to extremely liberal. Judging by what she experienced, from Athens to London, at that time, tectonic shifts may have been the only fixed variable of her young adult life.

Girton College, which became Huffington's new home, was an all-female institution at Cambridge. Huffington lived in a tiny room 'fit for a squirrel' and quickly grew accustomed to walking a 'half mile to the shower'. Cambridge was much colder and danker than Greece and this took no small amount of adjustment for Arianna. 'My time at Cambridge was a special, formative one,' she says. 'It was a shock for me, coming from a very loving, connected,

tribal Greek family and suddenly being in a Gothic building with endless corridors, putting shillings in my heater in
my freezing little room.'[1]

Male visitors had to follow strict rules when socializing
with Girton girls, and Huffington, striving to make friends,
even as she struggled to be understood through her heavy
Greek accent, was caught fraternizing too close to curfew.
'One night I had friends round quite late, although still
before midnight, and a porter came to my room and saw
there were men there,' she says. 'The senior tutor called me
in the next day and fined me one shilling per man. It was
worth it though – they were decent guys.'[2]

Of her distinctive accent, Huffington says it was
something 'I tried to lose, with no success'.[3] Cambridge
was particularly intimidating, she says, because it was 'a
world where accents really mattered'.[4] Huffington studied
Keynesian economics at Cambridge (named for the British
economist John Maynard Keynes, who believed that government intervention helped to keep economies stable).
But economics would turn out to be secondary to Huffington's rapt fascination with the university's prestigious
debating society, the Cambridge Union, whose chambers
she stumbled upon during a student-group fair. Huffington
describes herself as being 'transfixed' by the spectacle of
watching some of the brightest lights of the school's thirty-
one colleges engaged in sophisticated verbal jousting over
politics, philosophy and current events. 'I just threw myself
into it,' she says. 'I went to every debate. I must literally
have sat there with my mouth open.'[5] A long-established

mainstay for many of Cambridge's most rhetorically gifted students, the Union henceforth became Huffington's dedicated stomping ground. 'I would go to every debate, because I loved seeing the power of words and rhetoric moving people's minds and hearts.'[6]

Without fail, Huffington would show up for Union meetings – extremely lively affairs – and, like many of her contemporaries, jockey for attention. (The journalist Jane Mayer wrote in a *New Yorker* article in 2018 that the Cambridge Union 'is such a common path for ambitious future leaders that, according to one former member, its motto should be "The Egos Have Landed"'.)[7] For Huffington, understanding and conquering the clubby debating society, which she was told replicated the British House of Commons and followed parliamentary procedure, became her next great quest. 'I studied quite hard as a student, but my life was absorbed by the Union,' she says.[8] Discovering the Union was not something she expected, but it more than prepared Huffington for a lifelong journey of shaping the public discourse and influencing popular opinion – at first, among the Cambridge students and then on more national and international stages. 'So often, you know, in life there are these accidents that prepare you to the next thing. And for me, the accident was really discovering the Cambridge Union,' she says.[9]

By this time standing nearly six feet tall, cutting an elegant, aristocratic figure, Huffington could not help but stand out. Initially, the other students at the Union were not so welcoming. 'I instantly fell in love with the Cambridge

Union . . . but to put it mildly, the Cambridge Union did not instantly fall in love with me,' she says, likening it to an 'unrequited love affair'.[10] 'When I first went there and stood up to speak, people literally laughed at me. America has a much greater acceptance of accents than England. And everybody kind of assumed I would stop speaking after [a] couple more efforts. But I would stay until the end of the debate and I would stand up and speak and literally *learn* to speak [English].'[11] Huffington's height and overly formal clothing, in addition to her Greek mannerisms and ways of speaking – which could range from startlingly assertive to downright supercilious – put off many of the students. 'The charisma was there, but it was painful to listen to her,' one student told *New York* magazine. Huffington agreed. 'Sometimes I was called to speak after midnight, because I was so bad.'[12]

In *Fearless*, Huffington remembers she also brought a lot of teenage insecurities with her to university. In Greece, 'I was consumed by fears that I would never have a boyfriend, never be attractive to boys. I kept comparing myself to all my beautiful, diminutive classmates as I towered over them in my exquisite awkwardness. I kept getting As in school, but it didn't matter to me, because all I really cared about was how I looked. The good grades were my ticket out, but I still took a lot of those fears with me to Cambridge.'[13] At Union debates, students often dressed up, paying special attention to their appearance, diction and bearing. They would bring pre-written notes to make their arguments, constantly honing and polishing their presentations.

'Most of my happiness at Cambridge came not from my relationships, but from beginning to master public speaking, debating and the clash of ideas,' Huffington says.[14] It would be an ideal training ground for Huffington's long-term education in the art of public influence.

Another challenge Huffington faced was Cambridge's legendary class-consciousness. When referring to 'horseback-riding' in front of a group of other students, she was heckled. They were 'like, "What other kind of riding is there? *Donkey* riding?"'[15] As someone whose aspirations to attend Cambridge had been roundly sniffed at, Huffington remained undeterred and eventually mastered English while debating. Although she didn't recognize it at the time, the Union would be her passport to opportunities well beyond Cambridge, London and Great Britain.

As a rule, the Union witnessed many historic debates, with students inviting celebrated writers, leaders and dignitaries, both off-campus and on, to participate in heated, televised oratorical battles. In Huffington's first motion in a major debate, she declared, 'This house believes that technological advance threatens the individuality of man and is becoming his master.' (This echoes a position she would take decades later when launching one of her many entrepreneurial ventures.) She teamed up on the presentation with famed literary critic and Cambridge fellow George Steiner, who debated the point with Prince Charles, who also attended the Union debates. 'Prince Charles was speaking, although he did not take either side, because this was felt to be more royal,' Huffington recalls. 'Steiner got a standing ovation, which was quite rare at the Union. Afterward, he asked Prince Charles for an autograph, which surprised me. Steiner was the most popular lecturer at Cambridge, a guru don, so I felt a bit let down.'[16] Huffington was put out when her intellectual idols genuflected to something as incidental as British royalty.

During another televised debate, Huffington found herself pummelled by William F. Buckley Jr, a renowned conservative commentator and founder of *National Review*, a magazine for which she would eventually write, while arguing over the merits of the free market system – a crippling loss for Huffington, who hoped one day to get a PhD in economics. Describing it years later, Huffington said, 'He made mashed potatoes of me.'[17] Nonetheless, she found in it an important lesson. 'What I learned was that no one pays as much attention to humiliations and defeats as we do. I may have thought my career was over, but others were not as focused on one devastating evening.'[18]

At Cambridge, Huffington was able to meet with intellectual power brokers of the day and spent hours consorting with some of the most decorated scholars in the world in their sumptuous offices. 'Once, I read this huge book on poverty, *Asian Drama: An Inquiry into the Poverty of Nations*, for a tutorial with my fabulous don at Trinity, Dr Mitchell,' she says. 'He offered me a dry sherry, as usual, then asked how much of this book I had read. I said, "All of it." He said, "Really? That's more than the author has read!"'[19] Ever the networker, Huffington was even reported to have met and entertained UK prime minister

Ted Heath. At Cambridge, she told *New York* magazine, 'you meet everyone who's in politics on a level of equality'.

Photos and footage from this period of Huffington's life show her well-heeled and well-coiffed, decked in flowing dresses and beautifully brocaded, tailored clothing, her shiny locks meticulously styled. Against the drab seventies garb of the other students, Huffington might have been confused for royalty herself. No more was she the 'ugly duckling' of her awkward adolescent years. While her name – Arianna Stassinopoulos – and her laborious efforts at learning English continued to draw gibes (some of the students dubbed her 'Staryanna Comeacroppalos'), the Union was where she shed the last vestiges of her bashful, introverted side. At twenty-one, she became the first foreign president of the Union – and only the third woman ever to be elected to the position. In 2014, Huffington told the London newspaper, the *Telegraph*:

> I was never going to run for president, because I was so self-conscious about my Greek accent. People used to tease me about it all the time. One weekend I was in London and a friend put my name down in the candidate book for standing committee, one of the first rungs on the Union ladder. By the time I got back to Cambridge they had printed the ballot and I couldn't remove my name. I thought, 'This is going to be so embarrassing – no one will vote for me.' And then somehow, I actually got the most votes. Then I ran for

secretary, then vice-president, then became president for the Michaelmas term in 1971, my final year.

It is likely Huffington is grossly downplaying the amount of political savvy and willpower it took for her to capture the role of president. Historically, becoming president of the Cambridge Union requires a great deal of ferocious politicking, with candidates vying for endorsements within a cutthroat student body. While many of the other students had wealth and privilege on their side, they could not outmatch Huffington's hunger. 'She was smart and clever,' one London friend later told the *Washington Post*. 'And she was incredibly determined to make it.'[20] Huffington mainly credits her success at the Union to hard work and her efforts to overcome her strong aversion to public speaking. 'They say that public speaking is the greatest fear that many people have. The second greatest fear being death by mutilation. Every debate, I would research the subject and learn how to speak and eventually became president of Cambridge Union.'[21]

By the time Huffington took the helm of the Union, she had become a highly visible fixture on the Cambridge campus. Fellow students describe her possessing a lavish wardrobe and a high-end car. One former student who attended the university at the time, Chris Smith – later a minister in the Labour government of Tony Blair and member of the House of Lords – told the *Telegraph* in 2011 he recalls Huffington as 'a very prominent figure', known for driving her Alfa Romeo, an Italian luxury sports car, into the parking lot and leaving it across the double yellow lines, accumulating parking tickets. 'She was very striking and very glamorous, probably more of a socialite than a political figure,' he says. Her political leanings, even then, were inextricably linked with her social life. 'The liberal icon she has since become was not very evident in her student days,' Smith remarked. 'She was very much of the Right. I was regarded as being of the Left and, therefore, the enemy.'[22]

Huffington's prominence was amplified by her status as the leader of the Union. When she presided over debates, she sat on a raised platform at the front of the chamber, queen-like, in a well-worn, high-backed, wooden throne redolent of the British Coronation Chair, where monarchs sit to receive the crown. At age twenty-one, not long after Huffington took over as president, she met one of her intellectual idols, Bernard Levin, a nationally known journalist, critic and the gravitas columnist for the London *Times*. In 1971, both were invited to be panellists on the BBC's television programme, *Face the Music*, a classical music quiz. Huffington was starstruck when she heard that Levin would appear. 'I was there as a curiosity, a woman with a foreign accent, elected president of the Cambridge Union.' By contrast, Levin was a famous writer, well-known for his knowledge of music and theatre. During the recording of the programme, Huffington says, 'I was reduced to a bundle of inarticulateness. I'm still amazed that in my fog, I managed to recognize Schumann's Fourth Symphony.'[23]

Afterward, when Huffington learned that Levin planned

to speak at the church of a vicar they both knew, 'she asked to come along and meet me,' Levin told *New York* magazine. 'We all had lunch together. Sometime later, I ran into her again and asked her out.'[24] Although she had dated at Cambridge, Huffington says she was 'constantly doubting myself . . . it took me many years before I found myself as a woman.'[25] In her London days, Huffington was romantically linked to John Selwyn Gummer, now a British Conservative politician and member of the House of Lords (who told the press, 'I enjoyed her company enormously'); Simon Jenkins, who went on to become editor for *The Times*; and the former British politician David Mellor, a Cambridge friend who reportedly sent her poetry.[26] But it was Levin who would become what Huffington called 'the love of my life'.

Levin knew nothing about her before they met, but 'I had a major intellectual crush on him,' she says. Huffington prepped for their first date the way she got ready for Union debates. She pored over his columns in *The Times*, and studied his writings. 'I literally would cut his columns out and underline them and learn them by heart.'[27] Huffington wasn't alone; Levin was roundly considered one of London's foremost journalist–intellectuals, heavily influenced by the greats, particularly H. L. Mencken. Huffington loved his books, writings and collections of columns, which she found insightful, witty and stylistically brilliant. 'It was just like everything was so delicious about him,' Huffington once told the *New Yorker*.[28] As a student, she even kept a file of his work. 'No, I did not put pressed flowers in the file, but I might as well have,' she admits.[29] 'He was twice my age and half my size. I fell in love with him before I met him.'[30]

In her jittery preparations for a first date with Levin – who, at forty-two, was twice her age – Huffington spent the week cramming. She studied the current events in Northern Ireland, the Soviet Union and any other topics about which Levin wrote. She tried to memorize the musical canon of German composer Richard Wagner, one of Levin's favourites. 'I must have bored him to death, because for the second date, he took me to Covent Garden to see Wagner's *Die Meistersinger*,' she recalls. 'I spent the time between the dinner and the opera date reading about *Die Meistersinger*, and considering that more has been written about Wagner than anybody except Jesus Christ, there was a lot to read.'[31]

As the curtain rose at the close of the performance, Levin leaned in and confided to her, 'That's the opera I want to hear just before I die.'[32] A confirmed bachelor, Levin reportedly liked tall, glamorous women and courted them in highly stylized fashion, bringing sprays of flowers for them to wear on dates, as he 'needed them as companions at dinner or in the theatre', according to *The Times*. 'Arianna answered that requirement perfectly and had an intelligence to match.'[33] Huffington would seek the company of older men, because she often intimidated men her own age, London friend Diana Negroponte told the *Washington Post*. 'She is an imposing person. You have to be able to stand up to it. It's not easy living with a prima donna.'[34]

Levin eventually became not just Huffington's partner and confidant, but one of her greatest teachers. 'He was my mentor as a writer,' Huffington says.[35] He also taught her how to think, how to persuade and how to develop and defend her world views. When she breakfasted with him in his rented flat at Devonshire Place, Marylebone, 'every single morning newspaper and all the weeklies were spread on the kitchen table, with Bernard lapsing into rage, disgust, amazement or amusement, all volubly shared with me,' Huffington says. 'The only response to the morning news that he never felt was detachment.'[36]

Their first trip abroad together was to Bayreuth, in northern Bavaria, to see Wagner's *Ring*. 'Even though he was no longer a theatre critic, Saturdays were spent seeing two or sometimes three plays, starting off out of the West End,' Huffington wrote in a piece for the *Sunday Times* of London in 2004.[37] Levin took her to music festivals in Germany and Austria during the summers and brought her to France to sample cuisine at three-Michelin-star restaurants.

Intellectually, he could be a snob: they never once saw a film together at a cinema. Levin liked to dress up for the opera, wearing his trademark billowing cloak, inlaid with brightly hued silks.[38] And because he was a dedicated 'foodie', Huffington says, there were times she grew tired of his gastronomical obsessions. If they were at a Michelin-starred restaurant, sometimes 'I would order something very simple,' she says, 'And he'd look aghast.'[39] During a summer abroad, 'I found myself rebelling by ordering grilled fish and vegetables every time he waxed lyrical over one complicated French marvel after another.'[40] Levin had never learned to drive, so when he and Huffington spent their time together travelling as a couple, he was always the passenger and she, the driver:

> I did all the driving on these holidays and he kept me royally entertained with stories about the places we were passing, or the operas or the music we were going to hear or, God save us, the food we were going to eat. One day in Salzburg, he stayed in the hotel to write and I went shopping. I ended up being gone for hours and he ended up calling the police.[41]

When Levin travelled, his writing usually came along with him. Huffington would later pen many of her columns for *The Huffington Post* on the fly. 'Anything that he loved, he wrote about, whether it was a new play, especially a Tom Stoppard play, or lobster or Kiri Te Kanawa, or Glyndebourne, or Solzhenitsyn,' she wrote in the *Sunday Times* article. 'I remember really disliking his columns about food. It was one of our few arguments, because on personal matters his mode was not to argue but to withdraw.'[42]

Levin turned her on to a cavalcade of short-story writers, opera singers and little-known pockets of civilization throughout the European world where he would take her – with her driving. According to Huffington, he was the strictest of task-masters when it came to writing, bringing her a plaque for her desk that said, 'You can break every grammatical and syntactical rule consciously when, *and only when*, you have rendered yourself incapable of breaking them unconsciously.' Despite Levin's left-leaning and libertarian views, Huffington would remain a staid political conservative throughout the seven years they were a couple. Still, it is likely Levin also laid the foundation that made it easy for Huffington to swerve politically left or right, depending on her inclinations at different stages of her life. 'Bernard did say that going to bed with him was a liberal education,' she says.[43]

Her reign as Cambridge Union president during the early 1970s coincided with societal turmoil that spilled over from the 1960s and left many of her contemporaries questioning the twentieth century's more rigid, traditional values. In this political climate, it was inevitable that the Union would at some point debate the rising women's liberation movement. On this, it appears, Huffington had much to say. During a televised Union debate on the subject – and in her own writings and speeches of that period – she lampooned the notion that women should cast off their 'female' roles within the home in order to be 'liberated', insisting that rather than defending equal opportunity, equal pay and equal rights for women, the women's liberation movement 'attacks the very nature of women and, in the guise of liberation, seeks to enslave her'.[44] Responding to those who regarded her views back then as patently anti-feminist, Huffington said more recently that she feels her perspective on this was, to the contrary, quite prescient: '[It's] really very much where we are now as women. Which is, it doesn't have to be either/or, you don't have to give up being a mother or having a family in order to have a career. But at the time, it was very contro-versial, because having a family at the time was considered part of social conditioning.'[45]

Huffington's televised arguments at the Union created a stir. They also caught the attention of an ambitious UK book publisher, Reg Davis-Poynter. 'I never thought of being a writer,' she says. 'That was an accident . . . That was really the biggest starting point, because that's what led an English publisher writing to me and saying I would like to commission a book from you.'[46] Having only just learned English, Huffington was reluctant to accept the offer. She also was finishing her studies at Cambridge and trying to prepare for graduate school. 'I was twenty-two at the time. I had not thought of writing a book . . . I wrote back and said, "Thank you very much, I can't write."' The publisher wrote again and asked, 'Can you have lunch?'[47]

They met in London. Davis-Poynter offered her £5,000, 'which wasn't a lot,' she says, asking her to write a rebuttal to a best-selling feminist book he had just published, *The Female Eunuch*, by Germaine Greer. The pro-women's liberation movement treatise authored by Greer had done well, and Davis-Poynter was looking for a follow-up to ride off its success. According to Huffington, she was extremely hesitant. 'If it turns out you can't write,' the publisher told her, 'I will have lost £5,000. If you can, I'll have a book.'[48] She agreed to the contract and began the arduous process of writing, 'which put me on an entirely different career path', she says.[49]

*

In 1972, she graduated with a master's degree in economics, with honours. Recalling how her mother had never been educated, Huffington sought to extend her own educational dowry: she began a new slate of studies at the London School of Economics, preparing a PhD thesis on Mediterranean Countries and the Common Market, a precursor to the European Union. 'Entirely self-taught herself, [my mother] didn't care much if her daughters ever married, but cared deeply that we get university degrees,' Huffington says.[50] She may not have been tempted to return to Greece at that time, as it remained in the grip of a brutal military regime, a period marked by continual uprisings and deaths. It would not be until 1981 that Greece would join the European Union, seen as a saving grace by Greeks wary of any more warring in south-east Europe.[51] Upon leaving Cambridge, Huffington originally intended to go to graduate school at the John F. Kennedy School of Government at Harvard University, but, instead, remained in London. Levin may have had a role in influencing her decision to study at the LSE, as he had studied there and flourished under such intellectual giants as the British political theorist and economist Harold Laski and the Austrian–British philosopher of science, Karl Popper – both among the twentieth century's greatest thinkers.

Even for the legendary multitasker, this may have been one too many projects to juggle. Huffington never got her PhD but, in 1973, she released her book, *The Female Woman*, dedicating it to her mother, Elli. It was a runaway best-seller. In the book, Huffington set out her own brand

of feminism, flatly rejecting the popular idea of 'the liberated woman' in favour of what she dubbed 'the emancipated
woman', who sought equal status to men for 'distinctly
female roles', which included both a place in the home as
a mother – a role to which Huffington herself personally
aspired – as well as the right to lead in the workplace. 'The
main point of *The Female Woman*,' she has said, 'is that
we needed to give all women equal respect for the choices
they make. Nobody expected it to do as well as it did, but
suddenly, I had all these offers to write more books.'[52]

The Female Woman, whose cover consisted of an en-
larged, soft-toned, smiling photo of Huffington, her hands
serenely clasped, created an uproar. Huffington wrote
bitingly of women who saw 'virtue, altruism and sacrifice
as signs of weakness', and presented scientific, zoological
and chromosomal evidence to buttress her argument that
'men and women differ in every cell of their bodies' and
that though 'emancipation means the removal of all bar-
riers to female opportunities, it does not mean compelling
women into male roles by devaluing female ones.'

Some sections of the book remain controversial and
others now certainly seem dated, such as Huffington's
famous riposte to Greer, predicting that the women's liberation movement 'would transform only the lives of women
with strong lesbian tendencies'. Other sections have held
up better and, to this day, align neatly with Huffington's
abiding world view of womanhood: 'The truth is that there
is no contradiction between femaleness and independence; between femaleness and self-realization; between

femaleness and intelligence. Today's female woman integrates and fuses these qualities without strain, without inner conflict.'[53]

The polarizing effect the book's publisher had hoped for was achieved, with sales to match. *The Female Woman* drew blistering criticisms and bold plaudits. The US magazine *Kirkus Reviews* faulted Huffington for limiting the scope of her research on the women's liberation movement to mainly Greer and a few others, damning her with faint praise: 'This is by no means a stupid book . . .' was the most positive assessment it could muster. The *Guardian* was kinder, noting that Huffington had taken on the women's liberation movement 'single-handed' and was 'fighting it off as if from behind the last barricades of femininity'.

Huffington received her first taste of sustained national media attention and agreed to interviews for newspapers, magazines, radio and television. *The Female Woman* did so well, her publisher even sent her on a transatlantic book tour. At this point, she says, she was making enough money to begin to support herself. It was a position she never thought she would be in so early in her adult life. In *On Becoming Fearless*, she wrote of this time with some gratification. 'Until then, I had never been quite sure where the money would come from to pay my fees at Cambridge, or my rent in London. Would my father be able to send me what I needed this month? Would my mother's brothers be willing, once again, to help her give her daughters things they were not quite sure we really needed – like an education abroad?'[54]

Huffington was invited to speak at women's conferences, literary roundtables and to conservative groups. While in the US to promote her book, she was interviewed by Barbara Walters for the *Today* show. Huffington had no idea who Walters was. Being interviewed by an American media icon 'didn't mean anything to me' at the time, she recalls, adding that if she had been interviewed in Greece by a well-known TV personality, it would have been a lot more 'terrifying'.[55] Huffington, who was becoming very skilled at making fast friends, would not only see Walters again, Walters would one day be a bridesmaid at her wedding and the godmother to her first child. 'Arianna's whole life has been an act of will,' the *Guardian* wrote in 2014. 'She willed herself to Cambridge University, despite growing up Greek and poor with her single mother in a one-bedroom flat in Athens. She willed herself to the presidency of the Cambridge Union. She willed herself on to the national stage, age 23 . . . and it's just gone on from there.'[56]

The media whirl surrounding Huffington's first book was, for her, highly intoxicating. She received offers to write more books, requests to write articles and do media appearances, speaking on the plight of women in a changing, post-modern world. Huffington says her book was translated into twenty-five languages. In addition to the dozens of offers to keep writing about women, she was also asked to host a television show. In short, Huffington was inundated. 'And I knew one thing: I knew I had nothing more to say about women! I had said everything I knew. I had nothing else to say. And I didn't want to become a professional women's writer, I knew that . . . So I didn't know what I wanted to do. But I knew I didn't want to do that.'[57] As her book tour wound down, Huffington began to feel empty, deflated. Alone, in her hotel room, she had an 'existential crisis.'[58] A she writes in *The Fourth Instinct*:

> A bestseller published around the world had brought me things that I thought would take a lifetime to achieve: financial independence; offers to lecture, to write books, to appear on talk shows . . . Yet behind all my apparent confidence, there grew a cloud of uncertainty – a confusion between secular seductions and spiritual yearnings, between hopes for the ephemeral and glimpses of the eternal. I remember it as if it were yesterday. I was sitting in my room, in some anonymous European hotel, during a book stop on my tour. The room was a beautifully arranged still life. There were yellow roses on the desk, Swiss chocolates by my bed and French champagne on ice. The only noise was the crackling of the ice as it slowly melted into water. The voice in my head was much louder. 'Is that all there is?'[59]

This moment in the hotel room, Huffington says, at age twenty-five, would be her first step on a spiritual 'journey of a thousand miles'. She decided to turn down the professional offers to write about women and focus anew on a different project. Her first book had been the idea of her publisher. The next one, she decided, would be a book entirely of her own, a sort of call-to-arms on a topic she had found absorbing while at university and would continue to long after. 'I decided to sit down and write a book that I wanted to write, which was a book about the crisis of political leadership in the West. Sounds grand, right?'[60]

She locked herself in her Chelsea flat in London and embarked on a deep dive into 'the role of leaders shaping our world',[61] working all hours of the day and night. During this time, she remained fiercely in love with Levin, who would weigh in on her work and read through her pages. Huffington leaned heavily on Levin for guidance, and he gamely obliged, lending her 'a large part of his library' and reading 'every version of the book, from the slim first outline to the monstrous first draft'.[62] Levin's sway was immense in ways both large and small. In the book's opening acknowledgements, Huffington genuflects to his passion for classical music, thanking the Austrian composer Franz Joseph Haydn, as well as the Italian opera composer Giuseppe Verdi for providing Levin-approved background music to her labours. 'Most of the book was written to Haydn's 104 symphonies,' she writes, 'and I am deeply indebted to him for providing the perfect musical accompaniment and a better stimulus than any amount of black coffee. I am equally indebted to my neighbours for putting up through all hours of the night not only with Haydn's symphonies, but even with some of the more clamorous passages of Verdi.'[63]

In truth, Huffington's sophomore effort did not come

easily and she frequently worked herself into a state of exhaustion on the book. 'I would write until I couldn't stay awake, sometimes into the early hours of the morning,' she recalls in *Fearless*. Whether consciously or unconsciously, she felt enormous pressure to perform under Levin's tutelage and to validate her promise as a writer, researcher and thinker. And after her debut best-seller, it was a book 'I thought the world was incredibly impatient waiting for.'[64]

Once the writing was completed on her manuscript, Huffington says, 'I don't remember ever before or since having been as happy with the work I'd done. So, imagine my surprise when publisher after publisher rejected it.'[65]

It was almost like starting from scratch. Huffington pitched her book around to more than thirty publishers yet could not get a single one to accept it. 'By rejection 25, I was really concerned,' she says. At night, she lay awake, plagued by self-doubt and wondering if she had chosen the wrong career path. Just as she had in her childhood, when her father struggled to support himself in the craft of journalism and writing, she found herself once again worried about money. '"What if the success of my first book was a fluke, and I was not really meant to be a writer?" I would ask myself in the middle of many a sleepless night. And this was, after all, not just a theoretical question. It was also a crassly financial one. "How am I going to pay my bills?" I had used the royalties for my first book to subsidize writing the second and now that money was running out.'[66]

After dozens of rejections, she briefly entertained giving up on her manuscript and getting 'some kind of a real job'. The decision was agonizing, but she decided to keep trying, noting, 'my desire to write turned out to be stronger than my fear of poverty.'[67] Walking into a Barclays bank in St James's Square, Huffington met a banker, Ian Bell. 'With nothing more to offer than a lot of Greek chutzpah, I asked him for a loan. And with a lot of unfounded trust, he gave it to me,' she recalls. To this day, Huffington says she still isn't sure what made her walk into that bank and ask to speak with the manager. 'I've always been grateful to Ian Bell . . . I still send him a Christmas card,' she says.[68] 'That changed everything. It allowed me to keep things together for another thirteen rejections and then, finally, an acceptance.'[69]

In all, thirty-six publishers passed on Huffington's book before New York-based Stein and Day agreed to publish it – on her thirty-seventh try – in the US (Stein and Day went bankrupt in 1987). The book, *After Reason*, was at last released in 1978, a book the *New Yorker* years later called 'a byzantine polemic against "political salvationism"' that reflected Levin's 'libertarian politics and orotund style'.[70] It was one of Huffington's earliest *cris de cœur* over what she called 'the bankruptcy of Western political leadership', in which, she argued, both the political left and right did far too little to help society's impoverished. She also gave due credit to voters, whom she regarded as partly to blame for 'our hypnotized acquiescence in this organized sham.'[71] It received some good reviews, but did not sell well and, by Huffington's own appraisal, was far too pedantic and cerebral to match the sales of her first book. 'If you read it now, it's incredibly dense and very academic and not at all flowing. But I still kind of use it as a reference book, because there's so much research about leadership.'[72] The book was also published in England under the title *The Other Revolution*.

Though not the best-seller for which Huffington had ardently hoped, the book may have been more important to the trajectory of her writing and political career than her first. 'The book was like a seed planted in my twenties that finally sprouted in my forties when I became seriously engaged in politics,' she says.[73] Arguably more than any other book Huffington ever wrote, *After Reason* reveals the underlying bedrock that allowed her eventually to mesh her conservative and liberal values so seamlessly later in life. The book's introduction, which hints at the person Huffington was to become, is almost hauntingly prophetic:

Our lives in the past decade have been increasingly dominated by political unrest, too much government, the concentration of power in fewer and fewer hands, and seemingly unending revelations of executive and legislative misrule. The takeover of life by politics is the single most important social development of the post-war period, and the threat that it poses to freedom and democracy is the most significant topic of public debate. But at the same time, the individual, increasingly dominated by impersonal and seemingly irresistible forces, has been searching, more and more urgently, for a spiritual path out of the closing trap.

This book makes the connection between this territory of the spirit and our Western political predicament.[74]

Aside from its prescience about the West's rising political obsessions in the days before the internet and 24-hour news television networks, the book represents Huffington's own struggle to reconcile the worldly knowledge she had gained from Cambridge and the certainty she felt, instinctively, that there were deeper truths to be found. It also forced her to prove her own mettle when events did not align, as every step of the book turned out to be a Sisyphean task. The experience showed she had the strength, tenacity and skills to bring her projects to fruition, even when her vision was not embraced or encouraged by others. 'Abundant passion and abundant hope – not to mention abundant nerve – pushed me past my financial fears', in writing *After Reason*, Huffington says. 'It is impossible to be fearless about money if we don't value other parts of our lives and ourselves more than we value our bank accounts.'[75] The book, which she dedicated to her sister, Agapi, was the first in which she would test-drive many of her earliest political philosophies – ones she would revisit and revise many times over in the years ahead.

To earn a living, Huffington returned to writing, doing reviews for the *Spectator*, articles for the British editions of *Vogue* and *Cosmopolitan* and a column for the *Daily Mail*.[76] She also had a knack for finding the public spotlight, co-hosting *Saturday Night at the Mill*, a British talk and entertainment programme on the BBC, with television

presenter Bob Langley. After a dozen or so episodes, however, she left the show, as viewers chafed at her supercilious
manner. Considering how Huffington's early experiences at
the Union drew criticism of her accent, it's more likely this
was the real reason for her dismissal. She continued making
appearances in 1979 and 1980 on a handful of episodes of
Friday Night, Saturday Morning, another BBC talk show,
in which she was interviewed by British broadcaster and
television host Ned Sherrin, one of Levin's media buddies.

Huffington learned early on that the limelight could also
draw negative attention – and she quickly had to develop
shrewd strategies for striking back. One British publication, the satirical magazine *Private Eye*, which was fond
of calling her the 'Vast Hellenic Scribe' and the 'Gigantic
Greek Pudding', went so far as to accuse her of cheating
to get into Cambridge. Huffington sued, tapping libel
barrister and future British Home Secretary Leon Brittan,
and the magazine backed off its claims, apologized and
reportedly paid Huffington an undisclosed sum for its
transgressions.[77] Huffington was also careful to retain her
place in heavy circulation within London's social vortex,
attending, as *Vanity Fair* remarked, 'every party of distinction, on the arm of equally distinctive men, most notably,
Bernard Levin'.[78]

She also began working on a new book encompassing
both her Greek heritage and her newfound spiritual inclinations, *The Gods of Greece*, which, in light of her feverish
social life, fell fallow swiftly, not to be rediscovered for years

to come. While toiling on it, Huffington had a conversation with a publisher, who instead persuaded her to pursue a biography of Maria Callas, one of the best-loved opera singers of the twentieth century who had recently died in 1977. Callas was an American-born Greek soprano and, as the English publisher who commissioned the book, George Weidenfeld, later told *New York* magazine, his notion to ask Huffington to write the book had much to do with her Greek heritage and physical traits. 'As I looked at [Arianna] in the haze of the London morning sun, I thought, "She likes opera, she looks like Callas, it's an obvious combination."'[79] Huffington says that when Weidenfeld first floated the idea, she resisted it. She was more interested in writing about politics, spirituality and leadership. 'And he said, "No, no, no, you need to learn to *tell a story*,"' she says. 'And I probably wouldn't have done it if I didn't need the money. By then, I had run out.'[80]

Huffington's tireless ability to leap from one project to another did not negate the fact that her constant strivings could exact a human toll. From her early midlife crisis at the end of her first book tour, through the travails of writing and getting her second and third books to market, she did not forget that longing she felt for greater spiritual sustenance. Throughout the 1970s, she started to bring Levin along with her on these personal explorations. Still deeply in love, they began, very publicly, to search for answers to their metaphysical questions, or 'as one of my more skeptical friends put it, *groping*', Huffington says.[81]

Starting where she always did, in the realm of books and ideas, she headed to Watkins Books in London and picked up the collected works of psychoanalysts C. G. Jung and Sigmund Freud. She also acquired the writings of Bhagwan Shree Rajneesh, the controversial Indian spiritual guru, as well as Yogi Sri Aurobindo, the Indian philosopher and poet, and others. 'I read everything I could lay my hands on . . . I just stayed in my flat in London, reading the collected works of Jung. It was very painful,' Huffington remembers. 'It was like knowing there was another dimension to life and that I wanted to experience it, knowing that nothing else mattered as much. It took me over completely.'[82] She also devoted herself to 'meditating for a regulation half-hour every morning'.[83] Both she and Levin understood well how fatigue, disappointment and disillusionment could weigh heavily on them. 'It was not that my life was not working,' Huffington wrote in the British Sunday newspaper the *Observer* in May 1979 of her spiritual journey. 'It was that something in me was convinced that there was more in me and more of me to experience.'[84]

In the *Observer* article, she said she had been deeply moved by a quote from the 1968 novel *The First Circle*, by Russian writer Aleksandr Solzhenitsyn: 'If you wanted to put the world to rights, whom would you begin with? Yourself, or others?' Huffington wrote this quote down and decided that she 'wanted to begin living what I had just finished writing'.[85]

For Levin, a non-practising Jewish man, embarking on a

spiritual quest with Huffington may have held some appeal in warding off his own bouts of depression. He had tried other remedies before and found them wanting. Not unlike Huffington's father, he could be susceptible to melancholia and despair. Huffington recalls Levin vividly describing his dark moods as 'the black dog' and 'the dark lair where the sick soul's desire for solitude turns into misanthropy'.[86] Throughout his life, he spoke of 'the gnawing', she says. In the introduction to an anthology of his columns, he described it as a feeling 'that ultimate reality lies elsewhere, glimpsed out of the corner of the eye, sensed just beyond the light cast by the camp fire, heard in the slow movement of a Mozart quartet, seen in the eyes of Rembrandt's last self-portraits, felt in the sudden stab of discovery in reading or seeing a Shakespeare play thought familiar in every line'.[87]

The thousand-mile journey led Huffington and Levin down a road many of their friends and colleagues did not want to follow them down and did not fully understand. It was, however, in many ways, profoundly foundational to the person Huffington was to become. 'I began to see how basically for people to find themselves spiritually, there had to be an element of service, a dedication to something more than ourselves,' Huffington says.[88] Greatly influenced by these ideas, in *After Reason* she called for a 'spiritual revolution' of Western democracies to safeguard individual freedoms, decrying how 'the pursuit of happiness has been reduced to the pursuit of comfort'.[89] In essence, it was an argument for the need to bring the spiritual dimension into everyday life. It was almost as though she were writing the book to herself.

Caught up in the age of 1970s enlightenment, Huffington dabbled in dream analysis, neuro-linguistic programming, encounter groups, New Age programmes such as EST, started by American self-help guru Werner Hans Erhard (EST stands for Erhard Seminars Training, a precursor to the self-enlightenment group Landmark Forum), and Lifespring, considered a 'potential cult', while communing with channellers and mystics – including one medium supposedly claiming to be linked to a 3,000-year-old man.[90] She travelled to India, New York and California, among other spiritual hot spots, to meet with self-anointed gurus and to attend seminars. Huffington did not just wish to read and write about spiritualism, she wanted to experience it in a way that would transcend her books, texts and lecture halls. 'I knew that I was in danger of succumbing to a powerful dose of religion to the head, of becoming yet another theoretician of self-awareness,' she wrote in the 1979 *Observer* piece. 'I was living out of the tragedy of our culture, seeking to live life, to capture and understand it, through the mind alone.'[91]

Some of the more popular spiritual role models at that time whom Huffington and Levin followed became highly controversial later. Not long after Huffington spoke of Rajneesh in the *Observer,* Levin travelled to an ashram in Pune, India, to write about him – a bearded guru whom Levin described for the *Times* in 1980 as the 'un-deified' God who gave 'a powerful sense that he is a conduit along which the vital force of the universe flows'. By the early 1980s, Rajneesh and his hundreds of followers left India to set up a ranch in Wasco County, Oregon, where they were subsequently blamed in 1984 for the largest act of bioterrorism ever to be carried out on US soil, poisoning 751 people in a failed attempt to hijack local elections.[92] No one died, but three of Rajneesh's top deputies were sent to prison. The group's leaders also were accused of participating in or enabling a pervasive culture of sexual coercion and predation.

Rajneesh, who went by the name 'Osho', was jailed and deported back to India in 1985, where he died five years later.[93] Huffington's representatives have consistently denied she ever visited the Oregon ranch or was involved in Osho's spiritual movement but, based on Huffington's own accounts, she travelled to the western US frequently at the time and even rented a home in California. She has openly remained a fan of Osho's teachings, which she referenced on social media as recently as 2014, while running *The Huffington Post*, featuring an inspirational quote from Osho on her Facebook page: 'When I say be creative, I don't mean that you should all go and become great painters and great poets. I simply mean, let your life be a painting, let your life be a poem.'[94] In 2015, *The Huffington Post* also started hosting and promoting a lifestyle blog called the 'Osho Times', which billed itself as a 'blog from a meditator's perspective, exploring the essential questions of how to fulfill our potential'.[95]

This brush with Rajneesh was not Huffington's only

foray into the teachings of messianic spiritual leaders in the 1970s. She also flew to New York to attend the 'Insight' training seminars of the Movement of Spiritual Inner Awareness (or MSIA, sometimes pronounced as 'messiah'), founded by another spiritual leader, the late John-Roger Hinkins. A coal miner's son from Rains, Utah, and a former high school English teacher, Hinkins had slipped into a coma during kidney stone surgery in 1963 and awoke, nine days later, claiming 'there was another being in me'. Raised a Mormon, Hinkins established a New Age church in California, teaching his followers 'the greatest challenge is not outer space, it's inner peace – the last frontier is inside.' Huffington, according to the *Washington Post*'s Stephanie Mansfield, met John-Roger at a friend's flat in London in 1974 and 'immediately set out to read everything he had ever written.'[96]

Huffington found her Insight trainings revelatory, writing later in the *Observer*, 'What if we are, each one of us, powerful creators – creating, allowing or promoting everything that happens in our lives? What if, contrary to all our belief systems that say nothing of value can happen in less than 50 years of hard slog, something invaluably valuable can and does happen . . . ?' Adapting these teachings alongside Levin, Huffington helped bring Insight seminars to London and promoted them. 'Insight is one of the many ways we can come closer to our reality,' she wrote in the *Observer* article. 'It is a way that has worked for me and I wanted to let you know that it is now available in London and may work for you.'[97] This was one of the first – but certainly not the last – times Huffington crossed the line between journalism and evangelism.

Encouraged by Huffington, Levin also became involved with Insight, which evoked scepticism from London's cognoscenti when Levin and Huffington decided to host a private gathering about their shared spiritual awakening, inviting around eighty people to a café on Regent Street. British–American columnist and essayist Christopher Hitchens, covering the event, was unrepentantly scathing. 'Let the record show that in October 1979 . . . Bernard Levin achieved the total state of self-absorption towards which he had been moving for so long. The venue was the Café Royal: amid incense and vaguely Oriental music, flanked by his companion [Huffington], Levin rose and told a large invited audience how they could be changed by investing £150 in a 50-hour "Insight training" . . .'[98] So startled was England's media establishment, the incident was highlighted again in Levin's obituaries in 2004. One attendee, writing for the *Guardian*, noted the audience was left visibly shaken over Levin's conversion. 'It was a strange experience to hear this paragon of logic, sceptical of all humbug, trotting out stories that normally he would have scoffed at. At the end of it, my neighbour turned to me and said, "I feel I have lost a friend tonight."'[99] *The Times*, which had published a number of Levin's columns on his spiritual enquiries, including the visit to Rajneesh's ashram in India, bemoaned this period of Levin's career in his obituary, stating that Huffington's 'interest in mystic cults . . . was to lead him into one of the more embarrassing episodes of his journalism – his hyperbolic praise, through a number of columns of the self-promoting guru, Bhagwan Shree Rajneesh, over whom he drooled embarrassingly.'[100] While some of the spiritual teachings, the *Guardian* said, gave Levin 'a measure of confidence, so that he was no longer so vulnerable and no longer shuddered when strangers approached him in the street,' it added, 'there are those who believe that the edge of his writing was blunted thereafter.'[101]

Considering how mysticism was often associated with Rabindranath Tagore, the writer who founded the university in West Bengal where Huffington had studied as a teenager, and the fact that Tagore, who won the Nobel Prize in Literature, was embraced by literary giants such as William Butler Yeats and Ezra Pound,[102] it may not have seemed out-of-bounds to Huffington to go on her own spiritual quest.

Flouting their critics, Huffington and Levin would remain affiliated with Insight and John-Roger Hinkins's Movement of Spiritual Inner Awareness throughout their lives. Huffington was ordained by MSIA in Paris in the late 1970s as a Minister of Light,[103] and awarded the highest level of secret initiation, 'Soul Initiate', which confers upon its followers 'the divine line of authority', according to a detailed account of the event in a 1994 article in *Vanity Fair*.[104] Soul Initiates are required to pray the secret names of God given to them by Hinkins, seen by his followers as the Mystical Traveler, and the chosen one of God on earth. Ministers can renounce their ministry, which is fully accredited in California to perform baptisms and weddings, but Huffington has never been known to do so. When *Vanity Fair* asked her in the same article if she was still praying the names of God given to her by Hinkins, she said, 'These are sacred questions . . . I pray. I'm not going to discuss how I pray.'[105] Huffington confirmed to the *New Yorker* in 2008 that she still remained affiliated with Hinkins, who died in 2014 and who she called a teacher, friend and 'way-shower'.[106]

Huffington's third book, *Maria Callas: The Woman Behind the Legend*, was published in the UK by Weidenfeld & Nicolson in 1981 to rave reviews. A bidding war erupted for serial rights between *The Times* – Levin's publication – and the *Observer*. Huffington credited much of her early success with the book to the advocacy of the *Sunday Times* editor, Harold Evans, husband of journalist and magazine editor Tina Brown. 'He decided to bid for serial rights and the *Observer* decided to bid against him. It was one of those strange things that happen.' While Huffington had received a paltry £6,000 for the book, in the end, it had fetched £180,000 for serial rights. 'It was a big success,' she says. 'What was supposed to be a little opera biography turned into a big, international book.'[107] The *Sunday Times* did a five-week serialization, with Evans working closely with Huffington on the photos and narrative to put together 'a great spread', she says, calling him an 'amazing editor'. The book was also published in the US by Simon & Schuster in 1981. Huffington dedicated the book to Levin, writing in the acknowledgements, 'Without his unfailing support and understanding, and without the long hours he spent reading, criticizing and improving, I wondered sometimes whether there would be a book at all.'

The Maria Callas book was praised for Huffington's ability to persuade a number of her sources to turn over rare documents, including decades of letters written by Callas to her godfather, as well as collections of private, informal photographs from the opera singer's life. In addition to showing the depth of Callas' suffering despite her fame, the book, according to *Time*, brimmed with colourful anecdotes. 'The foibles are fun; the gossip, especially about international high life, is entertaining,' it said. 'Huffington has entered the complex and contradictory mind of Maria Callas in an extraordinary way, and the result is a powerful story told movingly, yet without exaggeration,' wrote John Ardoin, one of the authors of an earlier book, *Callas: The Art and the Life – the Great Years*. His co-author, Gerald Fitzgerald, however, alleged that Huffington had lifted passages from their 1974 book.

An article in *The New York Times* in 1981 stated that 'at least two music critics and the authors of two earlier biographies about Maria Callas, the tempestuous singer who died in 1977, have charged that parts of a recent best-selling biography, 'Maria Callas,' by Arianna Stassinopoulos, have been taken directly from those earlier biographies – a charge that Miss Stassinopoulos and her publisher, Simon & Schuster, vehemently deny.'[108] In more than one instance, Huffington's book included passages about various Callas performances that mirrored Fitzgerald's word for word, *The New York Times* reported. Giving one example, the newspaper observed that Fitzgerald, in his own book, wrote how Callas, in her delivery of a song in Verdi's *La Traviata*, 'bows to the father's demands in the tender "Ah! Dite alla giovine," which Callas sang with her face inclined to the floor, her voice a mere whisper that somehow filled the theater.' Writing about the same performance in her own book, Huffington's passage says of Callas, 'She sang "Dite alla giovine," her renunciation of her lover in response to her father's plea, with her face inclined to the floor and her voice a mere whisper that somehow filled the theater.'

Another writer, Henry Wisneski, who'd written a different 1975 book, *Maria Callas: The Art Behind the Legend*, told *The New York Times* that Huffington used passages from his book as well. 'She did lift from my book,' he said, but added that he did not see it as plagiarism, because the copying was not extensive. 'All books are based on somebody else's work,' he shrugged.[109] Huffington's English publisher, George Weidenfeld, confirmed Huffington had only seen Callas perform twice, which made it plain that she would have had to rely on others' accounts of Callas' live performances to describe them.[110]

Huffington strongly rejected the charges, insisting she never copied full sentences. 'People can make allegations left, right and center,' she told *The New York Times*, 'but I can assure you there is not a single sentence, word for word, that I have lifted from any book. These are serious allegations coming from interested parties, especially when my book is a best-seller.' She dismissed the criticism as 'disappointment by authors whose books on Callas did not do as well [as hers did]'.[111] The matter was concluded out of court with Fitzgerald receiving a financial settlement that Huffington later stated was 'in the low five figures'.[112] Huffington told the *Washington Post* in 1987 that she believed she succeeded in winning Fitzgerald over during the deposition by using her newfound powers of spirituality and persuasion. 'It was truly miraculous,' she says. 'I sat there trying to practice and literally expanded myself to see his point of view.'[113]

The Maria Callas book, which took Huffington two years and six drafts to write, chronicled Callas's lengthy and futile pursuit of Greek billionaire Aristotle Onassis, who ultimately married Jacqueline Kennedy, widow of US president John F. Kennedy, in 1968. As part of her research, Huffington unearthed two revelations: she discovered that Onassis had continued to see Callas after his marriage to Jackie Kennedy and even planned on leaving Kennedy for Callas shortly before his death in 1975 (although this never took place). She also found out that Callas had, at one time, been pregnant with Onassis' child, which was reported years later to have been stillborn.[114] Callas was left childless, bearing a sorrow from which she would never recover. Callas's life, Huffington believed, was a cautionary tale of what happens when a woman squanders her world-class talents to chase society friends and a man. When Callas died of a heart attack just two years after the death of Onassis, who never stopped loving her but had betrayed her, Huffington concluded that what she had really died of was a broken heart. (In a famous lament, Callas had stated: 'First I lost my voice, then I lost my figure and then I lost Onassis.') In the end, Callas did not honour herself, and she paid the price. 'Don't believe you can write somebody's biography without total empathy,' Huffington told *New York* magazine in 1983 after the book was released in the US. 'I learned from Callas that you can't live an unbalanced life.'[115]

The experience of writing about Callas left her chastened. Huffington and Levin, throughout her twenties, had remained very much in love. But as Huffington approached thirty, she found herself at a crossroads. She longed to have a family. Levin was not of the same mind. After the success of the Callas biography, Huffington came to the difficult realization that 'the man I was deeply in love with . . . wasn't going to marry me . . . I desperately wanted to have children. He wanted to have cats. So, I decided the only way I was going to be able to have children and have all I wanted would be leaving him. Which was very tough, because I was still very much in love with him.'[116]

Huffington would occasionally tease Levin about his adoration of cats, which he regarded as having achieved the perfect balance of ambivalence and affection. He once wrote, 'Above all, I love the detachment of cats, their willingness to be loved but not to respond beyond a certain, very clearly defined point; no cat ever gave its entire heart to any human being.'[117] Levin's commitment and intimacy issues, Huffington says, were not something he regarded 'as a badge of independence and freedom like many men, but as a character flaw, almost a handicap'.[118] In his book *Enthusiasms*, written in dedication to her just two years later, in 1983, he said, 'What fear of revealing, of vulnerability, of being human, grips us so fiercely – and above all, why? What is it that, down there in the darkness of the psyche, cries its silent No to the longing for Yes?' It was a No, Huffington says, 'that often coincided with retreating into depression'. In *Fearless*, Huffington spoke at length about weighing her trepidations above leaving Levin against her desire to have children:

> I know how hard I worked to gain Bernard's approval. Because on some level I feared that I had fallen short – that if it weren't for my shortcomings, we would be spending our lives together. Rationally, I knew that his intimacy and commitment issues were his and had little or nothing to do with me, but irrationally I feared that it was I who wasn't enough. And as a result, I stayed long after it was clear that I was no longer being true to myself.[119]

After living such a grand life with Levin in London, Huffington couldn't bear to remain if they weren't going to be together. When she finally decided to leave him, she knew she could not just move to another city. She wished to move to another country, preferably as far as possible, across the ocean. 'I still marvel at what reserves of fearlessness I must have tapped into to be able to leave him,' she says. 'And not just to leave him – the first big love of my life, as well as a mentor as a writer and a role model as a thinker, but also to leave London and to change continents. But I had to. Our lives in London were so inextricably intertwined that I couldn't live there any longer. A quarter of a century later, I can still feel how painful that decision was.'[120]

While Huffington's mother did not mind waiting to be a grandmother, there was pressure from other quarters of the family for Huffington to get married and have children. 'When I was growing up in Athens, my grandmother was always planning my wedding,' she says. 'And when I was 21 and not married, she came saying to me, I do not understand why you are not married. You're not so ugly that you couldn't find a husband.'[121]

Although she and Levin were just as in love as they had always been, in December of 1980, at thirty years old, Huffington boarded a plane in London and left for New York. 'There was no real plan – that is what was so interesting,' she says. She had only the belief 'my mother gave me that life always has more imagination than we have. That it's like our plan is always less interesting than life's plan. If only we can be open to what life brings us. I'm not saying it's enough to just be there and good things happen to you – you know? You need to deliver.'[122]

PART 3

NEW YORK AND BEYOND

'I think I am drawn to people who can make things happen. I'm drawn to people who are doers.'

As Arianna Stassinopoulos set out for New York, she received one piece of valuable advice from George Weidenfeld, her publisher in England. 'Don't bother with men,' he told her. 'You'll only make the wives jealous. Concentrate on the key women, and if you play your cards right, you'll be a success.'[1]

While Huffington said there was no real plan, that was not quite true. She was careful not to come to Manhattan empty-handed. She arrived with a black book filled with contacts, as well as letters of introduction from her London friends that quickly opened doors for her. One of Bernard Levin's long-standing chums, Fleur Cowles, the writer, artist and one-time magazine publisher, wrote to White House Chief of Protocol Selwa 'Lucky' Roosevelt – a former journalist who had married the grandson of

President Theodore Roosevelt – speaking of Huffington in glowing terms. Roosevelt told *New York* magazine it was 'the first time in 30 years that Fleur's asked me to be nice to someone'.[2] British media executive Lord Bernstein of Craigweil introduced Huffington to the social circles of New York's artistic upper crust – most of them much older than Arianna – including film producer Sam Spiegel; playwrights Adolph Green and Arthur Laurents; stage and screen actress Kitty Carlisle Hart; and liberal political activist Marietta Tree, a New York socialite known for putting in the late nights with the Paleys, the Astors and the Warburgs, when not attending Truman Capote's black-and-white balls.[3]

Lord Weidenfeld, who, like Arianna, was known for his 'expansive ambition', according to *The New York Times*, helped smooth the way for her Manhattan entry, linking her up with some of the most socially powerful women in America. In the 1980s, Weidenfeld collaborated with Ann Getty, wife of oil billionaire Gordon Getty, purchasing Grove Press and building what they hoped would be a Weidenfeld-inspired New York publishing empire.[4] Bankrolled by Getty's husband, the son of J. Paul Getty, the British–American oil tycoon and industrialist, the publishing partnership did not last, but Huffington soon became very close with Ann Getty, who would introduce Huffington to her future husband.

The daughter of a farmer from California, Ann Getty married into appalling wealth. In the 1980s, *Forbes* twice named her husband the richest man in America. 'By all accounts', *The New York Times* wrote, Ann was 'a shy and very beautiful small-town girl' who had eloped with Gordon to Las Vegas in 1964.[5] Over a short period of time, Ann became extremely fond of Arianna, taking her under her wing and lunching and shopping with her.[6] Through Weidenfeld, Huffington also renewed her acquaintance with Barbara Walters, the *Today* host, who was, at this point, one of the biggest names in American television. Walters began joining Huffington for her ritual morning calisthenics each day.[7]

The timing of Huffington's arrival in New York was hardly incidental, coinciding with the US launch of her Maria Callas book by Simon & Schuster in 1981. Her launch into society helped her garner early attention and book sales. With her mother, Huffington rented a town-house on East 61st Street, a beautifully brocaded duplex with a spiral staircase, once owned by American actress and author Cornelia Otis Skinner, who had died of a stroke in 1979. Huffington soon was throwing stupendous dinner parties, entertaining artists, writers, media figureheads, celebrities, theatre and fashion folk and social icons. Her elegant fêtes became a staple of New York's East Side, with everyone from news anchor Dan Rather to broadcasting titan Bill Paley to Spanish opera singer Placido Domingo – a close friend of the Gettys – dropping in.[8] Huffington mingled with French couturière Pauline Trigère and the former *Vogue* editor Françoise de Langlade, first wife of Oscar de la Renta (both now deceased), as well as Princess Michael of Kent, a member of the British royal family said to be a frequent guest of Huffington's. The two had known each other since Arianna's London days.[9] Speaking to the *New Yorker* later, Barbara Walters noted how Huffington had taken the city by storm. 'Boy, she came to New York and, little by little, you knew who Arianna Stassinopoulos was,' she said.[10]

Lush descriptions of Huffington's life abound from this period. Magazines and newspapers offered ornate descriptions of Arianna and her mother presiding over 'tables strewn with peaches and figs' (*New Yorker*); 'Arianna's eccentric mother, whom one friend recalls walking barefoot through the apartment, wearing a full-length mink coat, burning incense' (*Washington Post*); and, finally, an article from *New York* magazine from July 1983, announcing Arianna's newfound social dominance in Manhattan, titled, 'The Rise and Rise of Arianna Stassinopoulos' and subtitled 'How the East Side was Won'. It reported, 'Arianna Stassinopoulos has become, in record time, a fixture in East Side social life, and without the advantages of wealth, a title, or conventional beauty. She has done it because she has been working – studying, observing, hustling – for this moment for nearly 20 years.'[11]

Huffington went out of her way to arrange dinner parties for those she liked and admired. She brought women friends to her home to go through her closet, urging them to try on designer trappings. And, the *Washington Post* noted, she was known for sparing no expense in pampering herself, 'going to the best manicurist, the best masseuse'.[12] *New York* magazine's Jesse Kornbluth called her 'well over six feet of woman, hair and high heels', her 'maquillage porcelain-perfect, the designer gown with as much yardage as a Yankee clipper'.[13] She even had a male social secretary, the magazine said. In 1987, Huffington confided to the *Washington Post*'s Stephanie Mansfield that she believed everyone had a blueprint in life. When she arrived in New York, she said, 'I set this challenge for myself, that whatever dinner I was at, to be able to make some kind of real connection with whoever the "blueprint" sat me next to.'[14]

When the *Post* pressed on why Huffington surrounded herself with only the influential, asking whether she perhaps promoted others simply to promote herself, the New York gossip columnist, Liz Smith, who was friendly with Huffington at the time, told the newspaper Huffington had no qualms about brazenly going after what she wanted. 'Look,' Smith said, 'there are a lot of people in New York with naked ambition, but you at least try and put a fig leaf on it.'[15] Yet Huffington had no need of a fig leaf. Ambitious, yes, but equal parts intelligent, articulate, polite – and completely unflappable – she fascinated her new friends and made no apologies for herself.

Even with her unfailing charm, selling the Maria Callas book in the US was not at all easy at first. (For one, it wasn't clear to an American audience why they should care about a deceased, if world-famous, foreign opera singer.) Huffington caught a lucky break when the word got out that the book revealed how Aristotle Onassis, the billionaire lover of Callas, had planned to leave Jackie Kennedy for Callas just before he died. Huffington, who had previously sent out 200 signed copies of the Callas book without much response, initially found herself turned down by the *Today* show and *Good Morning America*. But when her revelation involving a former First Lady and the wife of assassinated President John F. Kennedy suddenly surfaced, the book's sales got a boost and, in rapid succession, *Maria Callas* landed on book-of-the-month lists, *The New York Times* best-seller list and attracted a movie deal. According to *New York* magazine, the film contract alone earned Huffington 'a fast $1 million', her biggest known payday to date.

Huffington also was still trying to write a new book and, despite earlier fallout from the Callas plagiarism scandal in 1981, she received an even larger book contract from Simon & Schuster in 1982, with a reported price tag of $550,000, to write a biography of the deceased Spanish painter Pablo Picasso.[16] At the same time, she was also hustling to finish *The Gods of Greece*, the holdover project from the 1970s she'd set aside to write her best-seller on Callas.

In Huffington's preface to *The Gods of Greece*, a handsomely illustrated coffee-table book that also touches on her spiritual leanings, published in 1984, she explains how the gods of the past are not only 'very much alive today,' but provide insight into the future:

Because they are so natural, so human in their divinity, they can help heal our culture's split between the earthly and the sacred, the secular and the religious.

In the Greek gods, the eternal and the divine are fully at home with the ephemeral and the earthly. The natural is divine and, therefore, nothing is accidental or meaningless.[17]

This connection between the divine and sacred, the human and earthly, would be another pivot point that would continue to transfix Huffington. She also told the *Washington Post*'s Mansfield how writing about Hera, the wife of Zeus, in *The Gods of Greece*, was, for her, deeply affecting. Hera 'was longing to be fully met, matched and mated', Huffington recalled. When she read this, she said, 'I started crying. It was such a deep longing in me.'[18]

Even after leaving London, Huffington stayed in touch with Bernard Levin, who would remain a long-distance partner and confidant for the rest of her life. Her departure, it turned out, had been very hard for them both. 'A couple of months after I left London for New York, Bernard called me to tell me that he had decided to take drastic action,' she wrote.[19] Drastic action, for Levin was taking a sabbatical from *The Times* as a columnist and the *Sunday Times* as a book reviewer, without setting a date for his return. Levin told her that he wanted 'to follow the beckoning light wherever it may lead'. He travelled to New York to see her, but just eighteen months later, 'He was back at *The Times*,' she noted. They would never reunite as a couple but, she says, 'we stayed in close touch.'[20]

Huffington was still very much hoping to get married and have children. In her romantic life, she was described by her friends as much more liberal-leaning than she had been during her Cambridge years, dating a wide variety of suitors who were very much her senior and, for the most part, anything but conservative. Some of her more well-known escorts were, according to press clippings of the time, Werner Erhard, founder of the New Age self-help movement EST; billionaire philanthropist David Murdock; magazine publisher and real estate developer Mortimer Zuckerman (who harboured aspirations of attaining Democratic political office); and California Governor Jerry Brown, also a Democrat, for whom Huffington threw at least one opulent dinner bash that expanded, according to one account in *New York* magazine, 'from one table for 10 to five tables for 46'.[21] Guests whispered to one another, 'Who's paying for this?' All three men were Huffington's senior by a decade or more (in the case of Murdock, by nearly three decades). One fellow student from Huffington's Cambridge days recalls, 'I never saw her with anyone her own age; all of her suitors were quite a bit older.'

For a brief time, Huffington was thought to be so serious with Brown – a much-sought-after bachelor of the 1980s who also courted singer Linda Ronstadt – reports were leaked to the press that wedding plans were in the works. The rumours soon fizzled, though, as no one could publicly confirm it. One of Huffington's friends at the time later told *Vanity Fair*, 'She very much wanted Jerry. She was a liberal Democrat then. She felt he could become president with her behind him.'[22] *New York* magazine's Kornbluth openly speculated in 1983, 'Could Arianna have floated the

Brown item because she had concluded that no marriage was possible, and a little publicity would be the most she could derive from the relationship?' Liz Smith, the gossip columnist, suggested this was true. 'I was told by someone very close to her that they were about to announce their engagement,' Smith told the magazine. 'I called Arianna. I'm fond of her. I would have printed that they were "just good friends" if that's what she said. But she didn't say that. She said they'd had a lovely friendship and that it had gotten serious. I printed that. So, it amuses me that they acted as if *I* am crazy.' Huffington brushed it aside, telling Kornbluth, she had 'no idea' who misled the media. 'She is so fearless, so optimistic, so *innocent* about her own motives,' Kornbluth marvelled, it was no wonder Huffington shrugged off every misstep as though it never happened.[23] Such was the vintage of her wiles. Throughout her career, this would become a hallmark of Huffington's success – overlooking obstacles and forging ahead.

Wedding rumours notwithstanding, the Brown headline offered Huffington no shortage of cachet when it came to her matrimonial potential. 'The desire to get into society and find a wealthy husband is not a bizarre one,' *New York* magazine said, but it wondered at Huffington's 'ability to keep up with this crowd on a writer's earnings'. Even with her book advances and the Callas movie deal, there must be 'taxes, agents' and lawyers' fees', among other expenses, for example, settling the Callas plagiarism suit. How did she pay for all of this, plus travel, the hotels, the gracious New York townhouse featured in *Town & Country*, the 'clothes, maids, limos, a secretary, two researchers and her own Xerox? Surely there must be a secret backer,' Kornbluth theorized. 'But Arianna Stassinopoulos scoffs at these suggestions,' he wrote. 'See her instead, she says, in a strange town, with incense burning and scarves draped over the lamps and Mozart coming from the tape recorder in her hotel suite as her Mont Blanc pen covers a sheaf of paper a night.'[24] Huffington, embracing her role as the modern Aphrodite, was already creating an ethereal and mythic version of herself.

Poring over dozens of cartons of research materials on Picasso, Huffington, in 1985, decided she had to get away from the city and its overwhelming diversions to focus on her next book. She left for Los Angeles, renting a Coldwater Canyon home in the Santa Monica Mountains, with a tennis court and swimming pool, that offered plenty of new distractions. She was able to afford such luxuries, she told the *Washington Post*, because 'I spent everything . . . I never saved in my life.'[25]

The new lodgings also allowed her to live closer to her California-based guru, John-Roger, with whom she frequently consulted about her life, and whose non-profit foundation was based in Santa Monica. In addition, Huffington became close with John-Roger's good-looking assistant, Michael Feder, though she denied later to the *Post* the relationship was serious.[26] In the 1980s, she, John-Roger and Feder travelled on junkets for the Church of the Movement of Spiritual Awareness. In an interview in 2016, Feder talked about how he had discovered John-Roger in 1982, and how much the church had meant to him and its other followers. 'I felt like we had the secret of life, the magical formula to having an amazing existence, and nobody knew about it. It was this little mom-and-pop organization, doing this little thing, and it was the best thing on earth. I wanted everybody to know about this . . . it's very addicting,' he said.[27] Back in 1987, Huffington talked about having a similar experience, saying that meeting John-Roger had been a turning point of her life. She said she'd 'contributed a lot of money to the movement' and that she had attempted to recruit her friends to it, but could only 'plant seeds'.[28]

In 1984, John-Roger reportedly presided over Huffington's baptism in the River Jordan, under the auspices of the Church of the Movement of Spiritual Awareness, joined and witnessed by a number of the other MSIA followers.[29] In 1985, Huffington accompanied him and Feder on a visit to Calcutta to present Mother Teresa with an 'Integrity Award' from John-Roger's foundation. According to the *Los Angeles Times*, John-Roger 'appeared in *Interview* magazine, awkwardly posed beside award recipient Mother Teresa', while 'Arianna Stassinopoulos, who was ordained an MSIA minister in 1978,' wrote in the preface of her interview for the publication that John-Roger was her 'way-shower and friend'. (In MSIA parlance, 'Way-shower' was a special, spiritual term used by John-Roger in reference to himself as the leader of his estimated 3,000 followers.)[30] In another interview, John-Roger declined to directly confirm if Huffington was acting as a minister in the MSIA church, explaining, wrote the *Post*, 'Each person has to work out all that information for themselves. If she wants to verify that, it's her business.'[31]

John-Roger's foundation acted not only as a spiritual movement, but also a charity and 501(c)(3) non-profit organization, granting awards and throwing annual black-tie dinners attended by celebrities and covered by *Entertainment Tonight*. Other award recipients included Stevie Wonder, Ralph Nader and Desmond Tutu. During one of MSIA's formal events, the *Washington Post* wrote, 'Actress Zsa Zsa Gabor told a reporter she knew all about John-Roger. "He teaches you to live with yourself," she said, adding with a smile, "And he teaches you how to become rich."'[32]

This focus on attaining personal wealth and influence played a primary role in John-Roger's upwardly mobile church, which sold its Insight training seminars to individuals, as well as to blue-chip companies like Lockheed Martin and McDonnell Douglas (later merged into Boeing). It even sold its programmes at one point to the US Social Security Administration.

Insight programmes promised to deliver personal growth and increased productivity to clients, with an emphasis on seizing opportunities.[33] John-Roger's mantra to his followers was, 'Use everything to your advantage.' Huffington who, as the *Post* put it, followed those teachings 'religiously', told the newspaper in 1987, 'There is something about being in the flow of life where you don't need to be pushy. You accept the cosmic timing. Everything is a stepping stone.'[34]

As in London, many of Huffington's close friends and associates in America struggled to understand how she had come to align herself so closely with John-Roger, who claimed to have 'come down through Christ' and, who, according to the church's more controversial dogma, ranked himself as higher than Jesus Christ. John-Roger was also known for occasionally encouraging his followers to believe that they were quasi-deities themselves, able to change the weather, dismantle nuclear weapons and act as direct instruments of God. At one Insight training, Feder said that John-Roger, who he called 'J-R', persuaded him to believe he could heal a man from multiple sclerosis. 'J-R stops, looks at me, and goes, "It's your turn,"' Feder says. 'I'm like, "What?" I get up, walk over to [the man], touch him a bit, I turn him around and the guy kind of straightens out. I'm so shocked. I look at J-R and he just nods his head and goes like, "Don't you get this? It doesn't matter who it is." It was such a huge teaching moment that I realized that if I could get out of the way of my own stuff and be present, the [Spirit is] willing to do the work.'[35] The idea of setting aside one's ego to directly channel the divine was a common lesson of John-Roger.

When questioned closely about what she had personally derived from her Insight teachings, Huffington likened it to rapid-pace psychoanalysis. Detractors of John-Roger, she said, were only objecting out of fear. 'Analysis is okay,' she told the *Post*. 'All that Insight is is really another form of it. Except that it's faster. It fit my personality. Dealing with something intensely and then dealing with the keys I was given through life, rather than going through something every week.'[36]

Ann Getty served on the benefits committee for the annual black-tie dinners of John-Roger's foundation, but a number of Huffington's other friends felt John-Roger seemed too eager to promote himself among the rich and powerful. 'I didn't particularly take to John-Roger,' Washington socialite Ina Ginsburg told the *Post*, who met him at Huffington's dinners. 'I don't see how anyone else would.'[37] Barbara Walters echoed those sentiments, telling the *New Yorker* in 2008 that Huffington's devotion to John-Roger had left her unsettled. 'I did not take to him the same way that she had,' Walters said. 'That caused a pause in our relationship and, I think, of some others.'[38]

John-Roger did not present the only uncomfortable guru situation. It was around this time, in the mid-1980s, that the Indian spiritual leader she and Levin had followed, Rajneesh, also known as Osho, and a group of his devotees were implicated in the mass-poisoning in Wasco County.[39] It appears Huffington is still a fan of Osho's, posting his quotes on her social media feed in recent years and, while she was editor-in-chief at *The Huffington Post*, publishing a laudatory article about him in 2016.[40]

While Huffington was influenced by a wide array of spiritual teachers throughout her life, John-Roger undoubtedly had the greatest impact. She revealed to the *New Yorker* in 2008 that she still relied on his church's guided meditations. 'The first day I spent with her, in San Francisco, she handed me an iPod, the contents of which included a guided meditation entitled "Innerphasing for Multidimensional Consciousness,"' the *New Yorker*'s Lauren Collins wrote. 'I clicked on it. A voice intoned, "Let go of any restrictions of limitations that you've placed on yourself and let God fill the space where the restrictions or limitations were."'[41]

Huffington's relationship with John-Roger would reverberate throughout her life. Despite the multitude of criticisms that have been levelled at the spiritual leader, it is abundantly clear she drew a great deal of inner peace and personal growth from his guidance. Discussing Insight training seminars shortly after she was reportedly ordained a minister in his church, Huffington wrote that, for her, the 'practical, day-to-day effect is a deep acceptance of life as a spiral, ascending, but with plenty of downturns, and a greater ability to detach ourselves from our life's melodrama and learn to hear the inner wisdom underneath our own and other's opinions.'[42] To this day, people who work closely with her say that this focus on big-picture goals over passing concerns remains a major pillar in how Huffington approaches life.

In 1985, Ann Getty introduced Arianna to R. Michael Huffington Jr., her future husband. Getty encountered the boyishly handsome Huffington on a trip to Tokyo in July of that year. Telephoning Huffington, she excitedly announced, 'I've met the man you're going to marry!'[43] Both Getty and Michael Huffington came from families extremely famous for their oil wealth. Michael was the son of a Texas multimillionaire, Roy Huffington, who amassed much of his fortune from Indonesian oil and gas drilling. Roy was the chairman and founder of the Houston-based company Huffco. Michael had graduated from Stanford University, received an MBA from Harvard and worked for future US president George W. Bush in Texas in 1979 and 1980. He'd even interned for Bush's father, the first-term congressman George H. W. Bush in 1968 (who would go on to become president in 1989). As of 1985, when he met Getty, he was director and executive vice president at his father's company.[44] While Michael Huffington was a businessman at the time, he harboured political ambitions of his own.

Getty arranged for Michael Huffington to meet Arianna at the opening of the San Francisco Opera in early September 1985. The two met in the parlour of J. Paul Getty's luxurious Pacific Heights mansion. Michael was dressed in black tie and Arianna was in her usual flowing raiment. To Michael Huffington, she was a woman of mysterious origin. Other than that she was an author, he knew very little about her. While sitting alone, sipping a drink, Michael says he saw Arianna enter the parlour. The two quickly moved away from the crowd to become better acquainted, taking seats on a French settee.[45] 'He came straight up to me and took me aside,' Arianna recalls, adding: 'He asked me, what was the most important thing in my life? I said, "God, my spiritual life." He said, "In mine, too."'[46]

By the next morning, the *San Francisco Chronicle* had run a picture of them on its society pages, the caption beneath reading: 'Arianna Stassinopoulos Looks Adoringly at Michael Huffington.' Arianna, accustomed to press coverage, did not bat an eye. But Michael, intensely private and wholly unaccustomed to the limelight, was quite startled by the fanfare. He spent the entire weekend with Arianna. When they parted, however, he hesitated to ask for another date and the moment slipped away. Arianna left for Paris. She continued to work on her Picasso book and the two did not see each other again for some time.[47]

It was Ann Getty who called Michael to see if he would escort Arianna to the grand opening of the 45-room, Georgian-style 'farm' of MetroMedia billionaire John Kluge and his wife, Patricia, near Charlottesville, Virginia. Arianna was flying in from France and the three met in New York to travel to Virginia on Huffco's private plane. Arianna was paired up with a Virginia senator at the dinner, but she instead spent the entire evening with Michael.[48] While she and Huffington strolled the grounds of Albemarle House, she told the *Post*, 'that was the time we declared ourselves to each other.' During the walk, 'I said to him, "You seem very mysterious." There's a part of Michael that doesn't immediately open up to everybody. He said to me, "I'll only fully reveal myself to the woman I marry."'[49]

The courtship progressed swiftly during the last quarter of 1985. There was a trip to the La Costa Resort near San Diego to visit Barbara Walters (Walters told Michael Huffington, not jokingly, that Arianna's friends wondered if he would be able to measure up – she genuinely did not see the match), and the Huffco Christmas party in Houston, to which Michael never brought a date, where he showed up with Arianna that December. (His parents, eager for grandchildren, were charmed by Arianna and, despite her not being a Texan, gave the thumbs-up.) 'I was most attracted to Arianna because of her intelligence and seductiveness,' Michael told the *New Yorker*. 'I had never met a woman like her.'[50]

Arianna, who had often had suitors very much her senior, found in Michael Huffington not only a man close in age – he was just a few years older – but someone who also towered over her in height, even in high heels. Michael was six foot three. He was also reportedly worth $250 million, according to the *Washington Post* in 1987.[51] (This turned out to be a highly inflated figure, as Huffington's fortune was tied up in the stock of his father's international energy business and Huffco had yet to be sold.) Arianna told the newspaper at the time: 'It wasn't that Michael has a lot of money, but I did think to myself, though, "Is he really all that?" It's the combination. I mean, starting with the fact that he's taller than me. I've always been conscious of men that are shorter than me.'[52]

They also had a great deal in common. Both Arianna and Michael had grown up facing steep financial travails. Both their fathers had regularly gambled and had a penchant for taking jaw-dropping risks. While Arianna had watched her father start up newspapers that folded, resulting in devastating losses, Huffington had witnessed his father, a Harvard-trained geologist and post-war 'wildcatter', sink all his money into drilling oil wells in the 1950s that, more often than not, were dry holes. Huffington did not grow up wealthy and his father shuffled him and his family from one dilapidated apartment to the next in a mad quest to chase oil throughout Texas and New Mexico, before finally striking a well in Borneo in 1972, transforming him, as *Esquire* put it, into 'one of the great Texas oilmen of the twentieth century'.[53]

The courtship was short, consisting of just a few months. Arianna's engagement was a *fait accompli* by New Year's Eve, when Michael Huffington visited her home in California, along with her mother and close friend, Oscar-winning actress and spiritual writer Shirley MacLaine. (Arianna was a devotee of MacLaine's New-Age mysticism and best-selling spiritual books.)[54] That evening, Arianna passed a wand around the table to her guests, asking each to make a wish. When it was her turn, Arianna wished to be pregnant in the New Year. Michael wished her wish would come true.[55] The couple were engaged before the end of January. *The New York Times* ran the headline, 'Arianna Stassinopoulos To Be Married', with no mention of who Michael Huffington was until the final paragraph of the item. Instead, the announcement catalogued Arianna's credentials and book projects.[56]

Aside from her parents, the first person Arianna told of her engagement was Bernard Levin. Through it all, he had remained her ideal partner and confidant. 'He flew to New York for the wedding a week early and was by my side right down to helping me place the 400 guests at the post-wedding dinner,' she wrote afterwards. 'The man I had so desperately wanted to marry and spend my life with was now helping me with all the logistics as I was about to walk down the aisle. It didn't make any sense and yet it was perfectly natural.'[57]

On 12 April 1986, just three months after becoming engaged, Arianna Stassinopoulos walked down the aisle in a candlelit ceremony at St Bartholomew's Episcopal Church on Park Avenue in New York. The wedding, former US Secretary of State Henry Kissinger famously remarked, featured everything 'except an Aztec sacrificial fire dance'. The ninety-minute, black-tie ceremony was accompanied by the tones of trumpet, flute and organ and the couple had crowns suspended over their heads. The guests invited included MacLaine, Lord Weidenfeld, Princess Michael, Pulitzer Prize-winning author Norman Mailer, fashion designer Carolina Herrera, *Cosmopolitan* editor-in-chief Helen Gurley Brown and an armada of Washington lawmakers, insiders and members of New York society. In addition to Levin, other former beaux of Arianna's in attendance were Mort Zuckerman and Jerry Brown. Barbara Walters and President Reagan's Chief of Protocol, Lucky Roosevelt, were among Arianna's bridesmaids, donning mauve silk dresses that made the gossip pages, as four syndicated columnists, among them Liz Smith, were also there. Arianna wore an $18,000 wedding dress. 'It was really like a royal wedding, in a way,' Ina Ginsburg told the *Washington Post*. 'I think [Arianna] tried to get Placido Domingo to sing, but he was in Europe.'[58]

Ann Getty paid for the reception, which reportedly cost $300 a head – a larger bill than she had expected – with caviar, smoked salmon, Dom Pérignon and veal Florentine served at the grand feast following the ceremony. At the reception, Michael Huffington's father, Roy, stood up and exclaimed, 'We had almost given up on Michael.'[59] Terry Huffington, Michael's sister and another bridesmaid, reckoned her brother had waited so long to marry because his expectations for a wife had been so high. 'I felt he was looking for the perfect woman,' she said.[60] Press coverage of the event was characteristically over the top. According to the *Post*, one publication, *Women's Wear Daily*, 'trilled' the limos were 'three-deep', and 'so romantic was the setting, one would not have been surprised if the voice of the turtle dove had been heard through the congregation, if not the land.' Arianna's mother, *Women's Wear Daily* reported, was seen after the nuptials relaxing and smoking a cigar. 'Now that I've got Arianna married off, I can go back to Greece,' she quipped.[61]

Arianna told the *Post* the marriage led to a period of her life where she finally felt 'in bloom' and that, despite being a writer long accustomed to fending for herself in the publishing world, she somehow felt she would be supported. 'I always knew I would be taken care of,' she told the *Post*. 'I always felt that I wouldn't have to worry about money.'[62] While some of her friends, like Walters, didn't understand the attraction between the couple ('Michael is a very nice man, but he certainly didn't have Arianna's spirit,' Walters told the *New Yorker*), Arianna was smitten, telling the magazine, 'the word that so many of my friends used about him was "adorable"'.[63] Together, the Huffingtons would ascend easily to greater heights, but their shared ambition would eventually lead to a series of debilitating setbacks that would result in the dissolution of their marriage.

After honeymooning for three weeks – which included the Caribbean, a sortie to the estate of Princess Margaret outside London and a trip to Venice on the Orient Express – Arianna was eager to get back to her still-unfinished Picasso book, which she'd put on hold for months during her courtship with Huffington. With an eye towards living a political life, the Huffingtons settled in Washington. Their close friend Lucky Roosevelt threw them an A-list bash at the F Street Club, welcoming them to Washington's society.[64]

Leaning on his Bush connections (the Huffington family was well known for its hefty donations to the Republican party), Michael received an appointment at the Pentagon as Deputy Assistant Secretary of Defence for Negotiations Policy under then-President Ronald Reagan. This, effectively, made him an arms-control negotiator. In her first year of marriage, Arianna became pregnant and she set up quarters on Q Street in Georgetown, where she hired a full staff and social secretary. To help make ends meet, Arianna continued to give paid lectures and make appearances. The couple lived in a palatial rented townhouse consisting of five storeys, with a glass elevator and a two-storey living room that opened out onto a garden, described in great detail by the *Washington Post*. The living room was decorated in yellows, beiges and pinks and, over the sofa, Arianna hung a picture of a woman with a crystal ball. On the table below, she placed a crystal ball – a wedding present from MacLaine. Next to the telephone, Huffington also laid a heavy pink candle. 'I come down and light the candle and chant inwardly,' she told the paper, referencing John-Roger, adding she would evoke the many names of God. When the *Post* pressed her about following the guru, Huffington protested, 'I'm not a follower of John-Roger, because it's not something to follow. He's a man who said very clearly that all the answers are inside.'[65]

Arianna's office was on the top floor of her Washington townhouse, where she worked on the Picasso book and also composed toasts for her dinners, often weaving in famous quotes. 'I make headings,' she told the *Post*, adding that she did not like to bring her notes to dinner, instead committing her toasts to memory, so as to appear spontaneous.[66] Levin, at one time, had written toasts for Arianna, so it is likely this habit was learned from him.[67]

In writing her books, Arianna would often pack the pages with similarly gleaned wisdom, but it was at these dinners where she would test-drive new ideas she would pick up, harnessing her guests as a sounding board. (A decade later, she would use the internet in the same fashion, as well as many forms of social media.) Huffington would even tape-record her dinner gatherings for later review, including for use in her own writings, according to some press accounts.[68] For much of her life, she told the

New Yorker, she studied people and how they interacted, socialised and absorbed ideas. 'When I was in England, I would literally, like, watch everything,' she said. 'I would watch pop-culture shows. I would read pop-culture magazines. I remember sitting there and watching *Laugh-In.* And I did the same when I moved to New York. I made a point of studying what I had missed.'[69] Washington, a place of ideas and passionate debate, had already become her favourite city, she told the *Post* in 1987. 'It's a little bit like being in college. People discuss things earnestly. Things matter. I like that intensity.'[70]

The Huffingtons enjoyed the high life, dining at the White House – First Lady Nancy Reagan was said to be delighted by Arianna – and getting named in W magazine's line-up of 'Nouvelle Society'.[71] When Michael Huffington turned forty, Arianna threw a star-studded fête, with author Norman Mailer abruptly announcing that Michael Huffington would one day become president.[72] (Huffington had become friendly with Mailer after he wrote his own screed on feminism back in 1971, called *The Prisoner of Sex,* a book even more controversial than Huffington's on the subject.)

The Huffingtons' time in Washington was unexpectedly short-lived. Arianna's pregnancy, which began in 1986, ended in stillbirth at nearly six months, in the spring of 1987. For days, she fought to save the child on a hospital table in her living room, her legs elevated. Her husband and her mother took up vigil nearby, praying.[73] The loss of the child razed her completely. 'There were all these fears, because I didn't quite know why I lost it or whether I would get pregnant again,' she says.[74] Arianna expected to have her baby in the summer of 1987 and then finish her Picasso book, now long overdue. In deep grief, she found herself unable to contend with a tangle of Washington society engagements she could neither shirk, nor fulfil. Once again, she reached out to Levin. She recalls how he came immediately:

> Bernard insisted that I not cancel the benefit I was chairing for the Folger Shakespeare Library in Washington. 'I'll fly out and do all the work for you,' he said. 'It will take your mind off losing the baby.' And he did fly out, and he brought [the actress] Maggie Smith with him, and he did do all the work for me, writing the most brilliant piece for Smith and [actor] Alec McCowen to perform. He once again was there for me and it was a huge success.[75]

Press reviews of the event were glowing. Arianna was grateful to Levin for taking the helm. But the loss of the child haunted her – a son she and Michael had named Alexander. She spoke to others about a terrible recurring dream while she was pregnant in which she saw the baby, but his eyes would not open.[76]

In the days following the miscarriage, Michael Huffington spent some time in New York, praying at an Episcopal monastery with his close friend, the best man at his wedding, Michael Bryan Becker.[77] Huffington later said he blamed Arianna's feverish schedule for the loss. Arianna, her mother and Agapi remained together in mourning. When he returned from New York, Huffington, who had not particularly liked his Washington job, was ready for a change. He wanted to cash out of his stake in Huffco and move with Arianna to California in the hope of eking out a more stress-free life.[78]

The couple looked at more than a hundred homes throughout the Los Angeles area before settling on Villa Ruscello, an idyllic, $4 million Mediterranean-style mansion in Montecito, California, set in four acres of cascading gardens, with a swimming pool, pool house, tennis courts and stunning views of the Pacific Ocean. They were severely financially overstretched at this point, according to Michael in an interview with *Esquire*'s David Brock, but the home, nestled in the hills of Santa Barbara County, was a bargain.[79] They couldn't resist purchasing it.

For Huffington, the arduous process of cashing himself out of his father's energy business would take some time, requiring him to tap into his Wall Street connections and work closely with his dad, Roy, while living in Texas, which also offered enormous tax benefits. Contacting global investment bank Goldman Sachs to assist in arranging for Huffco's acquisition, Huffington lived apart from Arianna for years while he toiled to finalize the sale. In 1990, he at last succeeded, offloading the company to a Taiwanese consortium for a reported $500 to $600 million.[80] Michael's share of the company, he told *Esquire*, came to around $80 million – a relief, no doubt, for the Huffingtons. He was still living in Houston, but the windfall would allow them to reunite in California in 1991, where Michael would take up residency and begin building the kind of life they had dreamed of, free of acute financial stress.

As Huffington laboured alongside his father in Texas, Arianna, back in Montecito, put the finishing touches on the Picasso biography, finally released in June 1988. Levin, turning sixty that year, travelled to California to keep her company. Arianna says Levin appeared to be struggling with some minor health issues, so she took him for a medical check-up. 'He had come to stay with me in Santa Barbara and we had made the rounds of doctors in Los Angeles to find out why he kept losing his balance or not being able to retrieve certain words,' she says. 'Looking back, it is astonishing that nobody diagnosed it . . .'[81] Levin was suffering from early-stage Alzheimer's, but it would be years before he would find out.

In the summer of 1988, Michael Huffington went with Arianna to promote her Picasso book across America. They also attended the Republican National Convention in New Orleans, where she unexpectedly fainted in mid-August. Arianna was pregnant again.

With news of her pregnancy, her life would change dramatically. It would be several years before Arianna would publish another book. The Picasso biography would also keep her hands full. With its release, she found herself suddenly embroiled in a heated debate with the international art establishment over her scathing analysis of Picasso's art and life. Published under her newly married name, Arianna

Stassinopoulos Huffington, the book, *Picasso: Creator and Destroyer*, first appeared as a massive, 30,000-word excerpt in *The Atlantic* magazine – owned at the time by Arianna's former beau Mort Zuckerman. Even before the book became available on shelves, the *Washington Post* wrote, it 'already has readers gasping at its revelations about the great man, even as they must wonder at some of the biographer's fanciful leaps of judgment'.[82]

The sneak peek in *The Atlantic* raised a furore, as the book portrayed Picasso as 'a mean-spirited womanizer and wife-beater whose creative output was one vast exhibition of his own tragic life', according to the *Los Angeles Times*. By way of example, the newspaper noted that the book described how 'Picasso once stamped out a cigarette on a mistress's cheek, and that one of his wives and one of his mistresses committed suicide', even as it revealed how the artist's paintings exposed an 'ever-shifting love life', in which Picasso's 'ugly characterization of a live-in lover was often painted at the same time as a beautiful representation of a new, secret mistress'.[83] The book was written in a highly charged, visceral fashion that played up the inherent sadism of the artist himself.

The New York Times, in a review, grudgingly recognized Arianna's detailed, if shocking, reportage of Picasso's cruelty to many of the people in his life who were closest to him – children, wives, relatives, mistresses and friends – while faulting her for describing the evolution of his art in 'the sketchiest of terms', as well as the book's 'hyperventilated prose' and 'melodramatic presentation'.[84] Renowned

British art critic Robert Hughes of *Time* magazine went so far as to hurl personal insults, calling Huffington 'the fraud Arianna Stassinopoulos'[85] and proclaiming the biography to be 'worthless as scholarship'.[86]

But the brickbats belied an agenda suggesting much of the backlash had to do with protecting the artist's legacy. 'I found myself in a battle with the art establishment,' Arianna recalls. 'My sin was that I had dared criticize Picasso as a man, even while acknowledging his artistic genius . . . The art world would not forgive me for exploring the destroyer part [of the artist].'[87]

Long before she had completed her manuscript for the book, Arianna met with Paloma Picasso, daughter of the legendary Spanish painter and a celebrated fashion designer in her own right (she would later collaborate with Tiffany & Co.). Arianna hoped to have access to the late Picasso's archives. Paloma made it known following their meeting that 'she was sorry she had ever spoken to Arianna', reported the *Post*, and 'she would not grant access to the Picasso archives'. Calling the rebuff a 'misunderstanding', Arianna told the *Post*: 'The art world tried to set Paloma and me against each other.' Not to be stymied, Arianna instead won over Paloma's mother, Françoise Gilot, who became a close friend while she researched the book. When Arianna married in 1986, Gilot gave her a painting made by a friend of Picasso's, depicting a dark-haired woman who looked uncannily like Arianna.[88] In fact, the two women became so close that, years later, when Arianna republished *The Gods of Greece* with Atlantic Monthly Press in 1993,

Gilot contributed the book's accompanying paintings and illustrations.

As a result of their friendship, Arianna became privy to private details of Picasso's life, many of which Gilot had not included in her own biography of Picasso (primarily because he had still been alive at the time it was published; Picasso died in 1973). In the past, Arianna had staunchly maintained the only way to write a biography was to do so with great compassion for her subject. She did this with Maria Callas. But with Picasso, she took a different tack, highlighting his intense psychological and physical abuse of the people in his orbit. Gilot, who had been the artist's mistress for nearly a decade and the only woman ever to leave him, encouraged Arianna to write the biography with a strong feminist slant.[89] The result was a much more personal and intimate portrait of the artist than perhaps many Picasso fans and art critics wished to see. 'If you challenge a cult figure, it's inevitable there'll be a reaction,' Arianna told the *Los Angeles Times*. 'Those who represent the established point of view don't want to have it challenged.'[90]

The biography was highly lucrative for her. But it also led to a fresh spate of claims over her lifting material for the book from the four-volume PhD thesis of heavyweight Picasso scholar Lydia Csato Gasman, who, in reference to Arianna, told *Vanity Fair*'s Maureen Orth in 1994, 'What she did was steal twenty years of my work.'[91] Gasman had been the first to come up with the 'creator-destroyer' reference to Picasso and felt that Arianna's book cannibalized large portions of her research, while scarcely crediting her in the source notes.

Gasman, now deceased, told *Vanity Fair* she had wanted to take legal action, but didn't file a copyright infringement suit, because her resources paled in comparison to the wealth of the Huffingtons. She did confront Arianna, though. 'I told her she was an intellectual kleptomaniac,' Gasman told *Vanity Fair*. At one point, she said, Arianna had cried, and asked, 'Don't you think I've added anything?' Gasman was furious and said that Arianna told her, 'I didn't mean it. I think like you.'[92] In the end, nothing came of it, and Arianna publicly denied Gasman's allegations. The book attracted an offer for a television miniseries and resulted in the film *Surviving Picasso*, released in cinemas in 1996, depicting the turbulent relationship between Gilot and Picasso, with Anthony Hopkins starring as the renowned painter. Arianna received half a million dollars for the film rights.

In the preface of her Picasso book, she wrote, 'I was both fascinated and appalled by his unparalleled power to invent reality in his life no less than in his art and to persuade [others] to inhabit the reality he had created, however big the gulf between it and truth.' And, she added, with no trace of irony, 'I was struck by his instinctive brilliance in using publicity to build his celebrity and then his legend.'[93]

PART 4

WASHINGTON AND CALIFORNIA

'Unless people are determined to remain skeptical about my transformation, there is enough evidence that this is real.'

With Picasso wrapped, Arianna devoted the next few years to nesting and to family. After she lost her first child, she says, 'I spent my next pregnancy utterly terrified. So much so that, even though I was 38, I refused to have amniocentesis, because it carried a tiny risk of miscarriage. Instead, I simply prayed that the baby would be healthy.'[1]

She gave birth to her first child, Christina Sophia Huffington, at California's UCLA Hospital on 1 May 1989.[2] Her husband, mother and sister were all in attendance and, just after the birth, Arianna wrote, she had an out-of-body experience. 'I was looking down at myself, at Christina, at the tuberoses on the nightstand, at the entire room. For I don't know how long, I hovered in that state of almost intangible peace.'[3]

With her daughter's arrival, 'My fear of childbirth finally

dissolved,' she says. Her second child, Isabella Diana Huffington, was born almost exactly two years later, on 15 May 1991.[4] At forty years old, Arianna's two daughters were the long-hoped-for dream of decades finally come true. Michael Huffington, still residing in Houston, returned at last to take up permanent residence in California following Isabella's birth. Arianna's mother and sister, who often lived with her throughout her adult life, stayed with her in Santa Barbara, helping to care for her growing family.

The Huffingtons were no longer in Washington, but politics was never very far from their minds. With Michael out of the oil and gas business, the couple began to look into his chances at running for office – in particular, taking a congressional seat in their home California district. The wider Huffington family's energy empire had long supported Republican causes in the US South-West and in California, where Huffco had based some of its operations, and the family had many conservative connections throughout the country.[5] Michael Huffington himself was a major donor to the Grand Old Party (GOP) and its leaders, like Georgia congressman Newt Gingrich, who was about to become the fiftieth speaker of the House of Representatives. Huffington had never run for public office before, but he had been involved in politics since working for George H. W. Bush in the late 1960s. With his wife's support, he decided to wade onto the national political stage. Such a path had always felt natural to Arianna. 'Ever since I could remember, I was interested in politics,' she says. 'And being Greek, you know, it comes in your DNA. I always considered my book on political leadership [*After Reason*] in my twenties as a demonstration of that, but it was really only when I got to this country and after I did my biography of Picasso that I got more involved.'[6]

Michael Huffington first ran for Santa Barbara's congressional seat against a long-serving conservative incumbent, Bob Lagomarsino, who had held the post for eighteen years. After spending more than $5 million – making it the most expensive House race in American history at the time – Michal Huffington won the 1992 election by just five points, shocking the GOP political establishment.[7] The Huffingtons packed up and moved back to Washington for a two-year congressional term that began in 1993. They also bought a second $4 million home in the conspicuously affluent Foxhall Road section of Wesley Heights.

Throughout Huffington's run, Arianna and Michael worked closely together to build his platform and craft his political positions. (Unlike many Republicans, Huffington was pro-gun control, pro-choice and supported the full gamut of gay rights and the rights of gays to serve in the US military, a reflection of Arianna's views.) Arianna managed the books, the press releases and even on occasion showed up for debates against Huffington's opponents, causing many to believe she was the sole mastermind of his campaign.[8] Michael Huffington scoffed at this notion, telling *People* magazine, 'I'm the guy who has the power drive here. I'm the guy on the front line. She ain't.'[9]

Following Huffington's win, Bernard Levin came to visit Arianna at the family's new home in Washington. It was 'the hardest time', she writes of Levin's difficult days battling Alzheimer's:

By then, I was living in Washington and he came to stay with me. The medium he had mastered – words – now kept eluding him. It was such a cruel turn of fate. The man who could recite entire Shakespeare passages without faltering was now struggling to find a simple, everyday word lost in the recesses of his memory. 'I fell to speculating,' he wrote once, 'about what it would be like to be a prisoner in reality instead of fantasy, and came to the astonishing and disturbing conclusion that provided I could read and write what I liked, and had a congenial cell-mate (or better still, a sentence of solitary confinement), I would not find it nearly so terrible as I surely ought to.' But the key things that would have made his prison bearable were reading and writing and now they were becoming tragically hard. And, increasingly, all that was left was the prison. 'I can't take this,' he kept saying. 'I'd rather be dead.'[10]

There would not be much more time left with Levin, but Arianna would continue to visit him in London to the end. During her final visit in which his personality was still fully intact, she met him for lunch and brought her daughters. 'He put on a show for the girls: the old Bernard: charming, debonair, funny, on top of the world. Christina and Isabella, who had known him since they were babies, since he was always in and out of our lives, were now old enough (12 and 10 at the time) to appreciate the glimpse of the old fire they got just before it was extinguished.'[11]

As Michael Huffington began his first term in the House in January 1993, a new US president, Bill Clinton, was also just starting his own first term in the White House. Eight months after taking his seat, Huffington announced he would run for the Senate against California Democratic incumbent, Dianne Feinstein. It would be a close and bitterly contested race, with fellow members of Congress, political pundits and the media targeting Arianna Huffington and her husband with a series of escalatory and vicious attacks. Michael was criticized, variously, for having almost no legislative record; for refusing to release his tax returns; for being a 'cipher' for his wife's political ambitions; and parlaying his millions into purchasing the kind of political power that might one day land him in the White House. 'Fueled by his father's money and his wife's ambition, Texas millionaire Roy Huffington Jr. is trying to buy his way into 1600 Pennsylvania Avenue in 1996, after brief stops in the House and the Senate', wrote *Vanity Fair*'s Maureen Orth in 1994.[12]

Arianna also was a subject of singular scrutiny. 'If anyone thinks she hasn't seen herself in the White House yet, then you don't know Arianna Stassinopoulos Huffington,' Peter Matson, her former literary agent, told

Vanity Fair.[13] Arianna, as far back as the 1980s, had been repeatedly queried about her possible interest in becoming First Lady of the United States, at one point telling the *Washington Post* she had certainly considered it. 'If you are meant to deal with it, you just know what you are to do,' she said.[14] Her striving, however, drew no shortage of sceptics, with one article in *Los Angeles* magazine labelling her 'the Sir Edmund Hillary of social climbers'.[15] The media onslaught would be some of the most virulent Arianna would ever face and, for the rest of her career, she would not forget its lessons. She and her husband responded by keeping a stoically united front. Appearing side by side in an interview with Charlie Rose in 1994, the Huffingtons spoke supportively of each other and their goals. They also unapologetically portrayed themselves as a conservative power couple to rival Bill and Hillary Clinton. Michael Huffington told Rose, 'We're together as a team, but we don't share power like the Clintons do. We share ideas, and we share our love for each other, and we share our children with each other ... For the price of one, you get two.'[16]

Another obstacle in the campaign was the media's intense examination of Arianna's decades-long affiliation with John-Roger. In her story for *Vanity Fair*, Orth noted that John-Roger was 'a self-proclaimed god' who had been accused by well-respected members of the press of engaging in 'mind control, electronic eavesdropping, and the sexual coercion of male acolytes' – all charges he denied, she said.[17] In the article, which was nominated for a National Magazine Award, Orth questioned Arianna about whether she had ever received payments from John-Roger in exchange for helping him find new recruits or introducing him to rich and powerful people. (An earlier *Vanity Fair* piece, published by Bob Colacello in the 1980s, had reported that some of the more prominent guests at Arianna's wedding had been apoplectic at being seated next to John-Roger and among his followers.)[18] Arianna denied receiving any payments and told Orth that her earnings came primarily from her books and lecture fees. 'Nobody's been a guru to me,' she said, although she did confirm public documents unearthed by Orth showing she still contributed money to John-Roger. When asked why she did so, Arianna answered, 'I believe in the work that he's doing with people – his teachings.'[19]

Near the start of the Senate race, in February 1994, the *Los Angeles Times* ran an article underscoring Arianna's spiritual mission within her husband's campaign, with the obscenely lengthy headline: 'Eyes on a Cosmic Prize: Arianna Huffington wants to do more than help her husband win a seat in the Senate. She is also trying to raise politics to a higher plane.' As part of Arianna's 'ideal future', it wrote, 'a "critical mass" of spiritually inclined citizens would succeed where government had failed, volunteering time and money en masse to care for the tired and poor.'[20] In a speech Arianna gave at a hotel in Costa Mesa, California, the location of the Huffingtons' campaign headquarters, she told the crowd, 'It is not enough for Clinton to fail for us to succeed. Ultimately, we need to provide the American people with an alternate vision . . . We do our part and God meets us halfway. That's why I'm a conservative. Because conservatives believe in the individual.'[21]

As her husband ramped up his campaign that year, Arianna released her book *The Fourth Instinct: The Call of the Soul*, which neatly bookended her earlier polemic, *After Reason*, published almost two decades earlier. Both books highlighted how a spiritual revolution could solve political and societal ills. The 'fourth instinct,' she wrote, was the longing of the human soul to fulfil a greater purpose than the three basic needs of survival, power and sex. Arianna told Charlie Rose the book's message strongly aligned with the 'overarching theme' of her husband's Senate campaign, since both she and her husband believed that 'volunteer, private-sector initiatives' could not only feed the soul, but also ultimately 'replace the welfare state'.[22]

When Rose pressed Arianna on the critics who charged that she was running her husband's campaign and personally wished to run for political office herself, she promptly dismissed the notion. 'My life before I married Michael was a public life to the extent that I was a writer, journalist, doing television,' she said, adding, 'My way of trying to influence what's happening is through ideas, through writing, through speaking, not through policy. And that will always be the case.'[23]

But the public remained unconvinced. As *Esquire*'s David Brock wrote afterwards of Michael Huffington's run for Senate, 'Many people made fun of him for being a dilettante, for being deluded, for being a puppet. These people paid a lot of attention to his ambitious wife, Arianna, and said that she seemed to be in control of Michael's mind, and they made more fun of him because she sometimes even showed up to debate his opponents in his place. "Where was Michael?" these people said. "Who is this guy?"[24]

During her husband's campaign, which ran concurrently with the release of *The Fourth Instinct*, Arianna recommended that all Americans in a position to do so contribute at least one hour of service a day. In her book, which brimmed with quotes from Albert Einstein, C. S. Lewis, the Dalai Lama, Joseph Campbell and the New Testament, she wrote, 'The greatest tragedy of the modern welfare state is that we have allowed it to deprive us of a fundamental opportunity to practice virtue, responsibility, generosity and compassion.'[25] In its summary of the book, *Kirkus Reviews* noted the multitude of quotations from legendary thinkers showcased in it. 'Our author seems to be whisking us around some great cocktail party where we meet fascinating people without getting a chance to know them. Thus, she gives an impression of glibness in spite of her sincerity. Profound ideas, superficially treated.'[26]

Throughout the media blitz, Arianna's appearances, stump speeches and rapidly rising public profile made her a bigger fixture in the public eye than ever before, especially as her husband's campaign was becoming one of the most expensive, at that time, in American history. Her appeal to the soul of the Grand Old Party, the *Washington Post* wrote, made her the 'would-be Tom Paine of the spiritual revolution'.[27] But Arianna's spiritual message was also drawing fire. The press coverage of Michael Huffington's run for the Senate grew particularly searing in the final days, taking what the *Los Angeles Times* called 'a weird hop' in November 1994 'with national media and Democratic spin doctors suddenly blasting Arianna Stassinopoulos Huffington, wife of Republican candidate Mike Huffington, for her involvement with spiritual teacher John-Roger and his Church of the Movement of Spiritual Inner Awareness'.[28]

For a full week, the highly popular 'Doonesbury' comic strip branded MSIA 'a cult' and referred to Arianna as 'Arianna-John, Minister of Light'. One comic strip, in October 1994, featured two Doonesbury characters discussing the Huffingtons, with one asking, '[Michael] Huffington's married to a cult minister?' To which the other responded, 'It's getting too weird to be a conservative.'[29] Arianna publicly distanced herself from John-Roger and MSIA, saying she was a devotee of the Greek Orthodox Church and emphasizing her Christian values to voters. Following her disavowal, an MSIA church leader called the media melee a 'witch hunt', telling the *Los Angeles Times* that Arianna had enough of a 'track record' with John-Roger's church that any question of her involvement would 'take care of itself'.[30] Explaining her behaviour years later, Arianna told the *New Yorker*, 'I was feeling very defensive. I was trying to explain something that I shouldn't have tried to explain. Because it was a different realm.'[31]

Michael Huffington's professional standing, like Levin's, was questioned in light of Arianna's spiritual leanings. (Privately, Michael Huffington confided that he disliked John-Roger and 'competing for his wife's attention with this spooky man who seemed to have a hold on her,' *Esquire*'s David Brock wrote.)[32] Yet her entire life, Arianna would never renounce her commitment to John-Roger and his teachings, or her unswerving faith in the critical importance of having an active spiritual life.

Ultimately, what turned out to be the largest setback in Michael's Senate race would not be MSIA-related. 'As the campaign drew to a close, Huffington's internal polling showed him a few points behind, but closing fast,' Brock recounted, who was, at the time, a friend of the Huffingtons. 'And then, news that Mike and Arianna employed a nanny who was an illegal alien made the front pages throughout the country. As soon as the story broke, he dropped six points.' The Huffingtons' nanny, who had been employed while Michael was still living in Houston in the late 1980s, was, by this time, a beloved member of the household. According to Brock, Huffington wanted Arianna to fire the nanny, but she refused. 'The indefatigable [Arianna] Huffington, whose failure to comply with the laws governing household help, probably cost her husband the election', Brock wrote in his 2002 book, *Blinded by the Right: The Conscience of an Ex-Conservative*.[33]

Michael Huffington spent $28 million in the race against California Senator Feinstein, but lost by less than 2 per cent of the vote – an election so close that it required a recount.

The midterms that year saw the Republicans take both houses of Congress by storm, but Huffington was not to join them, despite having spent more on his campaign than any other non-presidential race in American history. Afterward, Ed Rollins, the former Reagan campaign strategist who Arianna persuaded Michael to hire to help steer him to victory, remarked that the race did not bring out the best in the Huffingtons. But he reserved his strongest critique for Arianna, who he believed was willing to do virtually anything to win. 'She was the most ruthless, unscrupulous and ambitious person I'd met in 30 years in national politics, not to mention that she sometimes seemed truly pathological', he wrote in his 1996 book, *Bare Knuckles and Back Rooms: My Life in American Politics*. Rollins added, 'Her allure and style were only a veneer· the soul of a wily sorceress lurked underneath.'[34] Noting the Huffingtons nearly won the election – losing by only 160,000 votes in the end – Rollins credited their wealth as a major factor in almost beating Feinstein. 'You can fool all the people all the time,' he said, 'if the advertising budget is big enough.'[35]

Ever resilient, Arianna 'emerged afterward as a bigger name than her husband', according to *Playboy* magazine.[36] As Brock detailed in his book, she would soon become Washington's 'leading social light in the new GOP power structure'.[37]

By the close of 1994, Michael Huffington had spent well in excess of $30 million of his oil fortune on national elections and was finishing his term in the House. After Arianna worked so tirelessly to support her husband's career in Washington for the past two years, he agreed to double her allowance and stay in the capital through the presidential election of 1996 so that she could hire additional staff to embark on a career as a political pundit.[38] Over the next several years, Arianna would throw herself into a staggering array of media projects, encompassing television, radio, a syndicated newspaper column, book deals and even the occasional sitcom or film cameo. In 1996 she even made an appearance on an episode of the television series *Roseanne*.[39] Arianna passionately embraced the 'compassionate conservatism' movement, which sought to apply traditionally conservative views toward the improvement of the welfare of society. (She later told the *New Yorker* it was around this time she began giving 10 per cent of her income to charity.)[40] She also became a hostess to the right, holding what she called 'critical mass' dinners and salons at her Washington home – 'decorated as a gilt-encrusted Italian palazzo', according to Brock – with the aim of 'narrowing the differences between liberals and conservatives by identifying middle-ground solutions, beyond partisan labels, to social problems'.[41]

Arianna forged friendships with a wide cross-section of both Republicans and Democrats, urging conservatives to be more socially conscious and do more to help the needy. She was still opposed to big government and wanted even stricter US immigration laws (which was noteworthy, considering she had just become a naturalized American citizen herself), and she also began to strongly align herself with Republican Newt Gingrich, who, in 1995, became the

Speaker of the US House of Representatives. Gingrich had been named *Time* magazine's 'Man of the Year' for leading the 1994 'Republican Revolution' that ended four decades of a Democratic majority in the House. In addition, Arianna hosted a talk show on right-wing cable channel National Empowerment Television, which encouraged GOP grassroots movements, and joined Gingrich's conservative think tank, the Progress and Freedom Foundation.

Gingrich first contacted Arianna in 1993 after she gave a speech on C-SPAN titled 'Can Conservatives Have a Social Conscience?' In it, she encouraged the GOP to reflect on the Bible's promise that individuals will be judged by how they treat the most vulnerable of humankind. 'This is exactly what we should be doing,' Gingrich told her afterwards. He even integrated elements of Arianna's message into his own inaugural speech when he became House Speaker. Well into the 1990s, Arianna and Gingrich would bask in each other's support, though Arianna says she eventually became disenchanted with his time as Speaker, because Gingrich did not care enough about 'the fate of the middle class, jobs and what's happening to the poorest Americans'. She later told the news website *Politico* she felt that Gingrich merely paid lip service to creating a social safety net for society's most vulnerable after making 'these really powerful statements' on the issue. 'If he had followed through on his rhetoric, he would have been a very different leader,' she said.[42]

Political alliances, both on the right and the left, along with a steady stream of books and media appearances from the 1990s into the 2000s, would not only allow Arianna to bolster her public profile as a media commentator, but also would become the foundation upon which she would build *The Huffington Post*. Despite her husband's very public Senate campaign loss and the damaging exposés on the Huffingtons released during the election, Arianna would achieve such total media saturation that nearly all negative press would effectively be obliterated. To those who laughed at her and her husband (or, as Rollins did, went so far as to call them 'arrogant seekers of power'), Arianna simply laughed back, deploying a potent mixture of humour and disregard that neutralized any vestigial detractors. Morton Janklow, a top-tier New York literary agent who had known Arianna since her arrival in New York in the 1980s and negotiated the advance of her Picasso book, told *Vanity Fair*, 'There are two schools of thought about Arianna. One is that it's all deliberate and calculated and she's ruthless. The other is that she really convinces herself beforehand. She sells herself first.'[43] In the same *Vanity Fair* article, one of her friends, Eva Haller, a philanthropist and activist, observed of Arianna, 'It's like watching a magician appear and disappear and make things look better than they are.' Some of Arianna's 'friends are so envious and jealous,' she said, 'they can't appreciate the art form.'[44]

In one of the most effective countermeasures to her husband's campaign loss, Arianna appeared throughout the 1996 presidential election season on Comedy Central's *Politically Incorrect* cable television programme, hosted by comedian Bill Maher. As part of a running segment called

'Strange Bedfellows', she appeared as the bitingly witty, conservative foil to liberal comedian Al Franken, subsequently endearing herself to millions. The skit not only presented her in a new light, putting her comedic talents on display before a national audience, but also allowed her to openly play up both her intelligence and sex appeal. Appearing together in a bed covered with an American flag duvet, she and Franken wore pyjamas and posed as a politically divisive couple. Their conversations consisted mainly of poking fun at each other and arguing over the latest current events. Franken called Arianna an 'evil' Republican and made light of the foibles of her husband's campaign. Huffington would respond breezily by emasculating Franken. A typical exchange:

> Al Franken: 'I am in bed with the beautiful and evil Arianna Huffington.'
> Arianna Huffington (in frilly nightgown with pilgrim collar): 'We're not having sex!'
> Al: 'Not . . . yet!'
> Arianna: 'We want to stress that because basically although my role in the Republican party is to bring compassion to Republicans, I am not compassionate enough to have sex with Al Franken! . . . I actually get a tax-deduction for lingerie!'

Arianna Huffington later defended Franken when he was plagued by accusations of sexual misconduct, eventually stepping down as a US senator in 2018. She stated that

Franken had never acted inappropriately with her. (Referencing the #MeToo movement, in which women told their personal stories of sexual harassment and assault, Huffington wrote, in response to those who dismissed her defence of Franken, 'I thought the point of this moment was to believe women's accounts of their own experiences.') In the 'Strange Bedfellows' series, she and Franken debated a range of issues, not excluding immigration, during which Arianna – now a US citizen – would often shout, 'I am legal!' As part of the skit, she also lampooned American attitudes toward immigrants. Sitting in bed with Franken, she remarked, 'Most conservative women I know would not take a low-paying, low-scale, unpleasant job of being in bed with Al Franken . . . It had to be an immigrant doing it!'

Franken teased Huffington about the nanny scandal that derailed her husband's Senate run, announcing in one segment that the Huffingtons had hired an illegal immigrant to look after their two daughters, to which Arianna cut in, '*Not* illegal!' Huffington and Franken even appeared in bed with then-US congressman Barney Frank, a Democrat from Massachusetts. During the national conventions, Huffington says, 'We'd always start the morning deciding what the skit would be about, and Al said, "Let's invite Barney Frank to come to bed with us." I said, "Come on Al, he'll never do that!" He said, "Let's try." So, he actually called Barney. And Barney, his only response was, "Do you want me in my pyjamas or do you want me in a suit?"' (Frank later appeared in bed with Huffington and Franken, sandwiched between them, in a suit.) The segment, which concluded with Huffington and Franken kissing goodnight and turning out their bedside lamps, earned them a 1997 Emmy nomination for outstanding writing for a variety or a music programme. While Arianna continued to be a registered Republican and backed the GOP presidential nominee Bob Dole against the Clintons through 1996, she says her friendship with Franken – a Democrat who, in 2009, became a US senator for Minnesota – caused her to question her affiliation with the GOP. In an interview at New York's Paley Center[45] in 2011, Huffington talked about her gradual change of perspective:

> I was a Republican congressional wife for a while, and my views then were not that dissimilar to my views now, because my views on social issues – on abortion, gay rights, gun control – were always the same. The shift in my views was about the role of government. So, when I was a conservative, I really believed that the private sector would be able to step up to the plate and resolve a lot of the social problems we're facing. And then in my case, I literally saw first-hand, living in Washington, meeting a lot of Republicans, getting to know Newt Gingrich, et cetera, that it wasn't going to happen. That, in fact, we did need an activist government and the real power of govern-ment appropriations to be able to solve a lot of the social problems we are facing. And I started writing about this in a syndicated column I had at the time,

and so my shift happened very publicly, by criticizing a lot of what was happening week by week. And Al Franken takes full credit because he and I in 1996 did this 'Strange Bedfellows' segment . . . Who would have thought that he would now be senator and I a Democrat? . . . Al and I spent a lot of time preparing for the skits and discussing everything and, really, that was like the time when I began to shift in my political views, partly because of our discussions.[46]

Another contributing factor in her shift may have also been her divorce in 1997 from her Republican husband. Michael Huffington, who took some time off work to be with his daughters after leaving Congress in 1995, was increasingly dissatisfied with his life in Washington. After the Clintons won a second term in the presidential election of 1996, he told Arianna he wanted to return to California, according to Brock's *Esquire* article.[47] Arianna was enjoying Washington, however, and wanted to stay. According to Brock, the couple reached an impasse that soon turned into talk of divorce.[48] Michael also came out as bisexual to his family and people close to him, though Michael told Brock he had disclosed his sexual orientation to Arianna before they were married.[49] When the *New Yorker*'s Lauren Collins interviewed both Huffingtons in 2008, Michael told her, 'In December 1985, in my Houston townhouse, I sat down with [Arianna] and told her that I had dated women and men so that she would be aware of it. I didn't think it would be fair to her not to mention my bisexuality . . . And the good news was that it was not an issue for her,' he said. Collins added: 'When I asked Arianna whether she was aware of this when they married – in the past, she has said that she was not – she said that she and Michael now have an agreement not to discuss the issue.'[50] The divorce, finalized in June 1997, was, according to Huffington's lawyer, Marna Tucker, 'one of the most amicable' she'd ever witnessed.[51]

Arianna was now forty-six. As part of the divorce settlement, she purchased and moved into a $7 million mansion in the glamorous Brentwood neighbourhood of Los Angeles, above Sunset Boulevard, with her two daughters, sister and mother. Years later in *The Huffington Post*, Michael Huffington wrote that he had made the decision to come out shortly after his religious conversion from Episcopalian to the Orthodox Christian faith, which led to his own acceptance of his sexuality. 'Through the Orthodox faith, I came to realize for the first time in my life that God had created me in His image, and that His image encompassed bisexual and gay people,' he said. 'Two years after I became Orthodox, and one year after my divorce, I decided to come out to the public as bisexual. This was made into a big deal by the press, because I had recently been in the national spotlight as a Republican nominee for the U.S. Senate race in California. I did it solely on my own volition. And I did it joyfully, because I knew God loved me for who I was and wanted me to live an open and truthful life.'[52]

In the years to come, Michael Huffington would begin dating men again and would forge a new kind of relationship with Arianna. 'Not long ago, Mike had lunch with

Arianna', *Esquire*'s Brock wrote in January 1999, 'and she told him that he seemed happier than in all the years she has known him. And Mike told his ex-wife that he is beginning to date men again. And Arianna Huffington asked Michael Huffington to be careful.' Huffington would also become a film producer and gay rights activist, working to 'educate Americans about gay, lesbian and bisexual people', he said.[53] In 2013, Michael Huffington was a signatory to an *amicus curiae* brief submitted to the Supreme Court in the Hollingsworth vs. Perry case, laying the groundwork for California's legalisation of same-sex marriage.

While some chose to look at the Huffington marriage as one of wealth and convenience, Michael told the *New Yorker* in 2008 he did not think that was the case. 'I am 100 per cent convinced that Arianna and I married because we were madly in love with each other,' Huffington told Lauren Collins. 'However, I don't think it hurt that she was beautiful and I was wealthy. But beauty and wealth alone would not have brought us together in matrimony.'[54] For her part, Arianna says, she had planned to be married for life and it took some time for her to recover. In the years to come, she would work hard to create a new kind of relationship with her ex-husband, and characterized it as worth the struggle. It wasn't until 2010 that she would tell the *Harvard Business Review*: 'My marriage gave me the two most important things in my life – my daughters. The end of the marriage was painful, but now Michael and I are able to be friends and even take vacations together with our children.'[55] In another interview later in *HuffPost*, she said that while her marriage to Michael eventually turned into a friendship, 'it didn't start that way – it was a journey. I don't want to sugarcoat it. What was important to both of us was to become friends because it was so key for the children. [Our friendship] helped us co-parent.'[56]

Even so, Huffington faced an uncertain future with the dissolution of her marriage. 'It was a hard moment for the children, understanding what [the divorce] meant,' she said.[57] Huffington refocused on her work in media and politics, writing columns and continuing to make appearances. She also began writing her next book, *Greetings from the Lincoln Bedroom*, released in 1988 and riffing off her stint on Comedy Central. Doubling down on the satire, Huffington's book described a fictional trip through a chaotic and ruinous Clinton White House from her self-styled Republican perspective. A staid anti-Clintonite, Arianna pulled no punches, but the book would be the last in which she would primarily espouse conservative views. She appeared on the book's cover wearing an American flag dress, gesturing toward an idyllic White House in the background, the label 'Mature Audiences Only' stamped on its front. Increasingly, this would be one of Huffington's trademarks: satire as a form of political dissent.

With the Clintons in the White House from 1993 until 2001, Huffington became a vociferous critic of the Washington political machine, appearing regularly on cable chat shows, doing a cameo in the 1998 Bruce Willis action movie *The Siege*, and playing herself in the 1999 Ron Howard film

EDtv. In the late 1990s, Huffington was also a regular on the Los Angeles public radio show *Left, Right and Center*, where, as a Republican, she debated with fellow journalists representing the liberal and centrist viewpoints. Throughout this time, she wrote a syndicated column printed in roughly a hundred US newspapers twice a week.[58]

Finally – and crucially – with the advent of the internet, Huffington began to experiment online. She started her first venture, Resignation.com, in 1998 to protest the Clinton administration. The website highlighted statements made by public figures, political commentators and elected officials, calling for President Clinton to resign after his impeachment for obstruction of justice and lying under oath to a federal grand jury over his affair with Monica Lewinsky, an unpaid, 21-year-old White House intern. Huffington, the parent of two young daughters, found his transgressions beyond the pale for any sitting president, calling Clinton 'a man of staggering narcissism and self-indulgence, whom nobody dared gainsay, investing his energies first in gratifying his sexual greeds and then in using his staff, his friends and the Secret Service to cover up the truth'. On her new site she wrote, 'The message of Resignation.com is clear. Take responsibility, Mr. President, for what you have done to your party, your office and your country, and continue your "journey" of "reconciliation and healing" in private.'[59] Her site soon became an online community for conservatives, gaining attention in the mainstream press. Huffington told the *Washington Post* in December 1998 that, far from being disruptive, she believed if Clinton would resign, his vice president, Al Gore, could assume his duties in a 'seamless transition'.[60]

Huffington also created a personal website, AriannaOnline.com, to plug her work and blog her views. At the time, it was just another medium for her to get out her message and display her latest articles. Huffington scarcely realized how important the web would be to the future of her career. In fact, her first inclination toward it was much like her impulse to join the Cambridge Union more than two decades earlier. She genuinely enjoyed the process of debating with people online and becoming an influencer. 'I don't remember the first thing that got my attention [about the internet]', she says. But she does remember why she kept coming back:

> What fascinated me was the engagement, the fact that writers are no longer just writing and leaving the scene, but staying there to engage with the readers, and that the readers had a voice. Whether it was in chat rooms or forums or the early versions of what was happening online, something new was happening . . . I created a website, my own website, called 'Arianna Online,' and engaged with my readers. My columns would go up, they would comment, I would comment back.[61]

She did not see the internet or blogging as something she could turn into a business but, from the start, she did appreciate the web for its ability to reach a national – and even global – audience. 'I was just thinking of it as an extension of my journalism,' she told Harvard's Shorenstein Center on Media, Politics and Public Policy in 2013. 'I was writing two columns a week, and I wanted to begin to communicate with my readers. Not just read it in the newspaper, in the *Los Angeles Times*, or any of the other papers where my column was syndicated . . . I liked the fact that [readers on the internet] talked back.'[62]

It was while writing her columns, talking to readers and researching her next political book, *How to Overthrow the Government*, published in 2000, that Huffington began to definitively step away from identifying as a Republican. While she enjoyed influencing her readers, her readers, in fact, were influencing her. Huffington's book, released just before the nation's disastrous presidential election recount (between Democratic presidential candidate Al Gore and Republican contender George W. Bush), takes both Republicans and Democrats to task for ignoring America's poverty and debt levels, while arguing for campaign-finance reform. When asked in July 2000 by CNN about her shift away from the GOP, Huffington told the cable news network, 'I don't consider myself as being transformed from a conservative to a liberal. I consider myself being transformed from a conservative to a populist. Through the last six years of doing a syndicated column twice a week and through writing [my] book . . . I had to confront the data about poverty and about the failed drug war, about the corruption of our politics. Then, as a result, I became radicalized.'[63]

During the nation's presidential election season of 2000, Huffington helped organize the Democratic and Republican 'Shadow Conventions', with the aim of looking at issues often overlooked by the Republican and Democratic national conventions' wealthy donor bases.[64] Issues covered by the Shadow Conventions included 'the corruption of money in politics; poverty in the middle of our prosperity; and the failed drug war', she told CNN.[65] Anyone could attend the conventions live, or watch them on cable TV or the internet. The Shadow Conventions, which the London *Observer* called 'far more entertaining than anything' that took place at the national conventions,[66] featured presentations from politicians, celebrities and social activists.[67] More than 780 members of the media registered to attend, Huffington said,[68] with panellists including Senator John McCain from Arizona, actor Warren Beatty, the Reverend Jesse Jackson, and Huffington's Comedy Central friends, Bill Maher and Al Franken.[69] The purpose of the Shadow Conventions – which Huffington held again in 2012 – was 'to amplify the voices of those who will not be in the other conventions, are not on the contributor lists, do not buy access and whose issues are not on the table as a result,' she said.[70]

Huffington's sudden ascension as a liberal figurehead was met with scepticism. But she was quick to reject the label herself, saying her leanings were not classifiable. 'The reason why I would not describe myself as a liberal, is because I don't consider poverty and issues of those left out of prosperity to be issues that belong to the left, but issues that are central to our democracy,' she told CNN.[71] In an article for *Los Angeles* magazine, writer Steve Oney quoted a political consultant saying, 'Arianna is one of the most dedicated persons to developing a political profile that I've ever seen. She's gone through some remarkable changes, but one thing about her is that she is a consistent self-promoter.'[72] Huffington rejected the notion that self-promotion was the point of the exercise, saying she was taking a stand not on 'right–left' issues, but 'right–wrong' issues.[73]

By this time, according to *Playboy*, she had 'established herself as a progressive salonista in Los Angeles, holding regular parties at her Brentwood home to promote an array of ecological, political, philosophical and spiritual causes'.[74] Huffington had also created a new social circle for herself consisting of a 'a staggering and mostly liberal collection of powerful entertainment, media and political types', *Playboy* wrote, some of whom she would later recruit to blog for *The Huffington Post*. Huffington found no shortage of people to support her, saying, 'I did find myself welcome and embraced by new allies.'

In 2003 she received the Upton Sinclair award from the highly progressive non-profit Liberty Hill Foundation, to honour Huffington 'for the integrity and courage it took to transform herself', a formal acknowledgement of her change of heart, which included speeches against the criminalization of marijuana and the car industry for failing to embrace fuel-efficient vehicles, while dismissing her former GOP allies as 'fanatics'. Even Huffington's public radio show, *Left, Right and Center*, stopped introducing her as a Republican and started introducing her as 'beyond these categories, in the fourth dimension of political time and space'. Eventually, Huffington would refer to the year of her transformation as 1996, but that appears to be a bit of exaggeration, as she was still showing up as a Republican on Comedy Central at that time with Franken, and backing Bob Dole. A review of her media appearances shows that she continued to appear as a conservative political commentator as late as 1998, but her affiliation waned after that.[75] 'I was a Republican. Did you know that?' she told the Washington DC television network C-SPAN in 2003. 'I know that the statute of limitations may have run out, that you may be ready to forgive me since, after all, it was 1996 when I left the Republican party . . . It was a long time ago.' That same year the *Observer* noted it wasn't that long ago that she parted ways with the Republicans, but Huffington was unmoved. 'Unless people are determined to remain sceptical about my transformation,' she said, 'there is enough evidence that this is real.'[76]

While moving on from what Huffington called her 'Republican interregnum', she was dealing with a number of challenges at home, rearing her kids – Christina, now eleven, and Isabella, nine – as well as tending to her mother, Elli, who was in and out of hospital with congestive heart failure. On 24 August 2000, Elli passed away at home, surrounded by her daughters and grandchildren.[77] Huffington's father had passed away in May of the same year.[78] Huffington's mother had lived with her for most of her life – throughout her marriage, the birth of her children and her divorce, she says. Arianna later described the final hours of her mother's life as 'transcendent' and deeply moving, recalling how they had spent a day shopping at Santa Monica's international food market, which was 'like Disneyland' for her mother, and cooking up a feast. Elli sat down to eat and was still grazing on shrimp when she fell from 'a massive stroke', Huffington says.[79] Arianna tried to carry Elli to her bed. Instead of getting up, though, her mother told her to 'bring her lavender oil to put on her feet'. Arianna did so.[80] Huffington later wrote about what Elli instructed her to do next:

> She said, 'Do not call the paramedics. I'm fine.' Agapi and I felt completely torn. So instead of calling an ambulance, we called the nurse who had taken care of my mother at home. And we all sat on the floor with her, her granddaughters still going in and out of her room on their scooters making happy noises, completely oblivious to what was happening, because that's how my mother wanted it to be. The nurse kept taking her pulse, but her pulse was fine. My mother asked me to open a bottle of red wine and pour a glass for everyone. So, we all sat there having a picnic on the floor telling stories for an hour or more waiting for her to be ready to get up. There she was on the floor with a beautiful turquoise sarong wrapped around her, making sure we were all having a good time. It sounds surreal now, and it was surreal then. I had

the sense that something larger was moving all of us, keeping us from taking any action, so that my mother would have the chance to pass the way she wanted to pass. Then suddenly her head fell forward and she was gone.[81]

Huffington's mother died with no worldly possessions and no will, 'which is not surprising, considering her habit of giving things away,' Huffington notes, adding, 'The time we tried to give her a second watch, within 48 hours she had given it to someone else . . . Wherever she was – in an elevator, a taxi, an airplane, a parking lot, a supermarket, a bank – she would reach out to others.' When a stranger once admired Elli's necklace, 'my mother took it off, and gave it to her. When the astonished woman asked, "What can I give you in return?" my mother said, "It's not a trade, darling, it's an offering."'[82] These were the stories Huffington would revisit again and again about her mother. In 2017 she wrote: 'What she left us with was what she embodied while she was alive: nurturing, simplicity, unconditional loving and a connection with the sacred that was so complete that it felt like those dimensions of life were taken care of for all those who were blessed to be in her orbit. Which I still am – both in her orbit and being orbited by her.'[83]

The memorial celebrating her mother's life was filled with family, friends, food, flowers, poetry and music. 'We scattered my mother's ashes in the sea with rose petals, as she had asked,' Huffington wrote, adding that in her garden, 'We planted a lemon tree in her honor that has been producing juicy lemons ever since. And we installed a bench engraved with one of her favorite sayings that embodied the philosophy of her life: "Don't Miss the Moment."'[84]

Her mother's influence on her would continue to be profound long after her passing, inspiring Huffington's entrepreneurial ventures in the years ahead:

> [Elli] was a towering example of the joys of slowing down . . . she and I had an unspoken deal: Hers would be the rhythm of a timeless world, a child's rhythm; mine was the rhythm of the modern world. While I had the sense every time I looked at my watch that it was later than I thought, she lived in a world where there were no impersonal encounters and never a need to rush. She believed that rushing through life was a sure way to miss the gifts that come only when you give 100 percent of yourself to a task, a conversation, a dinner, a relationship, a moment.[85]

The same year Huffington won her Upton Sinclair award, in 2003, she released *Pigs at the Trough: How Corporate Greed and Political Corruption are Undermining America*, a *New York Times* best-seller that roundly eviscerated virtually every aspect of the American political and financial system, from corporate fraud to corrupt CEOs to anybody who attempted to use what she called 'sleazy, tax-cheating loopholes'. That year, as the war in Iraq commenced,

Huffington also organized a citizen-funded campaign called 'The Detroit Project', attacking the nation's 'Big Three' automakers (GM, Ford and Fiat Chrysler) and their backers in Washington for continuing to manufacture sport-utility vehicles and other cars with poor fuel efficiency. Until recently, Huffington had herself driven an SUV, but switched to a compact hybrid Prius when her close friend, environmental activist Laurie David (then-wife of Larry David of HBO's *Curb Your Enthusiasm*) chastised her for driving a gas-guzzler and feeding into America's oil dependence: 'If you aren't connecting the dots, who will?'[86] Huffington's response, as usual, was hardly mincing.

Her 'Detroit Project' attracted headlines and culminated in a not-so-subtle series of television ads suggesting that driving an SUV was tantamount to supporting terrorists and wars in the oil-rich Middle East. Following the 9/11 attacks of 2001, all references to terrorists in the media had become highly charged and many of the major television networks refused to run Huffington's ads, calling them too extreme. (One of the spots showed an SUV owner saying, 'I sent our soldiers off to war', while another featured a voiceover saying, 'This is George ... And these are the terrorists who get money every time George fills up his SUV.')[87] Once again, Huffington took the controversy in stride, explaining that the ads were meant as satire. 'There seems to be an epidemic of literal-mindedness at the moment,' she told *Mother Jones* once they aired, summing the ads up as 'really irreverence with a purpose – which I revere'.[88] The campaign received a glut of media attention and, shortly afterwards, lawmakers – including California Senator Dianne Feinstein, former opponent of Huffington's ex-husband – introduced legislation to close loopholes and end tax credits for SUVs.[89]

Huffington's political crusades naturally caused the media to wonder if she wasn't herself planning to run for office. In May 2003, when the *Observer* asked her about this, she batted away the notion. 'I think the system is too broken to bring about change through elective office,' Huffington declared. 'I think we have to change the system and then a lot of good people are going to gravitate to it again. Basically, if you run for office you spend about 80 per cent of your time begging for money. It takes a psychopathic personality to be willing to do that. American elected office has become a tomb for ideas.'[90]

In 2003, energy issues were of grave importance to Californians, as the state had suffered an electricity crisis that triggered rolling blackouts in 2000 and 2001 which tripled some residents' utility bills and were later blamed on energy companies like Enron and an array of manipulative trading practices. California governor Gray Davis, a benefactor of Enron campaign donations, was accused of turning a blind eye to the problem and not doing enough to defend Californians from energy fraud – in some cases, even entering long-term electricity contracts at wildly inflated prices that made the financial fallout in California worse. While Davis eventually spoke out, declaring that 'Someone at Enron should go to jail', the public perception was that his objections came far too late.

In mid-2003, a grassroots movement in California to remove Governor Davis from office and elect someone new to replace him gained momentum. Attracting national headlines, it would lead to the state's first-ever recall election. The field of candidates was enormous, with celebrities like *Diff'rent Strokes* actor Gary Coleman and porn star Mary Carey running alongside venerable public servants who sought to succeed Davis – some of them pouring millions into the movement, such as former California Republican representative Darrell Issa. The bar was admittedly low: Any California citizen able to collect sixty-five signatures from their own party and pay a non-refundable fee of $3,500 could run. In the end, the recall election ballot would ask voters two questions: should Governor Davis be recalled? And, if so, which of more than a hundred different candidates should replace him? Any candidate could win by simply getting the largest percentage of the votes.[91]

For Huffington, who had said many times she would not run for office, the opportunity was too tantalizing to pass up. On vacation in the Irish countryside that summer with close friends – former *New Yorker*, *Vanity Fair* and *Talk* magazine editor Tina Brown, as well as Brown's husband, Harold Evans, the editor who helped arrange the serialization of Huffington's *Maria Callas* book at the *Sunday Times* – Huffington floated the idea of making a run for governor.[92] At the same time, her former husband, Michael Huffington, was having similar thoughts. In fact, in September 2000 he publicly announced his interest in the role of California governor at a state Republican convention, saying, 'We only have so much life left. Before I die, I want to do something good for people.'[93]

But the Huffingtons did not have the blessing of their children, who did not want to see their parents running against each other. 'The summer before I started 8th grade, my mom and dad decided to run for governor of California – against each other,' their oldest daughter, Christina wrote in *Glamour* magazine in 2013. 'I hated the idea. Their divorce was painful enough in private; seeing it hashed out in public would be even worse.'[94] Citing his daughters' wishes, 'that they did not want their parents to run in this election – either one of us', Michael Huffington told the press he ultimately decided not to run.[95] But Arianna, stating she had only agreed not to run if her husband ran, announced in the first week of August 2003 that she would be entering the race, as an independent. 'I'm not, to say the least, a conventional candidate,' she proclaimed in her launch speech. 'But these are not conventional times. And if we keep electing the same kinds of politicians who got us into the same kinds of mess funded by the same special interests, we'll never get out of this mess.'[96]

It was a short run, but an extremely challenging one, with 53-year-old Huffington finding herself belittled and attacked on all sides throughout her campaign – especially by her most formidable opponent, millionaire action-movie star and leading Republican candidate, Arnold Schwarzenegger, whom her ex-husband went on to endorse, calling him 'a charismatic leader'.[97] While Warren Beatty and many in the liberal establishment – Hollywood environmentalists and social activists, in particular – cheered Arianna on, she struggled to maintain the media spotlight as a crush of candidates, quite a few of them celebrities, vied for the same office.[98] Among her supporters, Huffington counted thousands of fans of her work, she said, as well as backers of a website that suddenly went up in the summer of 2003, www.runariannarun.com, led by progressives that included Huffington's chief grass-roots organizer and future White House adviser, Van Jones. 'I never would have run if this were a regular election,' Huffington told the *Washington Post*, adding: 'This is the year that someone independent of the parties, with a grass-roots base, can definitely win as a progressive.'[99]

Assuring voters she would use none of her own money, but was 'running to win', Huffington deliberately appeared at the Los Angeles County registrar's office to file her qualifying papers at the same time as Schwarzenegger and his wife, Maria Shriver – working her way through the crowd of screaming Schwarzenegger fans. In a bold move to share his grand entrance, Huffington 'managed, while knocking down a bank of microphones, to squeeze herself next to Schwarzenegger, as he emerged from the registrar's building, putting her face in the frame with his and Shriver's that would be on many Sunday front pages', the *Post* wrote in August 2003. Afterward, when the newspaper asked her about how it went, Huffington, sipping ice water on the patio of her home in Brentwood, said, 'It went fine. It was very good.'[100]

Her characteristic unflappability notwithstanding, her detractors – even other progressives – could be harsh.

Democratic strategist Harvey Englander told the *Los Angeles Times* he felt Huffington's political views had whipsawed once too often. 'I do not believe she is a serious candidate,' he said. 'I think that all she's doing is trying to promote her new book. This is a person who has no ideological foundation, OK? The issues she was against three years ago, she's for today.'[101] At this point in her career, Huffington's command of the press, populism and punditry ensured she would almost always get in the last word against any critic. But she was unable to overcome the objections to her tax returns, which the *Los Angeles Times* reported in mid-August 2003 showed she had paid less than $1,000 in federal taxes, total, in the prior two years and no individual state income taxes. While Huffington did report a six-figure annual income from her best-selling books and other projects, her earnings, the *Los Angeles Times* wrote, were 'far outweighed by losses that she reported were incurred by Christabella Inc., the private corporation she owns and uses to manage her writing and lecturing businesses'.[102]

Against Huffington's strident criticism of corporate 'fat cats' and tax-dodgers exploiting loopholes both in her best-selling book, *Pigs at the Trough*, and on the campaign trail, the optics did not look good. When pressed by journalists, she said: 'I'm a working woman, and my income fluctuates', noting that her expenses exceeded her income in recent years because she had been researching books and working on television projects. To the *Los Angeles Times*, she dismissed the criticism – while also continuing to plug her book: 'I'm sorry, but if you don't see the difference between a tax loophole – which is used basically to shelter your profits, which is what I have been speaking out against – and a legitimate business tax deduction, then I suggest you read a copy of my book,' she said. 'I would be very happy to give you one.'[103]

More important than tax returns was beating Schwarzenegger's mega-celebrity before the recall election on 7 October. The two faced off at a televised debate in September among California's leading gubernatorial candidates, which included both Huffington and Schwarzenegger – a former Mr Universe who, at the time, had attained global recognition for starring in action-hero movies, including the extremely popular Hollywood *Terminator* series. The event was held at the Grand Ballroom of California State University in Sacramento, with all the candidates receiving their questions in advance. While there were five candidates taking part, Huffington and Schwarzenegger effectively took over the debate, trading barbs that had the crowd roaring while inspiring *The New York Times* headline, 'Live, the "Arnold and Arianna Show."'[104]

Expectations were low for Schwarzenegger, as he had declined to do other debates in the lead-up to the election and had little-to-no policy experience. But he proved surprisingly deft at cutting one-liners during his debut. The debate focused on California's fiscal crisis, taxes and immigration, with Huffington criticizing 'business tax loopholes' and accusing Schwarzenegger of being too cosy with

Republicans and tax-dodging corporations. Schwarzenegger responded, 'Arianna. Your personal income tax is the biggest loophole. I could drive my Hummer through it.' Huffington, in rebuttal, complimented him for memorizing his lines extraordinarily well.[105]

With its massive live audience and omnipresent television cameras – as well as the recall itself – the event was repeatedly likened to a 'circus' or a 'carnival' by the national press, which seemed preoccupied with the fact that two iconic, foreign-born Americans with thick accents were going head-to-head in what Huffington dubbed 'the battle of the accents'. (Schwarzenegger, who originally hailed from Austria, had an accent as heavy as hers.) When Huffington tried to link Schwarzenegger to issues of Washington's GOP and the current administration of George W. Bush, Schwarzenegger shot back at her, 'You need a little more decaf.' Huffington called Schwarzenegger 'completely hypocritical', noting his relationship with establishment Republicans would make it virtually impossible for him to address California's financial problems, at which point, Schwarzenegger repeatedly interrupted her. Huffington didn't give him an inch. 'Let me finish. You know this is completely impolite. This is the way you treat women,' she said, pointing a finger at Schwarzenegger. 'We know that – but not now.' The audience erupted with laughter, booing and hooting. 'She called his past proposals empty, cynical attempts to find his way to the governor's chair,' *The New York Times* wrote. 'He called himself Governor Arnold.'[106]

The moderator, Stan Stratham, repeatedly favoured

Schwarzenegger during the exchanges (for example, he allowed Schwarzenegger extra time during the debate to respond to an attack from Huffington but did not allow her the same when Schwarzenegger made a jab at her). Schwarzenegger's rejoinder to Huffington's allusion of sexism pandered to the crowd: 'I have just realized I have the perfect part for you in *Terminator 4*,' he said. The audience grew rambunctious again and the moderator largely lost control of the debate. Against the din, Stratham could be heard saying, 'Ladies and gentlemen, this is not Comedy Central, I swear . . .'[107]

In the days to follow, the debate would become a point of ridicule in the national discourse, with Schwarzenegger following up with more sexist remarks about his one female opponent – Huffington – describing her as 'a whining woman'.[108] Yet Huffington easily carried 'the heavy, if not overwhelming support of the entertainment industry', *The New York Times* noted in September 2003. 'Arnold Schwarzenegger may be Hollywood's own, but Arianna *owns Hollywood*.'[109] Still, Huffington wrote later in *Fearless*, the experience of running as a gubernatorial candidate was one of the few times in her life she felt truly laid bare, particularly as a woman. Throughout her career, she had often used her sex appeal to full advantage – leveraging it and wielding it as her own. No one could have ever said Huffington was a victim of her own seductiveness. To the contrary, she inhabited it with aplomb. Here, however, she found her gender being used to mock her: 'During the campaign, I was confronted with the fear of being caricatured and misunderstood. Of course, it's in the nature of political campaigns to turn your opponent into a political caricature. But I saw firsthand how different – and how much harder – it is if you're a woman, how much more exposed and vulnerable you feel.'[110]

In late September, one week before the recall election, polls indicated Huffington only had 2 per cent of the vote, with Schwarzenegger leading every candidate by at least 15 points. Huffington decided to withdraw from the race, but it was too late to get her name off the official ballot. She appeared on CNN's *Larry King Live* show, saying that while she'd hoped to be governor, she had never supported the recall. 'I'm pulling out and I'm going to concentrate every ounce of my time and energy for the next week fighting to defeat the recall, because I realize that that's the only way now to defeat Arnold Schwarzenegger . . . I've always believed this is not the way to run a democracy. But I also saw the opportunity provided to elect with a simple plurality an independent progressive governor,' she said.[111]

At the time she pulled out, Huffington was behind Democratic California Lieutenant Governor Cruz Bustamante, who carried an estimated 25 per cent of the vote, and Schwarzenegger, who led with 40 per cent. In the end, Californians voted to recall Governor Gray Davis and elect Schwarzenegger as their new governor. Huffington received the support of only about 1 per cent of the electorate – or 47,505 votes – when the results were certified on 14 November 2003. But the election had given her unprecedented name recognition across the state. It also did something else: it taught her the power of the internet, from which she later claimed to have raised roughly $1 million of campaign funds.[112] Throughout the race, Huffington frequently used the internet to get out the message, issuing statements, blogging and at one point even posting a video comparing herself to Schwarzenegger, titled, 'The Hybrid versus the Hummer'. The spot touted her progressivism and green credentials. None of it was enough to overcome Schwarzenegger's stardom, but it garnered heavy traffic that she would not soon forget. And it taught her a lesson: there was a great deal of mileage to be had out of the blogosphere.

In the meantime, Huffington still had Comedy Central on her side and, even as Schwarzenegger defeated her, she used it to get the last word. Appearing on comedian Jon Stewart's *The Daily Show* in October 2003, Huffington served as, variously, media commentator, political pundit and candidate in her own election. When asked how Republican contender Schwarzenegger managed to win an avalanche of support in a state as staunchly liberal as California, Huffington said that Schwarzenegger's campaign was 'a very elaborately produced masquerade', noting that Schwarzenegger himself 'ended up being a kind of very elaborate, very expensive special effect'. When pressed further by Stewart, she added, 'If you have $20 million to spend on wall-to-wall advertising, and you use the words the public wants to hear, and the media gives you basically a free ride, and the women you've groped come out too late, what do you do? You win.'[113] While Stewart seemed visibly shocked by the casual reference to Schwarzenegger's groping, he could hardly argue; in a *Los Angeles Times* article published that month, Schwarzenegger was accused by six women of subjecting them to sexual bullying and humiliation across decades. Huffington also told Stewart she thought California's electorate was willing to vote for a celebrity instead of a traditional politician because there was 'an incredible thirst to end business as usual . . . and incredible longing for change'. Already attuned herself to the populist headwinds swiftly overtaking post-9/11 America, Huffington would soon find a way to harness them. But going into 2004, she was not quite there yet.

In the immediate aftermath, the loss of the recall stung. And worse, Huffington's daughters – Christina, fourteen, and Isabella, twelve – were still very unhappy that she ran. The election and the negative press coverage it entailed, particularly over Huffington's tax returns and, in the final analysis, her child-support payments, had pitted her and her ex-husband publicly against each other. Her elder daughter Christina wrote in *Glamour* in 2013 that though her parents had 'both ultimately dropped out of the race . . . the experience was so upsetting that I decided to get as far away from Los Angeles as possible.'[114] In 2004, she enrolled in a boarding school in New Hampshire. The move was extremely hard on her and, feeling isolated, Christina recounted how she turned to alcohol and struggled with bulimia and cocaine for years. 'I missed my mom,' she wrote. 'We were always so close.' One of her and her mother's great loves was bonding over journalism and politics, she said.[115]

Christina said she always felt loved and embraced by her family – 'I wasn't one of those kids who got money, but was ignored . . . my parents showered me with attention and love', she wrote – but she was also plagued by teenage anxieties from having famous parents, and 'the irrational idea, which had always haunted me, that my parents would somehow get hurt or die'. It would take years for her to overcome these issues, but, with her family's support, she said, she was able to recover.[116] In her own writings, Arianna Huffington describes how her youngest, Isabella, around the same time, needed treatment for an eating disorder:

> My daughter, Isabella, was 11 years old when she started being obsessively careful about what she ate . . . It was when, at her 12th birthday party – with all her best friends around the table – she didn't touch her birthday cake that I realized we had a serious problem. As soon as I realized we were dealing with early symptoms of anorexia, I arranged to see a doctor, who basically told Isabella that if she didn't put on 10 pounds over the next two months she would be hospitalized . . . My fears were also mixed up with guilt. Was this my fault?[117]

Huffington says in *On Becoming Fearless* she worried the eating issues may have had to do with her. 'Did it have to do with the fact that I was also rejecting food to control my weight?' Fortunately, she writes, Isabella began eating again and regained her health. Huffington's fears eventually subsided, 'but I still remember as though it were yesterday a day when the children and I were in London on vacation a couple of months after the visit with the doctor. Isabella was getting her hair washed at a small hairdressing shop near the hotel. I looked in the sink and saw that it was filled with chunks of her hair. The sight of Isabella's beautiful red hair lying lifeless in the sink filled me with terror . . . That night, I couldn't help but fixate on every bit Isabella consumed at dinner.'[118]

While Huffington had encountered many challenges in the decade since her former husband first ran for office – the loss of two major elections, a divorce, the loss of both her parents, and the scares of her daughters' eating disorders – the loss of Bernard Levin, who died on 7 August 2004, was undoubtedly one of the greatest losses of all.

The last time she saw him, Huffington says, was about a year before he died.

'I was in London with my daughters. The Alzheimer's was by then sufficiently advanced that I could no longer talk to him on the phone. So, I called Liz Anderson, arts editor of the *Spectator,* who has been a true gift in his life, to arrange to see him. That was when she told me that Bernard's condition had so deteriorated that she had had to arrange for him to be moved to a home.

'We decided that he would be brought to the Berkeley [Hotel] where I was staying, so we could have tea

– another favorite ritual of his. "Arianna," she warned me, "he may not recognize you."'[119]

Huffington says Anderson's words did not prepare her 'for the shock of not being recognized, especially because Bernard looked exactly the same – as always, fastidiously dressed and mannered, except that he turned down tea and asked for water. And then, no matter what memories, nicknames, shared moments I brought up, there was no connection.'

To know that everything between her and Levin was effectively erased, was something Huffington could hardly bear. 'I went back to my room,' she says, 'and wept.'[120]

PART 5

BUILDING *THE HUFFINGTON POST*

'Although I had no idea how big it would get, I knew we were doing something that would work, because the old media ways were not meeting people's needs.'

Turning away from a career path that at one time seemed destined for politics and leadership on the national stage, for Arianna Huffington, was extremely painful. Her losses weren't just publicly devastating, but also deeply personal, encompassing both her career and family life – two of the things she valued most. She'd lost the California gubernatorial election, her marriage, her mother, her father and now her soul mate, Bernard Levin. Despite her many successes, the period from the late 1990s into the early 2000s had brought with it blow after blow.

Yet more than any other time in Huffington's life, this would be the turning point. She was nearly halfway into her fifties, but had no plans to stop working or retire. Instead, during the course of the next decade, Huffington would not only demonstrate her indefatigable ability to rebound, but to completely reinvent herself. And she would do so in a manner that even her most virulent critics would be forced to admit was nothing short of extraordinary. Without a husband, parents, or her long-time confidant, Levin, to lean on, Huffington would come into her own, relying only on herself. This was the time in her life that she would stop following and start leading. 'Out of difficult experiences, out of challenging experiences, you learn so much,' she said later. 'I just wanted to get back to work. I learned so much out of the cauldrons of these campaigns and being right at the center of American political life.'[1]

Huffington returned to where she began, to writing, the skill that, above all else, had always carried her through the turbulent times to her next incarnation.[2] At first, she focused on her usual editorials, articles and newspaper columns. But she longed for greater interaction and audience engagement, so she kept posting her work on her site, 'Arianna Online', and built up her readership. 'I had a syndicated column at the time about bloggers,' she says. 'I really loved what blogging was, which was being more conversational, being more intimate, responding to your readers and they respond back.'[3]

Huffington had, in the past, experimented with keeping personal journals, but blogging felt much more immediate. By posting online, she was journaling with a ready-made, live audience that offered instant feedback. All of this played very well to her talents and preferences, tracing all the way back to her Cambridge days. She loved nothing more than to test-drive ideas – and get a reaction. Just as with the Cambridge Union, she became completely engrossed with experimenting with her growing audience, seeking to cajole, influence, debate and, ultimately, win people over. 'Blogging became a new form of expression, and I loved how effective it was,' she says.[4]

With the rise of the internet and people increasingly moving their social networks online, Huffington, whose networking abilities had catapulted her to prominence throughout her life, saw an opportunity to reach more people than ever before. 'I saw what was happening online. Everything I was doing in the early 2000s let me recognize how the conversation was moving online,' she says.[5]

Curiously, the spark that ignited *The Huffington Post* – though Huffington did not know it yet – had already been struck. In 2003, when she was headed into her gubernatorial campaign, she met with the public-relations wizard Kenneth Lerer in New York. A former AOL-Time Warner executive and skilled media tactician, Lerer knew how to strategically use the press to build global brands like MTV, or even resuscitate the reputations of Wall Street titans, such as Michael Milken, the famed 1980s junk bond trader who went to prison. Lerer kept a very low profile but had a big-league reputation. For Huffington, it was just another meeting with a media strategist – one of many such meetings at the time. She was used to consulting with brand and image experts during her years as a political wife. Interestingly, Lerer was more hesitant. When his friend Tom Freston, co-founder of MTV and, at the time, head of Viacom, suggested Lerer and Huffington meet up for dinner with him and his wife, Kathy, Lerer almost said no. He considered Huffington to be ostentatious and flashy. He was the opposite. Lerer was familiar with her from her time as a Republican talking head in the 1990s, but that was about it. 'I didn't think I was going to like her,' Lerer told *The New York Times*. 'She's a big personality. I didn't know her. I wouldn't say I'm a shy guy, but I stick to myself.'[6]

It would turn out to be a most propitious meeting. Lerer was surprised to find that he and Huffington took to each other almost immediately. When they met with the Frestons at an Italian restaurant on the Upper East Side, he was bowled over by her charisma. 'I said, "She's terrific,"' he said. 'You know how you just hit it off with people instantly?'[7] The two kept in touch and, over time, they began speaking of creating an online platform that could offer fresh insights into American politics to counter the Bush administration's right-wing policies, and to showcase Huffington's own leftward views. Lerer, a classic New York liberal, had recently tried his own hand at online news and politics, launching a pro-gun control website called 'StoptheNRA.com', aimed at opposing the National Rifle Association (NRA) and supporting the extension of the Clinton-era assault-weapons ban. While ultimately unsuccessful – the GOP-led Congress let the federal ban expire – the site gave him his first taste of internet entrepreneurialism and taught him how to leverage the web to build audiences and gain influence.[8] With Lerer, Huffington would seek out new ways to shape and influence the national discourse. If she could not do it as a politician, then she would do it as an internet entrepreneur, progressive and thinker.

As Huffington began to formulate a plan to transform her personal website 'Arianna Online' into *The Huffington Post*, she opened up her Rolodex and started reaching out to her contacts and friends – from London to New York to Washington to California – asking them to engage in what she called 'elevated blogging'. Some of those who signed up early to write for her included long-time friend Mort Zuckerman; world-renowned journalist Walter Cronkite; celebrated filmmaker Nora Ephron; writer and comedian Larry David; Hollywood film director David Mamet; actresses Diane Keaton and Maggie Gyllenhaal; actors Warren Beatty and Alec Baldwin; legendary author Norman Mailer; and social critic and public intellectual Arthur M. Schlesinger.[9] 'Ever since I can remember, I loved starting conversations, just conversations about everything,' Huffington said. 'And the longing for conversations propelled me to want to start *The Huffington Post*, where people with something interesting to say can have a platform in which to say it. People from anywhere, well-known people, people nobody had heard of, and use the power of online media, use the power of the internet, which we're just beginning to understand.'[10]

One of her biggest challenges would be getting her friends to take a chance, she says. For one, many people did not understand blogging or feel comfortable with technology. While trying to recruit octogenarian Schlesinger as a blogger over lunch at the Century Club, she said he peppered her with questions. 'What is a blog?' he wanted to know. 'And what is blogging?' Huffington says, 'I found myself explaining [blogging] to a man who didn't do email, and who considered his fax machine a revolutionary way to communicate.'[11] (For those who were confused, Huffington had a very loose definition of blogging: basically, online writing that conveyed 'somebody's thoughts in real time, in a conversational way'. A blog could be 'sent by carrier pigeon [and it's still] a blog,' she once famously stated.) As was her wont, she quickly persuaded Schlesinger to be her first recruit. He had only one request. 'I barely use a computer,' he said. 'Can I fax you my blogs?'[12] Huffington, who was only too happy to comply, says, 'Some of the most important voices of our time were not going to be going online, unless it was made real easy for them.'[13]

Others felt hesitant because blogging was still considered to be a largely amateur activity, reserved only for writers who could not get published anywhere else. 'Blogging was supposed to be the caricature,' Huffington says, 'something done by people in their pajamas living in their parents' basements who were not really good enough to get a job.'[14] Her proposal was simple: join in the national dialogue without having to write the kind of long, formal editorials usually printed in the newspapers. What she was suggesting were quick drafts, composed on the fly, and she reached out to nearly everyone she knew to write them, even people she had only briefly met. 'Basically, my pitch was, "You wake up in the morning and you have something to say, I know you do, about the events of the day, about a movie you saw last night, about anything. But you're busy, you have a book to write, you have a company to run. Sure, you could write it for *The New York Times*, but you have to deal with editors and processes. You don't really bother. Just send it to us."'[15]

Tapping into her voluminous network, Huffington soon gathered a formidable line-up. Her powers of persuasion, says her former Comedy Central friend and now HBO talk show host, Bill Maher, were uncanny, if not irresistible. 'If Arianna wants to be your friend, I mean, give up, you're like a weak swimmer in a strong tide,' he told the *New Yorker*.[16] In her article-writing, as well as her books, Huffington had always enjoyed matching wits with the wealthy, powerful, well connected and intellectually bold. Relying heavily on her natural charm, she had also become adept at inveigling people to share their personal stories. 'She was dazzling – I saw her operate, melting the most reticent, unwilling-to-speak people,' one of her researchers told *Vanity Fair* after working with her on the Picasso book. 'I saw her disarm them totally. She has a determination that is beyond most human comprehension . . . I felt I had been lady-in-waiting to a Mack Truck.'[17]

In addition to luring great thinkers, celebrities and the people she admired, Huffington's vision sought to be both populist and egalitarian, including people of all ages and backgrounds on her site. She would offer no payment for her bloggers' contributions, but she would give them a robust platform through which they could convey their thoughts and ideas online and into the world. 'I decided early on that the internet, that new technology, was going to provide a new way of connecting people,' Huffington says. 'And although I had no idea how big it would get, I knew we were doing something that would work, because the old media ways were not meeting people's needs.'[18] From her earliest recruits, she aimed for boldface names and a diversity of viewpoints. 'In the months leading to the launch of *The Huffington Post*, I always knew that I wanted our group blog to include the best of the old and the best of the new,' she says.[19]

Her goal was to create an online space for ideas and conversations, allowing easy access to members of the wider media, corporate leaders and political commentators, in addition to moving 'the important conversations in the country . . . from living room and dining room to online. To expose people to the ideas I was being exposed to.'[20] Always evolving, Huffington, by this time, told *The New York Times* she identified as a 'progressive Democrat' who no longer cared very much for political labels. 'In a solicitation letter to hundreds of people in her eclectic Rolodex', the *Times* reported, 'Ms. Huffington said the site "won't be left-wing or right-wing; indeed, it will punch holes in that very stale way of looking at the world."'[21]

While Huffington hustled people to write for the site – positioning herself as its chief curator – Lerer, working mostly behind the scenes, undertook much of the team-building and careful brand management *The Huffington Post* would need to take off. (One of their earliest decisions was to name the site *The Huffington Post*. Lerer says he originally wanted to call it *The Stassinopoulos Post*, but added later, 'I'm glad I didn't.') They also engaged in fund-raising and enlisted some of the brightest minds in digital media. Huffington's background playing to both conservative and liberal causes came in handy when making her first crucial hires. And it showed she prized her staff far more for their digital media chops than their personal politics. Founding members of the team included Andrew Breitbart, a former researcher for Huffington who had since become the whiz kid behind The Drudge Report, a leading right-wing news site. After launching in 1995, it had become one of the most popular conservative news sites on the web. (Matthew Drudge, the political commentator behind the site, in fact, had introduced Huffington to Breitbart back when she was still a Republican, writing for Drudge's political team.) Breitbart later founded the far-right news site Breitbart.com, which he would later describe as '*The Huffington Post* of the right'. (Many disagreed, regarding Breitbart's site as xenophobic, misogynist and racist. Breitbart died in 2012.) Another major founding member of Huffington's team was Jonah Peretti, a graduate of the Massachusetts Institute of Technology's Media Lab, recruited to oversee the sophisticated technology that would underpin *The Huffington Post*. A sort of digital media wunderkind, Peretti would go on to conduct some of the internet's earliest and most successful experiments in 'viral' media and news aggregation. Peretti and Lerer would later become partners in *BuzzFeed*, a popular entertainment and news site, founded in 2006.

Some did not think the types of people Huffington wanted to have write for her site – mostly well-known public figures, pundits, academics, activists, politicians, humorists and celebrities – would have the ability to remain active in the blogosphere for sustained periods of time or hold readers' interest. Drudge told the *Times* he was excited about Huffington's new enterprise, saying 'the internet is still in its infancy, it's wide open', but doubted whether the rich and famous would have the drive, talent or sustained focus to write the kind of quality content that, day after day, would be able to captivate audiences. 'I suspect the Hollywood players will find it harder to maintain a compelling webspot' than to open big at the box office, he wrote to the *Times* in an email. 'There are not simply thousands of theaters you have to pack in – there are millions of internet users and eyeballs to dazzle.'

Another early concern was how to handle the unfiltered nature of the writings from contributors and bloggers that Huffington hoped would be streaming in. Answering her critics, she explained that all work would be fact-checked and copy-edited, and would seek to retain the writers' natural voices and the immediacy of their work. At the same time, much of what happened next was largely unplanned, with her team simply letting *The Huffington Post* forge its own path. 'It certainly is inspired by millions of people online who are writing away to their hearts' content,' Breitbart told *The New York Times* in 2005. Peretti added that the site would leave it to the individual – the bloggers themselves – to decide if they wanted to debate issues of the day with the readers who left comments. 'It's something we'll experiment with,' he told the *Times*. 'We want to make sure there's a productive, interesting dialogue and not just people ranting.'[22]

After watching her father repeatedly try and fail to keep his newspapers and various publications afloat, Huffington knew from the start that *The Huffington Post* would be a strictly digital news site. She didn't plan on going bankrupt, like her father, while launching, funding and sustaining a media company. And she sought others to back her financially. On a hike with her close friend Laurie David, she pitched the new start-up, hoping that David and her husband, Larry, would invest. 'A lot of the planning for *The Huffington Post* was done on hikes', Huffington writes in her 2014 book, *Thrive: The Third Metric to Redefining Success and Creating a Life of Well-being, Wisdom and Wonder*. (Huffington made a point of conducting much of her personal and professional business on the hiking trail, noting in *Thrive* that *solvitur ambulando*, translated from Latin as 'it is solved by walking', is one of her favourite phrases.)[23]

During the hike, David agreed to become one of Huffington's first investors. From there, Huffington rustled up additional early rounds of friends-and-family money, reportedly pitching in some of her own, along with Lerer. Huffington's early-stage investors provided around $1 million to $2 million of the seed capital needed to launch what would soon be known as 'The World's Internet Newspaper'.[24] It wasn't much for a new business looking to start up coast-to-coast operations, but it was a sizeable chunk of change for a fledgling news site. Including Lerer, there would be about a dozen angel investors in all, most of whom Lerer and Huffington would not name to the press. According to a 2005 article in *Vanity Fair*, Lerer and his family contributed the lion's share of the capital.[25]

Huffington's foray into internet entrepreneurialism started with half a dozen staffers based in a SoHo loft in lower Manhattan, managed by Lerer. Huffington and Breitbart worked on *The Huffington Post* from her Brentwood home in Los Angeles.[26] To bolster their meagre funding, Huffington and Lerer decided to raise revenue by selling advertising space on the website, receiving commitments from MTV and Sony, among others, landed mostly through their shared connections. Huffington also signed a first-of-its-kind advance deal with the company that syndicated her newspaper columns, Tribune Media Services, to procure extra cash. As part of the arrangement, the New York-based media group agreed to syndicate various parts of *The Huffington Post* and its blogs to newspapers and websites across the country.[27] With this in hand, Lerer hoped *The Huffington Post* would break even in its first year. Huffington, of course, set her sights higher: she wanted to generate a profit by the time *The Huffington Post* had reached its first birthday.[28]

With the dot-com boom in full swing from 1994 until 2001, Huffington and Lerer made a strategic decision to harness en masse Americans' anger over the Bush administration's leap into the 2003 Iraq War, as well as the election loss in 2004 of the Democratic presidential nominee, John Kerry, to say nothing of the mess that was the US election recount of 2000, which saw another Democratic presidential candidate, Al Gore, lose to Bush. It was a time in history when it was uniquely easy to fire up American liberals.

Lerer expounded on this just before *The Huffington Post* launched, telling *The New York Times* in April 2005 that the publication 'was born, in part, out of frustration with the elections – the last one and the one before that. A lot of people didn't know what to do after those campaigns, and this will allow them to enter the dialogue.'[29] Nick Denton, a fellow internet entrepreneur and founder of website Gawker Media (which folded in 2016), put it more bluntly: '*Huffington Post* was fueled by liberal rage against George Bush, Fox News and the right-wing media-political complex.'[30] The real intention of the site, Denton suggested, was to offer a counterpoint to the conservative-in-extremis American voter base rapidly gaining a chokehold on American politics.

True to form, Huffington sounded much more inclusive when explaining the site's genesis. 'The original idea behind *The Huffington Post* was to have all these voices that I was exposed to in my life online,' she says. 'I knew that a lot of the people who were my friends would never be online [without it].'[31] What she wanted, she said, was to bring new voices to the fore, whether they were sharp-edged or more nuanced. 'Sometimes you make a difference by helping to convince a few people,' she says. 'It doesn't have to be a difference at the national level. You help people articulate, no doubt, what they already believe. I totally believe in the tipping point, or the critical mass. For me, there are three different terms for the same thing: the tipping point, the critical mass and, also grace, the spiritual concept of grace. You do your 10 percent and then grace is extended, if this is what is to happen. If it is what is right.'[32] These terms came straight from the spiritual lexicon Huffington had been invoking for years, and increasingly carried over into how she expressed her political views.

Besides handling the complex logistics of a start-up, Huffington had to overcome the fresh objections of her teenage daughters, who were not at all enamoured of a news site carrying their surname. 'My daughters thought it was a terrible idea,' Huffington recalls of her plans to launch The Huffington Post. They 'hated it'. They especially did not want their name on it – in case it failed, she says.[33]

Launch day arrived on Monday, 9 May 2005, and, as her daughters feared, drew an avalanche of scathing criticism. 'We got terrible reviews when we launched,' Huffington says. 'One of them I've kind of learned by heart', because it listed nearly every career catastrophe she had ever had, before calling The Huffington Post a failure from which she would never recover. The review, written by Nikki Finke for LA Weekly and widely noted by members of the press at the time, went on to say:

Judging from Monday's horrific debut of the humongously pre-hyped celebrity blog The Huffington Post, the Madonna of the mediapolitic world has undergone one reinvention too many. She has now made an online ass of herself. What her bizarre guru-cult association, 180-degree right-to-left conversion, and failed run in the California gubernatorial-recall race couldn't accomplish, her blog has now done: She is finally played out, publicly. This website venture is the sort of failure that is simply unsurvivable. Her blog is such a bomb that it's the movie equivalent of *Gigli*, *Ishtar* and *Heaven's Gate* rolled into one. In magazine terms, it's the disastrous clone of Tina Brown's *Talk*, JFK Jr.'s *George* . . . No matter what happens to Huffington, it's clear Hollywood will suffer the consequences. It seems like some sick hoax . . .

A number of conservative publications, like the *National Review,* also piled in. Given Huffington's vociferous distaste of the American right, this was to be expected. One review in particular, by a conservative panning her site, however, must have rankled, as it came from Tribune Media Services, the same media company she had signed with to syndicate parts of *The Huffington Post*. In a piece entitled 'The Blog That Ate Real Journalism', political and social commentator Cal Thomas wrote:

The Huffington Post, an internet blog that debuted May 9 after a campaign that would have delighted P. T. Barnum, makes me nostalgic for the good old days of journalism. It isn't that its founder, Arianna

Huffington ... doesn't have every right to join the increasingly clogged blog superhighway ... The problem with blogs such as *The Huffington Post* is that they divert our attention from real and serious journalism ...

Ignoring the naysayers, Huffington pushed ahead as *Huff-Post*'s inaugural president and editor-in-chief. 'Really, the difference between failure and success is perseverance,' she says. It was the sort of aphorism that could have come straight from her mother. Even with the blistering reviews, readers flocked to *The Huffington Post* during its first days of going live out of curiosity – and to read whatever the various celebrity bloggers had to say about US politics, foreign policy, the Bush administration and the war in Iraq. From the start, the primary focus of *HuffPost* was politics. To anyone who hesitated to write for the site, Huffington would exhort, 'Put it in an email and send it to me and we'll publish it exactly as you sent it to us and you'll have entered the cultural bloodstream. You'll have entered the conversation. You don't have to do anything else. Then people can comment, react, take it to the next level.' This was her mantra and, she says, 'that's exactly what happened.'[34]

The site created buzz, with people clicking, reading and emailing articles to one another. 'The first day we launched was kind of a new day for blogging,' Huffington said, adding, 'It began the process of elevating blogging to something that, of course, we all do.'[35] A few members of Huffington's rarefied social circles also came forward, telling the press how much they enjoyed writing their thoughts online. The filmmaker and journalist Nora Ephron, who agreed early on to write for the site – one of approximately 300 high-profile people to do so – told *The New York Times* she welcomed the 'casual aspect' of posting whenever she felt like it. 'The idea that one might occasionally be able to have a small thought and a place to send it, without having to write a whole essay, seems like a very good idea,' she said. She felt it was also an opportunity to counter some of the nation's more right-wing media bluster. 'In the Fox [News] era,' she said, 'everything we can do on our side to even things out, now that the media is either controlled by [conservative media mogul] Rupert Murdoch, or is so afraid of Rupert Murdoch that they behave as if they were controlled by him, is great.' Still, there were times she just wanted to write about non-political things, she said, adding sometimes 'I may merely have a cake recipe.'[36]

Veteran *CBS Evening News* anchorman Walter Cronkite, well into his eighties by this time, was of the same mind, noting the beauty of the internet was that anything he might post could either be abbreviated or have no word limit at all. 'This gives me a chance to sound off with a few words, or a long editorial,' he told the *Times*. 'It's a medium that is new and interesting, and I thought I'd have some fun.'[37] Even the famously curmudgeonly Norman Mailer – with lots of prodding from Huffington – agreed to give blogging a try. (A few years earlier, he had been asked in an interview if he 'did' the internet. 'I don't,' Mailer had admitted. 'That would use up what I have left.') By mid-May, following the kick-off of Huffington's website, he was forced to grudgingly concede writing online had some utility. 'I'm beginning to see why one would want to write a blog,' he said. Some of the final writings of Cronkite and Mailer, both now deceased, appeared on *The Huffington Post*.[38]

Huffington was gratified to have another ambition realized when she launched her site: Some of the most brilliant minds in the world were weighing in on the political news of the day in real time. Schlesinger faxed in his first blog post, slamming a statement made by President George W. Bush that, Huffington recalls, was 'part and parcel of [Bush's] ongoing derision of negotiations, diplomacy and anything but unilateral cowboyism'. Having a well-respected historian speak up 'swiftly and knowledgeably' about how Bush's comments could be 'delusional', she says, was 'my dream come true'.[39] When Schlesinger died in 2007, Huffington penned a column for *HuffPost* with the memorable headline, 'Arthur Schlesinger, Jr.: Historian, Kennedy Court Philosopher . . . Blogger.'

A number of trademark features made *The Huffington Post* unquestionably successful. The very top of the site's home page displayed a 'splash' deck, which showcased the most riveting story of the day with a massive photo and a jumbo-sized headline that filled up the screen. This has remained one of the biggest traffic-generators and most instantly recognizable traits of the site. Another feature of *HuffPost* was its highly popular three-column, newspaper format, embedded with photos and divided into different sections that would, as the publication grew, cover not just politics, but also business, hard news and entertainment. 'It doesn't look like a blog,' Huffington said, predicting, 'it will become its own product unto itself.'

HuffPost also offered something traditional newspapers and many websites, at the time, did not: a comments section beneath the blogs and stories so that readers could have their say and, as was frequently the case, debate with each other, as well as with the writer of the article. Soon, hundreds of thousands of people were posting their comments to the site, resulting in the kind of spontaneous, widespread, conversational community Huffington had long aspired to see. 'Self-expression is the new form of entertainment . . . blogging is transforming our lives, changing the way in which we think, observe, critique and respond, just as it is changing the field of journalism,' she said.[40] For Huffington, the idea was not just to get attention but, as a lifelong networker, share it as extensively as possible. As her co-founder Lerer told the *New Yorker*, 'Here are the pockets: L.A., New York, D.C. Tell me somebody else who can bring those three cities together. With Arianna, it's not six degrees of separation – it's two.'[41]

Initially, the bulk of *The Huffington Post* was primarily bloggers posting thoughts 'on anything from the events of the day, to food, to movies, to anything at all', Huffington says. 'One of our sayings was, "If you have anything to say, say it on *The Huffington Post*."'[42] The site had bigger intentions, though. It sought to become a sprawling 'journalistic enterprise', she said, 'where we practiced conventional journalism, investigative journalism. At the beginning, the blogging part was the dominant part until we started raising and making money to be able to hire journalists.' Until then, the heavyweight names attracted web traffic and *HuffPost* rode the curiosity factor to generate more clicks. Huffington herself was the first to acknowledge she used celebrity names to her advantage, saying that when famous 'people who had never blogged before' wrote for the first time, it would cause readers to 'sort of sit up and look at it as something different'. Celebrities joining the blogosphere through her site, she said, 'is an affirmation of its success and will only enrich and strengthen its impact on the national conversation'.[43]

Her site offered 24-hour-a-day news aggregation, pulling the most important headlines and news stories off the web and rewriting or repackaging them on *HuffPost*, so readers – especially the news junkies – didn't miss a beat. While many media outlets, including Associated Press and *The New York Times*, objected to having their news, special investigations and photos taken, rejigged and spat back out by the *HuffPost* content machine, Huffington's site was hardly alone. A wide range of news portals – including major journalism organizations – across the media land-scape were already pushing the outer boundaries of fair use guidelines by 2005. News was prohibitively expensive to create, but once it was online, other websites could steal it and publish it for free. Huffington's team only differed in that it sought to endlessly redefine the cutting edge of doing so. 'Our promise to our readers, basically, is that we will bring you the best of the web,' Huffington stated.

'Whether we produce it, or we find it and curate it for you. And we present it with a certain flair.'[44]

Behind the scenes, *The Huffington Post* was doing a lot more than just that. It became a veritable skunk works for online media and viral content. Guided by Peretti and Breitbart, *HuffPost* mastered the art of search-engine optimization by affixing keywords to blogs and articles published on the site, so that they rose as high as possible on Google searches.[45] Back then, readers received much of their news via internet searches, as opposed to social media. In the years ahead, however, *The Huffington Post* would leverage the high wattage of social media outlets, tracking the rise of Facebook, Twitter and other global drivers of media traffic. Huffington's team also experimented with content, employing A/B testing – for instance, writing two different headlines, or more, for the same story to see which headline received the most clicks and the best response. The winning headline would be used most widely. Huffington's team would tease out the choicest bits of stories already published on the web and add peppier headlines or lead paragraphs to make them more appealing than the original. In this way, a major news site might publish a popular story, but then quickly lose the traffic to *HuffPost* when its staff rewrote it and then reposted it to read far more smartly.

Obsessively adjusting *HuffPost*'s content, measuring the results and repositioning content to create the best possible outcomes for readership, eyeballs and clicks became a critical factor in the site's success. 'I've always been interested in why ideas spread, in network theory and in why people share things,' Peretti explained to the *Independent*, which in 2012 dubbed him 'the nerd-genius'.[46] But he had never connected all the dots to turn his knowledge into a business before *The Huffington Post*. In a separate interview with Harvard's *Nieman Journalism Lab*, Peretti said that Lerer, a savvy venture capitalist, was 'the one that got me excited about doing business'. At first, Peretti said, 'I wasn't interested in *The Huffington Post* primarily as a business. I was like, "Oh, it's a cool new opportunity. It's something different."'[47] But that changed very quickly. Within a few years, Peretti grew adept at building analytics platforms for web content that traced in real time how consumers interacted with news headlines and other media, placing the site's most popular blogs and news exactly where people would see them most, and creating 'a viral advertising platform that sends more traffic to content that is actually working'. It is a method he would develop further and employ when he later started his own company, *BuzzFeed*.[48]

With so much news-aggregating and big names being floated on *HuffPost*, there was the occasional hiccup. Huffington would sometimes be too eager to land a celebrity blogger. Such was the case in March 2006, when she strung together a series of quotes from interviews Hollywood actor George Clooney had done with CNN and the *Guardian*, typed it up into a blog post with the headline, 'I am a Liberal. There, I Said It!' and added Clooney's name underneath. When it was released, the reaction was far from muted. 'If Clooney blogs, does that make it sexy?'

Denton's Gawker news site asked. But then Clooney himself asserted he had not written any of it. 'These are not my
writings,' he said in a public statement. 'They are answers
to questions – and there is a huge difference.'

The blog was taken down. Critics gleefully branded the
episode 'Clooneygate'.[49] Huffington blamed Clooney's
public relations representative for approving the blog after
she wrote it. Following a great deal of hue and cry from
media critics, readers and purist-bloggers – who primarily
argued that cobbling together a bunch of Clooney quotes
does not a Clooney blog make – Huffington finally issued
an apology. In a post titled 'Lessons Learned', Huffington
said she made a 'big mistake' by writing a blog as though
she was Clooney himself. She promised that it would not
happen again, because 'it diminishes the amazing work
of bloggers who, day in and day out put their hearts and
souls into writing their blogs'. It was by no means the first
time Huffington had got into a scrape for lifting material
or misrepresenting it. Yet by now she was a pro at assess-
ing – and answering to – her public. If fighting her corner
didn't work, she instinctively knew when it was time to
apologize. It was a talent she had honed over many years
and few could match. This is why no matter what kerfuffle
came her way, Huffington almost always knew what to say
to readers and fans to emerge a media darling once again,
largely unscathed.

While juggling the day-to-day operations of her site,
Huffington also managed to put together another book – a
feel-good title that doubled as a victory lap on the heels

of the launch of *HuffPost*. *On Becoming Fearless . . . In Love, Work, and Life* was the first book to come out since she'd founded her business and a notable departure from the taut grimness of *Fanatics & Fools: The Game Plan for Winning Back America*, released in 2004 shortly after she lost the California gubernatorial race. *Fanatics & Fools* had mainly consisted of a series of attacks on the GOP, propounding Huffington's transition from right-wing conservative to social progressive. By contrast, *Fearless* heralded her arrival as a media 'disrupter', bringing old media (traditional newspapers and legacy media) together with new media (digital and the social web). 'I watched *The Huffington Post* come alive to mixed reviews, including some very negative ones,' she recounted to *Forbes* in 2014. 'It's an illustration of one of my deepest beliefs, which is that we must dare to take risks and to fail, as many times as it takes, along the way to success.'

Huffington's book *Fearless* is where she boldly assumes the mantle of the pioneering businesswoman – proud, fierce, regal and unstoppable. In it, she tells the stories of her life, her mother's life and the lives of her daughters and friends about how to deal with fears over love, career, personal appearance, ageing, illness, finances and becoming a leader. She also asserts that Americans, from citizens to CEOs to political leaders, need to do a better job of confronting their own fears and standing up for their convictions. Huffington populates the book, which departs from politics to focus on self-improvement, with many passages from her stable of famous female friends and acquaintances, including Diane Keaton, Nora Ephron and other prominent women from the television, film and entertainment industries. Her daughters, at this point aged fifteen and seventeen, inspired her to write the book, she said, adding that she wanted to give them and others a 'road map for achieving fearlessness in every aspect of our lives, a straight-to-the-point manifesto'.[50]

By now, Huffington's celebrity friends were not only contributing regularly to her books, but also writing positive reviews for them. In *Fearless*, Keaton both contributed a short chapter and offered a review of the book for its back cover. 'There is no one else in the world better suited to write about fearlessness than Arianna Huffington', she wrote. Huffington's world, while increasingly wide, was also becoming an increasingly closed circuit. She dedicated her book, which came out in 2007, to her late mother, her daughters and to 'Kenny Lerer, my *Huffington Post* partner, whose love and support have made my own journey more fearless'. Her ascent as a leading light in the media cosmos was sealed in May 2006, exactly one year after starting up *The Huffington Post*, when Huffington was named among the 'Time One Hundred', *Time* magazine's list of the world's hundred most influential people 'whose power, talent or moral example is transforming our world'. It would be the first time her name would appear on the list, but not the last.

Speaking to this author in summer 2006 from her home offices in Brentwood, California, Huffington, then fifty-six years old, said she believed that fearlessness was the No. 1

reason for her success. 'If you are any kind of woman who wants to launch any venture, you need to develop your fearlessness muscle,' she told me. 'It's something you have to do and something you have to face if you want to succeed. It gets easier, the more you do it.' She estimated at that time that she had accumulated 'well over 700 bloggers' for *The Huffington Post* – all unpaid – with the site fetching roughly 2.9 million unique visitors a month by mid-2006 and 35 million page views. More noteworthy, *HuffPost* had quickly become the fifth most popular weblog overall on the internet and the most popular 'analysis and opinion' site, as measured by web hits. It would dominate the rankings for years to come.[51] That year, even Huffington's ex-husband began blogging for her site.

During our interview, Huffington said that she felt she was living out her dream. I asked her what she now saw herself as – a politician, an activist, businesswoman, or writer? 'Obviously, I see myself as a journalist who tries to speak truth to power and try to bring into online journalism all the values of fairness and accuracy that are so important,' she said. 'Also, I want to challenge the conventional wisdom and bring in a lot of new people who have given up on politics.' Taking a page from Bernard Levin, she was also fond of writing on the fly. 'I am writing about all the things that I love and the thoughts that I have when I wake up in the morning and throughout the day,' she said. 'Often I dictate into a machine, or to a person, because I am so much on the go.' She described her blogging style as akin to speaking to a close friend or a confidant: 'I believe that blogging has an informality and an intimacy to it. It's sort of how you might email a friend and that allows you to reach people. Keeping it that way is key. It is extremely fun to write about things you are passionate about and care about. I write every day . . . it's at various times.'

Throughout the interview, Huffington's graciousness and optimism were apparent. In every statement, she conveyed great expectations, positivity and hope. Even in its infancy, *The Huffington Post*'s traffic was already beating many other major news organizations' sites and, according to Huffington, it was doing so with only a dozen or so paid staffers. Speaking to one of her employees at her Brentwood home, I learned more about Huffington's work habits. 'She's a dynamo,' the employee told me. 'She goes to bed at night at midnight and then gets up at 5 a.m. the next day. She outdoes the younger people she works with. She's extremely intelligent, with a positive spirit about her. Nothing gets her down. Whenever we get stressed out, she always says, "That's past, let's just move forward." She's inspirational for us.' To hear her employees describe it, Huffington hardly ever rested. In 2006, her home was carved up into a workplace with the upstairs for Huffington's staff of four and the downstairs for herself. Huffington told me she considered blogging a full-time job, and also a labour of love.

But was it profitable? Huffington would not give any dollar figures, or discuss how she supported herself while keeping *HuffPost* humming, but she said she made enough off the site to be self-sufficient. Even so, the site had not yet met her goal of producing earnings. Ad sales, however, were doing well. 'If you get enough visitors, then you can sell advertising,' she explained, 'and there's more and more advertising online these days.' (In the early days, many of the advertisers on *HuffPost* were other media or technology companies – Bloomberg News, eBay, HarperCollins and Google – targeting tech geeks and news addicts.) Writing books, Huffington said, provided her with some additional income, but she emphasized that she did not rely on this to make ends meet. In effect, she was facing a modern-day version of many of the same perilous decisions her father had to make while balancing the mission of journalism with the need for funding. There was just one key difference: she was doing it within a rapidly changing online media environment few yet fully understood, let alone had been able to master.

By August 2006, *HuffPost* needed more money and Huffington and Lerer commenced their first round of commercial fund-raising, with their original angel investors investing again, as well as two venture capital groups, Tokyo-based Softbank Capital, which focused on internet companies (it was once the biggest shareholder in Yahoo), and Greycroft Partners, a New York firm run by top Democratic fund-raiser Alan Patricof, a venture capitalist investing in early-stage digital media. In addition, another former AOL executive – the creator of MTV, Robert Pittman – bought a stake in *The Huffington Post* around this time, according to the *Guardian*. Pittman was co-founder of the Pilot Group, a private investment company that looked for opportunities in new media. (Gawker had once quipped, in another one of its celebrated one-liners, 'Bob Pittman Will Buy You Now.')[52]

The investors contributed $5 million in all, allowing *HuffPost* to pursue an expansion of its site and the hiring of additional staff to provide more original reporting and journalism. Lerer and Huffington strongly believed that the quality of the journalism on the *HuffPost* site would be crucial to its long-term success. As Lerer was fond of saying, 'Content is king.' As part of *HuffPost*'s evolution, Huffington also widened the scope of the site beyond politics to focus on health, wellness, the environment and work–life balance issues. 'After the first year, we started adding sections and the traffic started growing and so my dream started getting bigger,' Huffington says. 'But we were still a start-up.'[53]

Above all, Huffington wanted to be able to expand the site wherever it needed to go, including adding powerful images and video, as well as new sections highlighting her work. 'There is always so much happening in the internet universe,' she said. One section based on *On Becoming Fearless* covered relationships, wealth-building and fashion. While Huffington was by no means a tech geek, she noted that while the site's political news drew more male readers, a broader range of lifestyle topics attracted a larger female contingent.[54] With a strong connection to her audience and what they wanted, she continued writing articles, blogs and editorials for the site in primarily a journalistic capacity. But because the site bore her name, it was also an extension of herself – and what she wanted. And what Huffington wanted was not to be bound by any limits, local or global.

Before the end of 2006, she had captured the world's attention, landing a coveted '*Playboy* Interview'. In a lengthy Q&A, *Playboy* magazine described Huffington as a 'noted biographer, a political wife, an outspoken columnist and a TV talking head' who had 'morphed over the past few years from a conservative voice and major voice in the Republican Party into a Democrat who has run for office'. It then went on to say that her 'most impressive shift' was leaping 'from mainstream media to the web with *The Huffington Post*, her news-aggregating multi-blog brainchild'. The magazine called her site the go-to outlet that 'breaks news stories and relentlessly pursues crucial issues long past their mainstream media expiration date'.[55]

By the time the *Playboy* magazine article rolled out, Huffington was a household name, able to inveigle nearly anyone of public stature to write for her site, including political leaders preparing for the 2008 presidential election. In a 2007 article titled 'Arianna Calling!', featuring a pictorial of Huffington fielding phone calls and running *HuffPost* from her luxurious study in her Brentwood home, *Vanity Fair* wrote, 'With *The Huffington Post*, Arianna might finally have it all: Attention, influence, and the chance to showcase her ideas and those of her interesting friends in the biggest dinner party she's ever thrown.'[56]

With the next election top of mind, *The Huffington Post* began another round of fund-raising for the site in 2007, drawing an additional $5 million. Softbank, Greycroft and the rest of the previous investor group participated. As a private company, *HuffPost* did not need to reveal who paid for what share of the company, but everyone in the group would have known that bowing out of the latest fund-raising spree would have lowered the value of their individual *HuffPost* stakes.[57]

The site, at this point, had raised an estimated $12 million in all since its inception, attracting more than 900 contributors and bloggers. Huffington announced that the site would be sending hundreds of volunteers into the field to report on the coming presidential race, as well as break news and offer opinions and analysis on the competing candidates. *HuffPost* also teamed up with Yahoo and *Slate*, an online news and entertainment magazine, to host two web-only presidential debates, which allowed voters to ask candidates direct questions live and rate their performances.[58] The debates would be hosted by PBS's Charlie Rose. When he asked her in 2007 to reflect on her journey from Greek immigrant to internet entrepreneur, she told him, 'I came here as an outsider . . . I did different things . . . I wrote books, I wrote columns, I spoke . . . My latest endeavour, in the internet, which had many naysayers saying it's not going to succeed, succeeded . . . It involved risk which is sort of an essential element of leadership. You have to be willing to risk.'[59]

A new risk would soon be changing the game. The rise of social media platforms like Facebook, Twitter and others were beginning to direct a surge in traffic to *The Huffington*

Post, with users increasingly posting and sharing *HuffPost* news on their personal media feeds. This multiplied the number of ways in which readers could find stories on *The Huffington Post* website, which was now aggregating stories from around the world twenty-four hours a day and receiving hundreds of thousands of comments from readers every month.[60] In 2007 *HuffPost* expanded its news coverage to include business and entertainment, attracting more than 3 million unique viewers a month and more than 70 million page views – and prompting *The New York Times* to report that *HuffPost* had become 'a well-known, oft-cited news media brand in the blink of an eye'.

With Lerer recruiting yet more talent to *HuffPost* at its SoHo headquarters, Huffington focused on tirelessly chasing down celebrity contributors and presiding over the growth of the business from her Los Angeles home. She was working eighteen-hour days, seven days a week, and trying to keep up with both the east and west coasts. One day, Huffington's sister Agapi, who was with her at the time, said she heard a thud in the next room and found Huffington lying on the floor of her home office in a pool of her own blood. 'I was right there,' she told the London *Telegraph*. 'I was in bed with a cold when I heard this horrendous thump. I hurried into Arianna's office and saw her bleeding on the floor. I was so scared that I fainted.'[61] Huffington had collapsed. 'I hit my head on my desk, I broke my cheekbone, I got five stitches on my right eye,' Huffington recalls.[62] It was a 'painful wake-up call'.[63] After multiple tests at the hospital from brain scans – for a possible tumour – to heart sonograms, Huffington received her diagnosis: burnout.

Shortly before the accident, Huffington says she was visiting universities with her eldest daughter, Christina (both of Huffington's daughters would attend Yale). She had just returned home to catch up on her work. During the college tour, she says, she and her daughter had made a deal: 'Our ground rule was that I would not be on my devices, that I would be fully present with her. I literally returned home completely sleep-deprived.' Long known for her superhuman endurance, Huffington was forced to reassess her approach to her career. After getting by on four or five hours of sleep a night, she 'began the journey of rediscovering sleep' and realized she needed closer to eight hours a night, she says.[64] Although she would continue to struggle with maintaining a work–life balance, the experience would stay with her, later inspiring a book, as well as a new business venture, in her late sixties. 'Building *The Huffington Post,* I had bought into the mythology that everything was dependent on me, and I had to do everything, at the expense of sleep, health,' she says. In hindsight, Huffington says she realized she had ignored the many warning signs. 'It was a question of coming to in a pool of blood and realizing nobody had shot me.'[65]

Huffington was not the only one working around the clock. Her entire staff – as well as Lerer – put in very long hours during the first two years of *The Huffington Post*'s launch. Lerer steeped himself in the details of the site's technology and worked closely with its young, underpaid staff to improve its appeal to readers. He wrangled with writers and editors over the headlines, presentation and story angles to get the site maximum attention. He could be a demanding and hands-on boss, according to *HuffPost* employees. But he also worked as hard as they did.

He 'was known among the twentysomething staffers as a benevolent slave-driver, expecting 12-hour workdays, seven days a week, but often staying in the newsroom himself past midnight to tweak headlines, photos and video, while calling in his directions as many as 20 times a day', according to an article in *The Daily Beast*.[66] Katharine Zaleski, one of *HuffPost*'s first recruits and a senior editor, told the *Observer* it was not unusual for her to receive calls all day from Lerer in the early days to do things like rewrite the top headline of a story. 'He was the kind of boss who would make you do something, or you'd put it up and say, "This is crazy, this headline makes no sense," and then he'd say, "Trust me, just trust me." And then, oh my God, it would be a huge hit.'[67]

Lerer, a Brooklyn-born college dropout,[68] started his career working not only on political campaigns, but also in journalism – at one point even writing for *New York* magazine – before entering the white-shoe world of public relations.[69] He went on to work for big corporations, like Warner-Amex (parent company of MTV and a precursor to Time-Warner), which became his first major client when he opened his own PR firm in 1986. From there, he became known as an image man with a knack for making – as well as resuscitating – people's reputations by way of his virtuosic ability to shape public opinion through the press. In helping junk bond trader Michael Milken resurrect himself after going to prison for securities fraud, Lerer commenced a media campaign and charged Milken a $150,000-a-month retainer.[70]

Lerer's method in working on brands and reputations was to play the long game, according to the 1989 book *Den of Thieves*, by author James Stewart. In it, he describes how Lerer's firm set about repairing Milken's reputation by telling its staff the goal 'was to turn public opinion from outrage to neutrality to acceptance – and finally, to admiration'. The campaign to rejuvenate Milken's reputation, Stewart wrote, 'was remarkably effective'.[71] Stewart also says Lerer would contact reporters at major newspapers to dangle small bits of information: 'Lerer would call these reporters frequently, working the phones as he played Nintendo in his office, or calling from his car, planting story ideas worked up by members of his staff,' according to Stewart. 'Occasionally, he dribbled bits of "exclusive" information to his current favorites. Lerer once called it "breast-feeding" the reporters.'[72] This was how modern-day public relations often succeeded in shaping and reshaping public opinion.

Other clients of Lerer's firm included AOL, Microsoft, NBC Television and MTV. Lerer's approach was to roll out a steady 'drumbeat of announcements', such as advertising deals or expansions to new regions, timing it 'in such a way that there was a calendar-spaced set of announcements used to stoke the growing pace, to do deals and get warrants in other companies,' a source told *The Daily Beast*, adding, 'He was always orchestrating stuff . . . He was a master at creating friendly relationships with the media.'[73] By all accounts, Lerer also could be a stabilizing force in the midst of corporate chaos, able to ground and steer difficult conversations towards resolution. As one executive who worked with him recalls, 'I can remember some pretty intense, highly intense, volatile meetings where there were conflicting points of view. Things were really rattling around the table. And I'd look at him and call on him and he was just calm, straightforward, extremely poised while everyone else around the table was losing it.'[74]

Lerer's keen understanding of how brands were built through the media, his overall collectedness, and his proclivity for finessing members of the press, worked well at *The Huffington Post*, and helped put it on the map. Combined with Huffington's star power and creative energies, the site's rapid growth may well have been inevitable. Lerer and Huffington were an excellent match: she was an extrovert and he preferred to stay behind the scenes. Both were well-connected multi-millionaires (Lerer made his first big payday when he sold his PR firm, which he co-founded). Both preferred to be their own bosses and move freely through the world. Most importantly, neither liked to play by convention. 'An avowed loner and devoted husband and father who hates large meetings and avoids wearing ties, [Lerer] found that he was increasingly miserable having to play corporate politics', reported *The Daily Beast*.[75] This made *HuffPost* a perfect place for Lerer, who sought to use the realm of internet entrepreneurialism as a testing ground for generating influence and profit.

Within just a few years of *The Huffington Post*'s launch, publications such as *Business Insider*, *Bloomberg* and *Vanity Fair* began publishing ever-higher valuations for the company, which, in turn, attracted more investors to it, many of whom hoped to one day reap a profit.[76] In September of 2007, *Business Insider* gave *HuffPost* a valuation of $60 million, largely based on the expectation that the site would report profits in the following year.[77] It didn't. But media reports of the company's burgeoning value continued apace.

In December 2008 a third round of fund-raising at *HuffPost* drew the site's first large investor, Oak Investment Partners of Palo Alto, California, which paid $25 million for a stake in the company, pushing *HuffPost*'s overall estimated valuation to nearly $100 million.[78] While Huffington maintained there were no plans yet to sell the site, by December 2010, *Bloomberg* estimated the site's valuation at $300 million to $450 million. *Vanity Fair* put it at $350 million in January 2011.[79] Given Lerer's known skill with the press, his fingerprints were suspected of being on the media's consistent reporting of the rising value of *The Huffington Post*'s business. While Lerer stated he was not responsible for providing any of the numbers reported to the media, many speculated that he or Huffington, with their numerous connections to the press, were in a position to do so.[80]

From 2008 on, Huffington presided over the expansion of *The Huffington Post* ahead of the next presidential race, launching more local editions of the website covering New York, Chicago and Denver, followed later by Los Angeles, San Francisco, Miami and Hawaii, among others.[81] The site was by now attracting blue-chip advertisers such as Starbucks, Home Depot and Volkswagen. Bolstered by more funding, the site hired additional reporters and, as part of Huffington's focus on health and work–life balance, set up a lounge at the Democratic National Convention offering conventioneers free yoga classes and facials.

Huffington played an outsized role in how *The Huffington Post* covered the 2008 presidential election, whose candidates included Barack Obama and Hillary Clinton – both of whom were vying to lead the Democratic ticket – as well as Republican presidential nominee John McCain. *The New Yorker* wrote assiduously about Huffington's approach to the political landscape at that time, as both a pundit and a businesswoman. 'Throughout her career, Huffington has demonstrated a gladiatorial appetite for verbal combat. Her assessments of Bill Frist, Karl Rove, Dick Cheney, campaign finance, the drug war, the war in Iraq – even at a time when questioning the war against terrorism wasn't popular – have been unflinching', wrote Lauren Collins in a lengthy profile of Huffington. She observed that *HuffPost*'s giant front-page headlines had a penchant for being extremely effective, citing a particular one about McCain during the 2008 global financial crisis: 'AS ROME BURNS . . . MCCAIN CAMP TALKS LIPSTICK, PIGS,

WOLVES, MOOSE, FISH, SNOW MOBILING AND SEX-ED FOR KINDERGARTNERS.'[82]

Huffington's aggressive approach, along with consumers' historically enormous appetite for political presidential news during election seasons, led to a spike in traffic at *The Huffington Post* from around 3.8 million unique visitors in February of 2008 to 5.1 million by the August. The leap saw *HuffPost* surpass the traffic of its conservative foil and predecessor, The Drudge Report, for the first time, according to the *New Yorker*, which called *HuffPost* 'a triumph'.[83]

During this time, Huffington was nothing if not vocal in her support of Obama, who won the Democratic nomination over Clinton before going on to clinch the presidency. (Huffington, whose historic dislike of the Clintons was well known, strongly disagreed with Hillary Clinton's support for the Iraq War.) Even so, both Obama and Clinton dutifully wrote for *The Huffington Post* throughout the election season – such was the power and sway of Huffington's site. With *HuffPost* now the most linked-to blog on the internet, neither candidate could afford not to speak directly to its readers, known for their passionately liberal political leanings.

Riding the coat-tails of the presidential election in 2008, Huffington published the book *Right Is Wrong: How the Lunatic Fringe Hijacked America, Shredded the Constitution and Made Us All Less Safe (And What You Need to Know to End the Madness)*, returning to her roots as a polemicist. The book takes the American conservative right to task, as well as the Bush presidency, asserting that

radical elements were taking over the Republican Party –
an observation that turned out to be extremely prescient.
Although Huffington noted that, by this time, she hadn't
been a member of the GOP for 'almost a dozen years', the
book gave her the opportunity to explain in more detail
why she left:

> People often ask me what caused me to change course
> so radically. In truth, my 'conversion' wasn't as dra-
> matic as it might have appeared. On all the so-called
> values issues – abortion, gun control, gay rights – I
> have the exact same progressive positions today that
> I've always had. The biggest shift in my thinking has
> been in how I view the role of government. I used to
> believe that the private sector would address the prob-
> lems of those in need. But then I saw, up close and
> very personal, that this isn't going to happen.[84]

Her shift in thinking, Huffington says, came when she
realized in the late 1990s 'how unfounded was my belief
that the private sector – especially conservative multi-
billionaires who wail about wanting less government
involvement – would rise to the occasion and provide the
funding needed to replicate social programs that work.'
She also says she noticed, over the years, that 'when I tried
to raise money for poverty-fighting groups and community
activists', it was far easier to raise money 'for the opera or
a fashionable museum than for a homeless shelter or free
clinic. So, I came to recognize that the task of overcoming

poverty is too monumental to be achieved without the raw power of annual government appropriations.'[85] The book, dedicated to Huffington's daughters, appears to be one of Huffington's first not to be copyrighted under her own name, but under the private company named for her daughters, Christabella Inc. Such vehicles are often used to safeguard profits while shielding the owner from losses and offering tax benefits.

The same year, *The Huffington Post* also released a book, *The Huffington Post Complete Guide to Blogging*, assembled by the editors of *HuffPost* and featuring an introduction by Huffington herself. The book offers tips and best practices for bloggers, billing itself as 'an A to Z guide to all things blog, with information for everyone from the tech-challenged newbie looking to get a handle on this new way of communicating, to the experienced blogger looking to break through the clutter of the internet'. While publicizing the book in December 2008, on Comedy Central's *The Daily Show*, Huffington buttonholed the programme's host, Jon Stewart, backstage, demanding: 'When are you going to blog for me?'[86]

While on air, Huffington and Stewart discussed the global financial crisis, which was in the process of devastating most Western economies – and blogging: 'We just started a whole series called 'Blog the Meltdown,'' Huffington said, referring to the crisis. 'You know, you've lost a job? You have time to blog. It's very cathartic.'

'I cannot believe that you just put a positive spin on the financial crisis,' Stewart said.

'You don't know what it will lead to,' Huffington said. 'I am a blogging evangelist.'

Stewart asked her about her interests. 'My obvious passion is politics,' Huffington told him, adding that a 'secret passion' of hers was cheese. 'Another passion of mine,' she added, 'is sleep.' That comment, unbeknownst to Huffington at the time, hinted at things to come.

At this point in her career, Huffington was thoroughly enjoying herself. While there was still the occasional dust-up over her continuing affiliation with John-Roger, these instances were getting fewer and farther between. They did not completely disappear, however. In late 2008 a report from Gawker bearing the headline 'Arianna's Mandatory Cult Meetings' described how two *Huffington Post* employees were instructed to attend an Insight training seminar in Westlake, California, with *HuffPost* footing the bill and covering the air fare. Some of Huffington's staffers expressed concern. One person told Gawker it became 'kind of a joke in the office', with employees tossing out references to being 'brainwashed by the creepy cult'. Still, in an election year – and particularly amid the throes of the global financial crisis – such headlines did not linger for long, vanishing swiftly in the slipstream of the news cycle.

In fact, Huffington's domination of the national conversation as the head of *The Huffington Post* was, at the time, unassailable. Her preferred presidential candidate, Barack Obama, not only handily won the White House, he won the largest share of the popular vote by a Democrat since 1964. Huffington was also largely shielded from the travails of the financial crisis, as she had successfully recruited thousands more people to her army of citizen bloggers – some of whom were breaking national news. While she was frequently slammed by the press for disrupting the for-profit media industry and capitalizing on the work of unpaid writers, she rejected such criticisms. She also was attempting to work on solutions to create more original, paid content for the web that could be disseminated far beyond the reach of just her own website. In early 2009 she launched 'The Huffington Post Investigative Fund', a non-profit, collaborative, journalistic unit focused on a variety of investigative projects that worked closely with editors, writers, freelancers and a number of university partners. The fund, Huffington said, had raised nearly $2 million to back 'serious investigative journalism'.[87] In 2010 the fund merged with the Center for Public Integrity, a non-profit investigative journalism organization based in Washington.

The steady number of alliances, deals and ventures helped nudge traffic to *The Huffington Post* to nearly 8 million unique visitors a month by July 2009, representing a more than 50 per cent increase from the beginning of 2008. In the same month, Arianna Huffington was named No. 12 on the *Forbes* list of the 'Most Influential Women in Media', a few slots below her old friend Barbara Walters. She also ranked more than once in the upper half of the *Guardian*'s 'Top 100 in Media List'.

Huffington was a progressive advocate for society's most vulnerable, but was also a 'limousine liberal', according to the *New Yorker*, who – like her late partner Levin – preferred to be driven rather than to drive, and was used to networking on friends' private jets and yachts.[88] As such, Huffington could be susceptible to indulging herself. In 2009 Gawker reported her profligate spending at *HuffPost* could occasionally become a problem, citing Huffington's request for a private jet when the website was still not yet turning a profit. 'After one infusion of fresh capital, Huffington was heard internally telling staff that everyone's lives would be greatly improved "once we get the jet"', the website noted, adding that *HuffPost*'s financials could in no way support a jet. In addition, Huffington was scrutinized for frequent stays at the high-end Mercer Hotel when she came to New York, rather than simply renting an apartment. According to Gawker, her travel preferences were said to be 'exactingly cushy: first class, aisle, bulkhead seat on a three-class plane only, fully refundable and nonstop'.[89]

Despite these gibes, Huffington's sister, Agapi, said success had changed Arianna for the better. After Huffington's very public comeuppance in the California gubernatorial race, her attitude and approach to life had become much more light-hearted, Agapi said. 'I think she's much more comfortable in the world,' she told the *New Yorker*, 'whereas before she felt like she had to protect herself. I think she has shed a lot of layers . . . Even when I see her on TV, I think she's much softer. Why? She doesn't have to prove herself anymore, in any way.' Huffington's former husband, Michael, made a similar observation. 'Arianna has definitely changed since she launched *The Huffington*

Post. She is calmer, happier, and has clearly hit her stride in something in which she excels and enjoys.'[90]

Many still wondered, however, what it was that drove Huffington through her many incarnations. She was wealthy, admired, an accomplished businesswoman and internationally renowned. 'I honestly think that Arianna believes she was put on this earth to make a difference,' said Sugar Rautbord, one of Huffington's oldest friends who attended her 1986 wedding, in an interview with *Vanity Fair*. 'If she can't be president, or senator, then she'll be part of this great Greek chorus trying to change people's opinions.'[91]

Huffington had come far in many ways, but she was still much like the young woman of her Cambridge days, hoping to head the debating team – only now she sought hegemony over the conversation on a global scale.

PART 6

GOING GLOBAL

'Anything I can dream of now, we can do it within *The Huffington Post*.'

On 10 November 2010, Huffington attended a media conference in New York that, without warning, would lead to her next metamorphosis. On stage was AOL Chairman and Chief Executive Tim Armstrong, a former Google executive, who was speaking on a panel about 'Digital Darwinism'. The talk focused on how disruptive technologies and the digital economy were changing traditional business practices. During the discussion, Armstrong described how his challenge at AOL was that while the company had enormous brand awareness and customer loyalty, it had almost no brand identity. Huffington was moved by Armstrong's words about his company's obstacles. 'I was immediately struck by his clear-eyed assessment of his company's strengths and weaknesses, and his willingness to be so up front about them,' she says.[1] She and Armstrong chatted briefly after the panel and arranged to meet again the next day.

For both of them, crossing paths marked the beginning of a series of conversations that would continue on the east and west coasts for weeks, eventually culminating in the merger of their companies. 'We talked not just about what our two companies were doing, but about the larger trends we saw happening online and in our world,' Huffington recalls. 'I laid out my vision for the expansion of *The Huffington Post*, and he laid out his vision for AOL.' She was thrilled to find they had much in common. 'We were practically finishing each other's sentences,' she says.[2]

Overlapping with Huffington's merger talks, *The Huffington Post* turned an annual profit for the very first time in December 2010, reporting earnings of just under $1 million on revenue of $31 million.[3] With most of the media and publishing industry in transition and rapidly losing money with the rise of social media and free news online, this milestone proved that *HuffPost*, under Huffington's leadership, was able to be competitive. In the space of just six years, the site had become one of the world's top-ten news destinations – and was finally minting money.[4] In the final quarter of 2010, Huffington had also launched a new vertical on her website, 'HuffPost Divorce', which received glowing reviews. The section's tagline, 'Marriage comes and goes, but divorce is forever', was inspired by Huffington's close friend, Nora Ephron, who collaborated with her on the page.[5] Calling Huffington the 'queen of web content', Jason Keath, CEO of Social Fresh, a New

York social media and digital marketing company, told *Newsday*, 'She doesn't apologize for things', adding that he was curious to see what Huffington could achieve with more capital behind her. 'As fast as she moves and as fond as she is of staying ahead of the game, having the resources to take more chances will be interesting,' he said.[6]

The website's earnings were particularly impressive in light of the fact that, as *Vanity Fair* writer William D. Cohan, put it, '*The Huffington Post* was not founded to be a business that generated enormous profits. Before it became the 154th most popular website in the world, its goal was chiefly political.'[7] Huffington's personal website had evolved into a celebrity blog and then a legitimate news portal that had trumped the hopes even of its founders. By late 2010 her site boasted 26 million unique visitors a month, with almost 4 million of them actively leaving comments on its pages and an estimated 100,000 unpaid bloggers writing for it.[8] *HuffPost* was now a hot property – and Huffington, as its editor-in-chief, suddenly found herself in an unparalleled position to make a deal.

Huffington and Armstrong met at her home in Los Angeles for lunch in early 2011. Armstrong told her he wanted to buy *The Huffington Post* and put all of AOL's media properties and content under a newly formed division to be called the Huffington Post Media Group, naming Huffington as its editor-in-chief. Looking back, Huffington says the appeal of Armstrong's proposition stemmed from their 'aligned visions' to build a well-capitalized, global media juggernaut. Armstrong, she says, recognized the fact that 'when you acquire a new company, you have to let it follow its own DNA'.[9] In the past, she noticed that smaller enterprises like *HuffPost* could easily be swallowed up by behemoths such as AOL. 'Small companies often get ruined by big companies,' she says, adding that start-ups 'need to be able to be themselves' and not be forced to take on the identities of their masters.[10] Huffington was also acutely aware that if *The Huffington Post* was to expand locally – with more cities hooked into its news pipeline – as well as globally, she would need more than the slim profits that her site generated. She would need to have the solid financial backing of a company much larger than hers and a carte blanche to match. With a market capitalization at the time of around $2 billion, AOL was more than able to provide both.

Despite its astonishing success, *HuffPost* needed a quantum leap. Huffington kept reminding herself of what Harvard Business School professor Clayton Christensen famously called 'The Innovator's Dilemma' in a book of the same name. The book explored 'how even very successful companies, with very capable personnel, often fail because they tend to stick too closely to the strategies that made them successful in the first place, leaving them vulnerable to changing conditions and new realities,' she says. 'They miss major opportunities because they are unwilling to disrupt their own game.'[11] As *HuffPost* expanded, she says, she and Ken Lerer 'obsessed' over the innovator's dilemma in trying to constantly get ahead and stay ahead of the competition. In the world of online entrepreneurialism, businesses either grew or shrank, and Huffington wanted *The Huffington Post* to be available everywhere in the world, accessible to millions, in multiple languages. Armstrong, for his part, wanted a driven editor-in-chief with a strong editorial voice, like Huffington, who could breathe new life back into AOL's lagging media properties, which were failing to capture the same traffic, readership and buzz that *HuffPost* seemed to attain effortlessly.[12] As a technology platform, *The Huffington Post* was adroit at pulling readers from Google and Facebook onto its site, making *HuffPost* the kind of traffic magnet AOL needed to grow its own readership, bolster its online-advertising business and boost revenue.

During their talks, Huffington says Armstrong made plain that 'he got the innovator's dilemma and was willing to disrupt the present to, if I may borrow a phrase, win the future.'[13] Together, Huffington and Armstrong agreed, they could build a content machine much greater than what each of them possessed. Huffington soon found herself in a whirl of negotiations, 'many more meetings, back-and-forth emails and phone calls about what our merger would mean for the two companies,' she says. 'Things moved very quickly.'[14] In the end, Armstrong was willing to pay hundreds of millions of dollars not just for *The Huffington Post*, but also for Arianna.

Huffington needed to convince *The Huffington Post*'s board to agree, however, and this would be harder. While Lerer, her founding partner, was content to green-light the deal, Fred Harman, representing one of *HuffPost*'s biggest investors, Oak Investment Partners, was more reticent. Eric

Hippeau, *HuffPost*'s chief executive officer, also wanted to wait, hoping to prep *The Huffington Post* for a much more lucrative opportunity – an initial public offering (IPO) that could reap a bonanza. 'Our goal was an IPO rather than building up the company to be acquired by another media company,' Harman told *Forbes* in 2011. If the board could just be patient for another year or so it might be able to cash out with as much as a billion-dollar payday. 'Even when Tim put a pre-emptive offer on the table, Eric and I were still inclined to roll forward as an independent company, out of the belief that *The Huffington Post* could continue to rapidly scale and be the dominant social news company on the web,' Harman said.[15]

Huffington, who also got a vote on the small, four-person board, was unmoved. She wanted to create one of the most formidable news portals in the world in the hope of rivalling – or surpassing – *The New York Times*. Recalling conversations with Huffington at that time, executives of *HuffPost* would describe her as irrepressible. 'There was a bucking bronco whenever someone said, "No, you can't do that,"' *HuffPost*'s chief revenue officer, Greg Coleman, told *Forbes* in 2011. 'I know Arianna very well . . . She wanted three things: a big bag of gold, a big, fat contract, which she deserved, and . . . unilateral decision-making over her world. And that is where you're going to have some problems. Arianna hates to be managed.'[16] The debate over whether to join forces with AOL notwithstanding, a simple truth about Huffington emerged that her colleagues were well-advised not to miss: Her desire to enrich herself off

HuffPost paled in comparison to her hopes of taking over the news cycle globally with her eponymous brand.

Huffington got her way. *The Huffington Post*, bearing her name, was built on her A-list Rolodex and personal connections. Her board and investors had little choice but to allow the deal to go through. 'AOL and Tim Armstrong represented a platform and partner for Arianna to greatly accelerate her ambitions of industry dominance for *The Huffington Post*,' Harman told *Forbes*. 'And simply put, nothing was going to stand in the way of that.'[17]

Huffington and Armstrong signed the deal, valued at $315 million, in February 2011, during the half-time show at the Super Bowl's Cowboys Stadium in Arlington, Texas. 'It was my first Super Bowl, an incredibly exciting backdrop that mirrored my excitement about the merger and the future ahead', Huffington wrote in one of her blog posts after the merger.[18] At the press conference announcing the deal, a reporter half-jokingly asked Huffington if she'd paid any attention to who was playing at the game (the Green Bay Packers beat the Pittsburgh Steelers). Huffington responded, 'Will.i.am' – a performer from the Black Eyed Peas, the band that performed at the halftime show.[19] Armstrong said the merger underscored his conviction that online news, if properly nurtured, could grow. 'The reason AOL is acquiring *The Huffington Post* is because we are absolutely passionate, big believers in the future of the internet, big believers in the future of content,' he said.[20] Some in the media – particularly *HuffPost*'s less internet-savvy competitors – were vocally less impressed. *The New*

York Times's then-executive editor, Bill Keller, stated that AOL's 'buying an aggregator and calling it a content play is a little like a company's announcing plans to improve its cash position by hiring a counterfeiter'.[21]

AOL paid $300 million in cash and the rest in stock for the news site. Huffington personally received around $21 million, about $3.4 million of which was in options to vest across a twenty-month period.[22] Huffington owned around a 14 per cent stake in *The Huffington Post* at the time of the sale, according to Cohan's account in *Vanity Fair*. 'Since she had put none of her own money into *The Huffington Post* at the start,' he noted, 'this was a sweet payday.'[23] Huffington also received a multimillion-dollar employment contract from AOL to take the helm as president and editor-in-chief of Huffington Post Media Group, which included $3 million in equity grants, such as stock options and restricted stock units.[24] A confidential memo circulated among the AOL board of directors' transaction committee while Huffington was still negotiating her post-merger contract terms, spelled out exactly how crucial she was to the merged company's success. It stated: 'Arianna Huffington, in particular, is a critical element to *HuffPost*, its identity and her name is a key [intellectual property] asset . . . A departure by Arianna Huffington could have a significant detrimental effect on the company's business.'[25] Privately, Harman told *Forbes* that Armstrong initially wanted to hire Huffington away from her own website. According to AOL executives, he was entranced by how she persuaded so many bloggers to work for her for free.

In an interview with *Forbes*, a former AOL employee said, 'It was always, "Arianna does it. That's what she built her business on. Why don't we do it too?".'

While *The Huffington Post*'s board had initially been divided on the merger, its investors profited mightily from the sale. Alan Patricof, the media venture capitalist who had invested in *HuffPost* through Greycroft Partners, earned six times his initial investment from Huffington's deal with AOL. 'I wish I'd put in more,' he told *The Daily Beast* in February 2011.[26] Lerer, Huffington's friend and business partner, had withdrawn from active management of *The Huffington Post* in 2007 but now enjoyed 'the hype normally accorded a Powerball winner', noted *The Daily Beast*, estimating Lerer's profit from the AOL transaction as *The Huffington Post*'s second-biggest shareholder and chairman came to 'as much as $50 million'.[27] But the largest fortune reportedly went to Harman's Oak Investment Partners, which was believed at the time to own roughly a quarter of *HuffPost*, earning it close to $80 million. The merger marked the end of the board's involvement with *The Huffington Post*. Lerer and *HuffPost*'s CEO, Eric Hippeau, stepped down and went on to form the investment firm Lerer Hippeau Ventures,[28] which would continue to back early-stage companies, including news and entertainment site *BuzzFeed*, the site of fellow *HuffPost* co-founder Jonah Peretti, where Lerer served as chairman for a decade before stepping down in 2019.

As a result of the AOL merger, some of *The Huffington Post*'s earliest staffers, including former news editor

Katharine Zaleski, became 'instant millionaires', according to *The Daily Beast*. In an interview with the publication, Lerer denied any involvement in orchestrating the AOL merger, stating: 'Arianna deserves the credit. I haven't been involved, except as chairman, for three-plus years . . . Arianna was the main architect and the driving force behind the deal.'[29] Tom Freston, who had introduced Huffington and Lerer eight years earlier, suggested Huffington's outsized success had led to 'a new Arianna piety among the sort of bigwig male moguls who once regarded her as a lightweight', in the words of the *New Yorker*. He told the magazine, 'They're fascinated with her. They respect her for building a business out of nothing but her wits and determination.'[30]

There was one fly in the ointment: *The Huffington Post*'s unpaid bloggers were galvanized by news of the merger, with many fretting that they would lose their editorial independence if AOL became their new parent company. Others were unhappy that the site's founders would not be sharing a slice of the deal's handsome profits. While Huffington and Lerer promised around 200 employees at *HuffPost* that they would share somehow financially in the merger, the site's volunteer bloggers were made no such promise.

A class-action lawsuit filed shortly after the merger closed demanded at least $105 million in damages (one-third of the price tag of the merger) as compensation for *The Huffington Post*'s bloggers. The suit, filed by *HuffPost* blogger and New York labour activist Jonathan Tasini, sought payment from AOL, *HuffPost*, Huffington and Lerer on behalf of what he said were 9,000 of the website's unpaid writers. 'Arianna Huffington is like a slave owner on a plantation of bloggers,' Tasini said to *Wired* in an interview in April 2011. 'The truth is, without the bloggers, there was no *Huffington Post* and there would be no sale to AOL. She has decided to rob all these bloggers of a fair share of this profit-making venture.'[31] Others piled on, such as the *Los Angeles Times*'s Tim Rutten, who embraced the blogger-as-serf metaphor, stating, 'To grasp *The Huffington Post*'s business model, picture a galley rowed by slaves and commanded by pirates.'

The lawsuit, combined with a separate and ongoing legal battle initiated by two political consultants who alleged that Huffington and Lerer stole their original idea for *The Huffington Post*, led to a number of headaches for the *HuffPost* founders after the merger. While Huffington did not deny she knew the political operatives suing her – James Boyce and Peter Daou – because they were among roughly 'three dozen people' invited to her home to brainstorm ideas in 2004 for a political media organization, she did not agree that *HuffPost* owed its origins to them. Dismissing the suit as 'laughable', Huffington and Lerer issued a joint statement, saying, 'We have now officially entered into bizzaro world', adding that the plaintiffs had 'absolutely nothing to do with creating, running, financing or building *The Huffington Post*'. In fact, Huffington and Lerer noted that 'for months now, they have been trying to extract money from us; they are filing the lawsuit of course because we did not agree to any payment.'[32] A judge was not so quick to dismiss the lawsuit, which dragged on for years, eventually ruling in 2014 the case could go to trial. Huffington, once again, found herself in the unenviable position of being accused of capitalizing on someone else's intellectual property. Instead of hashing it out in the courtroom, she settled the matter the same year for an undisclosed sum. In a statement afterwards, *HuffPost* repeated that the claims were 'without merit', while Boyce, one of the two plaintiffs, in a startling about-face, pronounced that Huffington 'deserves all the credit in the world for making [*HuffPost*] a far greater success than anyone could have imagined'.[33]

In the meantime, the blogger-led lawsuit was also scuttled. In 2012, US District Judge John Koeltl rejected claims by Huffington's unpaid bloggers, writing that 'no one forced' them to file written works for *HuffPost* with no expectation of being paid. 'The principles of equity and good conscience do not justify giving plaintiffs a piece of the purchase price when they never expected to be paid, repeatedly agreed to the same bargain and went into the arrangement with eyes wide open', he wrote.[34] John Coffee, a professor at Columbia Law School, in an interview with Reuters, summed up the bloggers' posts as 'the electronic equivalent of someone writing a letter to the editor'. The quid pro quo between unpaid bloggers and *HuffPost*, he suggested, was that Huffington had agreed to provide and finance a highly visible, national media platform for the bloggers, in exchange for their work. 'You are rewarded by publication, not by payment,' he said.[35] *The Huffington*

Post, in its own statement, said, 'Our bloggers utilize our platform to connect and ensure that their ideas and views are seen by as many people as possible. It's the same reason hundreds of people go on TV shows – to broadcast their views to as wide an audience as possible.'[36]

The blogger lawsuit, though unsuccessful, showed once again how Huffington's pioneering business model was upending even a swiftly changing media landscape, raising questions about how writers should be treated by organizations that, in some cases, preferred not to pay them. Even before the settlement, *The New York Times*'s Nate Silver argued in 2011 that the *HuffPost* to-pay-or-not-to-pay conflict arose from what he believed to be a fundamental misunderstanding of *HuffPost*'s business model. 'One reason that *The Huffington Post* gets a lot of criticism for not paying its bloggers is because most people think of it as a publishing company, when really – like Facebook – it is more of a technology company. Whether the content is paid or unpaid, the site is able to generate a comparatively large amount of revenue from it because of things like search engine optimization, and the way that its editors use their page space', he noted, adding of *HuffPost*, 'It isn't pretty . . . but it's innovative and effective.'[37] The lead plaintiff in the suit, Tasini, said he hoped his legal action would 'spark a movement and an organizing effort among bloggers to set a standard for the future, because this idea that all individual creators should work for free is like a cancer spreading through every media property on the globe'.[38] In response to the various critiques, Huffington vigorously defended her website's policy of not paying bloggers, saying that many media organizations relied on unpaid contributors. 'There's got to be a distinction between everybody who works for a media company and everybody who blogs for a media company,' she said.[39]

Huffington's arrival at AOL's New York headquarters as the head of the newly formed Huffington Post Media Group saw her take charge of a massively expanded newsroom in early 2011. Folding in AOL's own media operations, her 200-strong staff swelled to roughly 1,300 journalists and editors – more than the *Wall Street Journal* or the *Washington Post*.[40] She now presided over all of AOL's media properties, including AOLNews.com, TechCrunch, AOL Music, StyleList, Engadget, Moviefone and Patch Media – the last of which was a network of about 800 hyper-localized US news sites Huffington hoped would help *HuffPost* expand its coverage to new cities and reach new audiences. Contrary to what many of *HuffPost*'s bloggers had feared, AOL had no intention of whitewashing or restricting their independent voices to suit its corporate agenda – though the merger did upend the *HuffPost* platform in ways that dislocated some of *HuffPost*'s bloggers as Huffington made changes. Following the merger, AOL laid off hundreds of its veteran news staffers to make way for Huffington to hire her own fresh recruits.[41] Meanwhile, Huffington integrated roughly thirty of AOL's content sections into *HuffPost* and joined AOL's top brass as a member of its executive committee. For Armstrong, Huffington's takeover of AOL's sprawling media properties came as a relief. 'Everybody at AOL said you could see this weight lifted from Armstrong's shoulders, because he's not a media guy,' one *HuffPost* executive told *Vanity Fair*.[42] For Huffington, the AOL merger meant the achievement of goals that would have otherwise been years away for her, if not completely unattainable:

> What it has meant was that a lot of my dreams for *The Huffington Post*, which we had to achieve sequentially – because we didn't have a lot of resources – we now can sort of work on all at once. My priorities for *The Huffington Post* before the acquisition were to grow internationally, because no company has really grown to its fullest potential without expanding internationally; Facebook, Google, you know, over 70 per cent of the traffic comes from outside the United States. Video – we wanted to expand our video offerings, we wanted to expand original reporting and we wanted to expand all our social engagement tools, you know, invest in technology – all these things have been happening all at once.[43]

Huffington received a generous budget and embarked on a series of bold moves in creating her dream newsroom. She hired journalists from *Newsweek*, *The New York Times*, *USA Today* and other major media organizations known for their high-end, original content, offering pay packages that were unheard-of for journalism at the time – some editors' salaries reportedly topped $300,000 a year.[44] She also favoured recruiting young journalists from Ivy League universities who, according to *The New York Times,* would work for a 'pittance'.[45] At the same time, she sought to build a newsroom inside *HuffPost* that would showcase her personal vision of spiritual health and work–life balance, renovating the AOL newsroom to add nap rooms, which she says were very popular; a gym; refrigerators stocked with plenty of fruit, yogurt and snacks, as well as weekly meditation, yoga and breathing classes. At some point, she even installed a hammock, although most journalists would agree nothing could be more incongruous in a deadline-harried newsroom. Well into the *HuffPost*'s AOL metamorphosis, an article appeared in *The New York Times* magazine titled 'Arianna Huffington's Improbable, Insatiable Content Machine', featuring a large photo of Huffington, sitting cross-legged in the centre of a group of young, glossy-haired staffers, her head tilted in the air, eyes closed, arms outstretched, apparently leading a yoga exercise. 'Since the news is nonstop, there is definitely the temptation for editors, reporters and engineers to try to match the 24-hour news cycle,' Huffington explained, 'but at *HuffPost* we do a lot to prevent burnout.'[46] In an effort to reduce newsroom stress, Huffington made it non-mandatory for employees to check their email on weekends or on vacation – 'Once we see an email, we feel obligated to answer it,' she said – and offered employees up to three paid days off a year for volunteer work, plus a matched payment of up to $250 a year for each employee's charitable giving.[47]

More notably, Huffington moved ahead on her long-planned international expansion of *The Huffington Post*, opening bureaus throughout the world. Beginning in May 2011, she started with *HuffPost Canada*, followed by *HuffingtonPost UK* in July and, by early 2012, a French edition, *Le Huffington Post*, her publication's first non-English-speaking news portal. From there, *HuffPost* rolled out editions in Quebec, Spain and Italy in 2012, and Japan and Germany in 2013, prompting a number of media outlets to crisply remark that Huffington was charting a path to 'global domination'.[48] She did not deny this, but preferred to liken her growing global network to a series of 'laboratories' where she would experiment on what kind of content and news her readership liked best.[49] By 2014, *HuffPost* created *WorldPost*, bringing in globally renowned contributors like former Google CEO Eric Schmidt, British Prime Minister Tony Blair and the musician Yo-Yo Ma. Many of her international launches were done in partnership with media players local to each country. In 2014 *HuffPost* also launched its Brazilian, Indian and Arabic editions. In 2015 it introduced *HuffPost Australia* and, in 2016, launched *HuffPost South Africa*, among others.

It was in 2014 when Huffington finally introduced *HuffPost* to her native Greece. The goal, she said, in a blog post, was to 'be telling the stories that matter most in Greece and, just as important, helping Greeks tell their stories themselves'. She added, 'As *HuffPost* has grown, I have returned over and over in my mind to the traditions and wisdom of my home country. For my Greek ancestors, philosophy was anything but an academic exercise. Asking the question, "What is a good life?" was a daily practice in the art of living.'[50] This was a theme she would return to again and again. In an interview with *People*, she said, 'The thing about Greece is just how easy it is to make connections with people here, how easy it is to meet a stranger and feel like they're a friend – that's the special Greek gift. Greeks invented the notion of "philoxenia" [love of strangers] and don't make the same kind of distinctions between friends and strangers. And that's just a great way, a rich way, to live life.'[51]

Huffington was able to learn a great deal by experimenting with the international editions of *HuffPost*, which she did use as media labs. She noticed that Germany was more focused on video than many of the other regions, while Japan and South Korea led in mobile traffic. 'It's not just the US that leads', she noted in 2015. 'In Korea, 90 percent of *HuffPost*'s traffic comes from mobile. And Japan, where 72 percent of traffic is from mobile, has built the largest *HuffPost* audience outside the US.'[52] Where traffic came from could sometimes be surprising, and Huffington would tinker with *HuffPost*'s model to increase readership wherever she could. In an attempt to launch in China, *HuffPost* encountered a number of roadblocks and had to contend with strict government controls on the nation's media. In the end, Huffington said, it meant *HuffPost* would have to focus mainly on lifestyle and entertainment news. Aside from global expansion, Huffington also worked with AOL to loop a wide variety of verticals into *HuffPost*'s site, such as content from AOL's media properties like 'AOL Black Voices' and other *Voices* sections. Within a year of her arrival at the merged company, *HuffPost*'s verticals leapt from eighteen to around sixty, with 'HuffPost Politics', 'HuffPost Green' and 'HuffPost Gay Voices' ranking No. 1 in unique visitors in each of their categories.[53] Huffington, in 2012, also dipped her toe into the subscription-based online magazine business, launching *Huffington*, a weekly digital product offering exclusive, feature-length stories with infographics, video and multimedia pieces.[54]

The results of all this activity were not just striking, they were immediate. By May 2011, Huffington achieved her ambition of outstripping the web traffic of *The New York Times*, with *HuffPost* pulling in 35.5 million unique visitors a month, representing the merged traffic of her site, as well as AOL's properties, compared with *The New York Times*'s traffic of 33.59 million unique visitors a month.[55] Huffington's new media triumph over old media meant her disruption of the legacy news business was complete. By January 2012, with *HuffPost*'s traffic still rising, she couldn't help but exult over the rapid results of her site's marriage to AOL. 'As impressive as these numbers are, more important to us are the core values that are part of our DNA', Huffington wrote in the blog summarizing her first year's progress, ticking off a list of milestones, including 1,000 stories published a day, 6 million comments a month and an 'estimated' 1,874 naps taken in the nap rooms. 'We've been rewarded with one of the most active communities on the web, and over 130 million comments since we've launched.'[56]

Huffington was not only busy expanding her newsroom, she also released – and somehow promoted between 2010 and 2011 – her latest book, *Third World America: How Our Politicians Are Abandoning the Middle Class and Betraying the American Dream*. The book chronicled the struggles of Americans following the 2008–9 global economic crisis, the worst economic downtown since the Great Depression. 'I deliberately chose that title to be very jarring,' she said. 'You know, we don't associate America with the Third World. But I chose it, because I really believe that we are on this trajectory, where the middle class is crumbling. And the middle class is the foundation not just of American prosperity, but American democracy and democratic stability . . . By providing the data and the stories to back it up, I'm hoping that we will bring the sense of urgency that . . . is missing.'[57] Many Americans, Huffington wrote, could no longer support themselves without relying on some form of government aid. 'One out of every six Americans is on government anti-poverty programs', she said in her book. 'More than 50 million Americans are on Medicaid, 40 million receive food stamps, and 10 million receive unemployment benefits.'[58] When American banks were on the verge of potential collapse during the economic crisis, both Democrats and Republicans worked to bail them out, she noted. Yet when Congress considered a bill that would have allowed millions of Americans to stay in their homes by negotiating a mortgage modification, the bill failed. 'You know, we've all been screaming many ideas . . . Republicans, Democrats . . . from the payroll tax holiday to a really serious infrastructure and jobs program, to a green bank to an infrastructure bank, to tax credits for small businesses . . . The ideas are out there. What is missing is that sense of urgency and the political will.'[59]

Drawing from her own experiences growing up in a destabilized and militaristic Greece, Huffington also argued 'that overspending on war at the expense of domestic issues and the alarming decline of the middle class are troubling signals that the US is losing its economic, political and social stability – a stability that has always been maintained by the middle class', according to *Booklist* in a starred review of her book. Huffington believed the Reagan era had prompted the great American decline, with its disparagement of government-funded, social safety nets. She also laid blame at the feet of the nation's subsequent presidents – Bill Clinton, George W. Bush and Barack Obama – for consistently supporting the interests of the wealthy over the middle class.

Springboarding off these themes in her book, Huffington announced in early 2012 that *HuffPost* would be sending dozens of reporters and editors across the US during the 2012 presidential election season to 'highlight and define the economic and personal challenges facing the waning American middle class and the disenfranchised poor'. One of the biggest advantages of running her own media outlet, Huffington said, was 'being able to obsessively cover a story for as long as you think it matters'.[60] She also began to make a concerted effort to avoid covering the news through a strictly liberal-leaning lens, instituting a new tagline, 'Beyond Right and Left', and seeking out views from other parts of the political spectrum. 'Mainstream media tend to just mouth the conventional wisdom, to see everything through the filter of right and left,' she said. America's political polarization, she felt, was preventing people from crossing the political aisle to solve the nation's problems.[61]

War and political instability continued to be a focus – and it greatly benefited *The Huffington Post*. In 2012, national and foreign affairs correspondent David Wood became the first journalist at *The Huffington Post* to win a Pulitzer Prize for his series exploring 'the physical and emotional challenges facing American soldiers severely wounded in Iraq and Afghanistan during a decade of war'. He received the national reporting commendation. After the many barbs Huffington had weathered in her seven years as editor-in-chief of *HuffPost* about running a 'traffic-chasing sensationalism' blog, here was confirmation her site was capable of, as *Forbes* put it, 'society-changing journalism'.[62] Huffington was electrified, as was the newsroom. In an interview with *Forbes*, she noted that 'ever since we launched *HuffPost* we've wanted to use narrative storytelling to put flesh and blood on data and statistics'. Wood's articles sought to bring forward the plight of 'returning veterans and what happens to them,' she said, including suicide, adding, 'These are major facts and stories that need to be part of the national conversation.'[63] In 2012 *Forbes* also included Huffington on its list of the 'World's 100 Most Powerful Women in Media'.[64]

Huffington's ability to run a Pulitzer Prize-winning, global news team while also continuing to write books and still spend most of her days and nights jetting to parties, business meetings, talk shows, summits and lectures relied heavily on a tight-knit group of staffers she called the 'A-team'. This group of around a dozen people kept her schedule on track and helped, as *The New York Times* wrote in 2015, 'keep her in perpetual motion'. A-Team jobs, according to the *Times*, were 'known to be all-consuming, but also for those who last, a ticket to a promotion later on. While some stick around for years, many A-Teamers endure only about 12 months before calling it quits or asking to be transferred.'[65]

Huffington's work–life balance was made slightly less onerous by her decision in late 2012 to purchase a three-bedroom, 4,200-square-foot, luxury loft in New York's trendy SoHo district, valued at £6.5 million ($8 million), which made her work commute easier. She lived here, in addition to keeping her Brentwood mansion in California.[66] Besides the professional and social demands placed on her, she also was a mother, who, as she pointed out, struggled with the many of the same issues as any parent. 'Is there a meeting I can skip and go be with my daughter for something? Is there a party I will miss to go be with my child? It's these little tradeoffs that working mothers have to make every day,' she said in an interview shortly after the AOL merger. 'What's hard is sometimes I feel they take the baby out and they put the guilt in. As a working mother, I feel I've been perpetually guilty. And that's really one of the things we need to learn. That, somehow, it's never going to be perfect.' What's most important, she said, is that 'our children feel unconditionally loved. That's what my mother made me feel and I think it's the greatest gift we can give our children. Because the world judges us every day and if there's someone who loves us unconditionally, whether you succeed or fail, it is the most precious foundation for living life.'[67]

Following the AOL merger, Huffington also pushed several less-popular initiatives, some of which were prohibitively expensive. Not wanting to focus strictly on things like war, the decline of the middle-class and America's political dysfunction, she announced in 2012 she would begin showcasing 'the abundant displays around the country and the world of empathy and innovation in turning around lives and strengthening communities'. So began the 'Good News' section of *HuffPost* and the 'Greatest Person of the Day' feature. In a note to her staff, Huffington elaborated, saying, 'We want to show that the era of "if it bleeds, it leads," is over.' She also hoped to get more people to share *HuffPost* stories on social media like Facebook and Twitter, but to create more 'shareable' content, stories had to be less negative. In an unguarded moment, she told *The New York Times* 'You're not as likely to share a story of a beheading. Right? I mean, you'll read it.'[68] Meeting with her team in New York, she said, 'We're going to cover the good news. We're not going to just cover what's not working. We're going to cover what's working and we're going to dominate this. This is going to change the way people do journalism, change the way journalism works in the world.' Trained to uncover injustice, wrongdoing and corruption, many of her writers and editors were floored. 'Understandably, when you tell a roomful of people who think of themselves as journalists something like that, everybody was like "What the fuck?"' one of her staffers told *Vanity Fair*. Talking about the initiative, which she eventually dubbed 'What's Working', during a live interview at New York's Paley Center, Huffington explained that she believed most of the media was unnecessarily negative in its coverage of the news, remarking:

> One of the things that I say is, the media distorts what is happening, constantly, and that's made it much harder to deal with solutions. Because everything is presented in terms which polarize people. I feel we have a big responsibility not to just put the spotlight on what's not working, which we do every day, but also on what is working . . . Every day, we make things work . . . If we don't do that, we're letting people down.[69]

Huffington was trying to reshape journalism in her own vision, but some of her staff questioned her approach. How would they justify putting news through a rose-coloured filter and churning out fluff pieces masquerading as 'news'? The development could easily counteract the hard-won credibility *HuffPost* had received from its Pulitzer. A number of staff members, according to *The New York Times*, 'fretted that "What's Working" could result in a steady drip of pallid, upbeat stories (e.g., 'How Hugh Jackman's Coffee Brand is Changing Lives')'.[70] Huffington, for years, had favoured hiring hard-driving, Ivy League-trained journalists, as well as seasoned news veterans from the most prestigious newsrooms. Now, these same journalists wondered what they had signed up for – and whether Huffington's own lack of journalistic training might hinder their ability to do their jobs. 'I do believe she thinks of herself as a transformational figure,' a former *HuffPost* editor told *Vanity Fair*. 'She thinks that she is Oprah plus Jesus or something, I don't know. She genuinely, in her heart, believes that she can change the way journalism is done.'[71]

More problematic to AOL's management was the launch of 'HuffPost Live', a round-the-clock, internet broadcast network that sought to rival the cable news channels. 'This is not TV, with its set schedules, overproduction and rigid commercial breaks,' Huffington said in announcing the project in one of her blog posts. Instead, it 'will be more relaxed, more free-flowing and much more spontaneous and interactive', viewable from a computer, smartphone or tablet with conversations and stories from the writers, editors and bloggers of *The Huffington Post*. The goal, she said, was to create 'the most social video experience anywhere'.[72] The initiative attracted a handful of deep-pocketed founding partners, such as Cadillac and

Verizon, but the cost of the project was inordinately high and soon led to tensions with AOL's management and its CEO, Armstrong. Huffington's ideas were becoming grander and more unwieldy. 'HuffPost Live' was one of the biggest to date, costing around $12 million according to one former executive, who leaked to *Vanity Fair* that the project was considered 'a disaster . . . nobody was watching it'.[73] In early 2016, AOL scaled back the project and, in March of that year, 'HuffPost Live' aired its final segment.

How Huffington managed her budget mattered a great deal to AOL, as Armstrong had purchased her site to attract advertisers and generate both revenue and earnings for the company. Just before he'd approached her to purchase *HuffPost*, AOL's New York Stock Exchange-listed shares were trading at around $26. When the merger was announced, AOL's stock price lost 30 per cent of its value in a single day, closing just above $21 on the first day of trading following the news. Huffington convinced him that *The Huffington Post*'s business was about to skyrocket. But after bringing Huffington on board, he'd watched the price drop to around $11 a share by September 2011. *HuffPost* wasn't meeting the financial targets Huffington set ahead of the merger. Her expectations for *HuffPost* were for it to earn $10 million in 2011 on revenue of $60 million; $36 million of earnings in 2012 on revenue of $115 million; and up to $73 million of earnings on revenue of $203 million by 2015. That is not what happened, mostly because the rapid expansion of *HuffPost* was outpacing its earnings.[74]

Armstrong and AOL soon realized that as tireless as Huffington was, she had her limits. 'No one else could give a commencement speech at Smith one day, meet the prime minister of Japan on Tuesday and debate the Middle East on MSNBC on Wednesday,' an executive who has since left the company told *The New York Times*. 'But that doesn't mean she knows the ins and outs of running Moviefone.'[75] Huffington's distractions went far beyond just professional and social engagements. Keeping one foot firmly in the television and entertainment camp, she was regularly doing appearances on *Real Time with Bill Maher*, *The Tonight Show with Jay Leno*, *The Daily Show*, *Charlie Rose* and *The Colbert Report*, among others. She made cameos on *How I Met Your Mother* and *Family Guy* and, from 2008 to 2013, did the voiceover in her native Greek accent for *Family Guy* cartoon spin-off *The Cleveland Show*, as wife of 'Tim the Bear' (the wife, of course, was named 'Arianna').[76] In 2011 Huffington also made headlines for getting into a spat with former *Huff-Post* co-founder, Andrew Breitbart, whom she barred from writing for *HuffPost*'s home page after he publicly attacked the former White House adviser Van Jones as 'a commie punk', a 'cop-killer-supporting, racist, demagogic freak' and other assorted names. Issuing a statement about the reason behind the decision, *HuffPost* said Breitbart's comments violated 'the tenets of debate and civil discourse', although some in the press groused that the main reason for Breitbart's ousting was that Huffington and Jones were friends.[77]

Slowly, AOL began easing AOL's media properties away from Huffington's purview, until, by April 2012, no more AOL sites were left in her portfolio, except for *The Huffington Post*. Huffington also stopped attending AOL executive meetings. It was widely understood by AOL's management that Huffington, as the namesake of *HuffPost*, needed to remain the figurehead of the site. Even so, AOL moved an executive into *HuffPost* headquarters specifically to keep an eye on Huffington's spending. Not one to be reined in, Huffington reportedly began shopping *The Huffington Post* around to potential buyers with the hope that she might persuade one of them to purchase the site away from AOL for as much as $1 billion. While she was unsuccessful, it did get the media to start talking about *HuffPost* in the context of a $1 billion buyout – which was very much to Huffington's benefit. Between 2012 and 2015, publications such as *The New York Times* and the *Wall Street Journal* actively discussed her efforts to fetch a billion-dollar price.[78] Conventional wisdom held that buying *HuffPost* for a billion dollars was likely inadvisable, as Amazon CEO Jeff Bezos had just purchased the *Washington Post* in 2013 for $250 million.[79] Still, the outsized success of competing digital media sites, such as *BuzzFeed* and *Vice Media* meant the question warranted further examination.[80] After carefully sifting through *HuffPost*'s financials, *WSJ*'s Dennis K. Berman suggested in June 2015 that the billion-dollar valuation was probably too high, but that there was no denying Huffington, in the space of just a decade, had built a media empire of admirable scale. That said, she had not yet been able to both expand and generate *HuffPost* earnings consistently. Berman wrote, 'Coaching legend John Wooden put it best: Never mistake activity for achievement.'[81]

If AOL's CEO Armstrong was at all concerned, he didn't let on at *The Huffington Post*'s bash at the Gramercy Park Hotel's Gramercy Terrace rooftop garden, where old and new media luminaries gathered to honour *HuffPost*'s tenth anniversary in 2015. Among them were Martha Stewart; Gawker CEO Nick Denton; *HuffPost* co-founder and Buzz-Feed CEO Jonah Peretti; former *HuffPost* executive Greg Coleman, who went on to become *BuzzFeed* president; and Goldman Sachs Chairman and CEO Lloyd Blankfein, who helped broker the AOL–*HuffPost* merger. When asked how long it would be before *HuffPost* turned a profit at AOL, Armstrong retorted: 'What makes you think it's not profitable already?' The response from attendees was swift: Armstrong was gently reminded that he himself had stated that *HuffPost* was not profitable in 2014. Armstrong briefly reconsidered, saying *HuffPost* was still in the process of expanding overseas. 'We could make it profitable right now, if we wanted it to be,' he told the crowd, according to the *New York Post*. 'Our investors are happy, so we are going to keep investing.'[82] In 2014 *HuffPost* garnered revenue of $146 million, breaking even, according to *The New York Times* magazine.[83] The biggest challenge facing *HuffPost* was not the cost of overseas expansion, but the same one that confronted all digital media start-ups: it relied almost solely on online advertising for revenue, because it did not charge a subscription to its readers. While *HuffPost*'s ad rates were gradually inching higher – mostly due to higher-priced video ads, according to *WSJ*'s Berman – the fact remained that the price tag of digital display ads was constantly encountering downward pressure, because there was a near-limitless supply.[84] *HuffPost*'s answer to the profitability conundrum was directly tied to its expansion. 'Any difficulty turning a profit . . . is considered a temporary problem that will eventually be fixed by the sheer size of the readership', the *Times*'s David Segal wrote in 2015, citing a person familiar with *HuffPost*'s finances.[85] In other words, with ad rates low or even falling, eyeballs needed to go up. While Huffington's interest in ubiquity was, by now, legendary, this confirmed her relentless drive for expansion had just as much to do with turning a profit as with extending her global brand.

Huffington's push paid off. By August 2014, *The Huffington Post*'s web traffic topped 100 million unique viewers for the first time, making it the No. 1 news site in the US, according to Huffington. Describing her elation in a blog post later that year, she wrote:

It's the same feeling I get when I walk into our newsroom and see how a group of five has become a team of hundreds, or when I visit one of our 11 flourishing international editions. It's a lump-in-the-throat combination of gratitude; amazement; satisfaction at what we've accomplished; surprise at how fast it all happened; nostalgia for the early days, when we celebrated every small spike in traffic; and delight in knowing that, without question, our best days still lie ahead.[86]

She was right. By mid-2015, *The Huffington Post* claimed an extraordinary haul: more than 200 million unique visitors a month globally.[87] *HuffPost*, against all odds, had held onto its high perch as one of the nation's top news destinations, with more than 850 journalists and editors, along with thousands of bloggers, writing up to 2,000 stories a day. Huffington, still firmly in charge of her newsroom – as well as *HuffPost*'s fifteen international editions – proudly posed in a photo in 2015 with seventy-five regional *HuffPost* editors-in-chief and business executives from around the world, proclaiming to digital news site Digiday that she planned to be in fifty countries by 2020.[88] When asked during the Paley Center interview if she ever saw herself leaving *The Huffington Post* to reinvent herself again, she quickly dismissed the notion – while also alluding to her next venture:

> Anything I can dream of now, we can do it within *The Huffington Post*. Like one of my passions is how we disconnect from technology. I know it's an ironic, paradoxical passion, but I really believe [it], because I'm so invested in technology, because I'm so surrounded by it. I also see the dangers, and I see how dangerous it is for us not to learn to disconnect, you know, the addictive nature of technology. I see it in my children,

I see it with myself. And that's why I have made a point of creating sections on *The Huffington Post*, the health and living section, the Women's section, the Parents' section, that deal with all these issues of what we call 'unplug and recharge'.[89]

Drawing from these themes of living a more healthy and balanced life, Huffington published her next book in 2014, *Thrive: The Third Metric to Redefining Success and Creating a Life of Well-being, Wisdom, and Wonder*. She dedicated the book, which debuted in the No. 1 spot on *The New York Times* best-seller list, to her mother and copyrighted it, once again, under the Christabella LLC name. *Thrive*, a spiritual inquiry into the life well lived, cemented Huffington's trajectory as a self-styled wellness guru – a metamorphosis toward which she had been moving for decades. The book, heavy with gilded names and personal anecdotes from Silicon Valley CEOs, Ivy League scholars, various global leaders – even deceased thinkers like Nietzsche, Jung and Thoreau – is filled with tips on how to fight 'time famine', embrace 'digital detox' and the many benefits of so-called 'Blue Zones' – regions of the world with the highest life expectancies, like Okinawa, Japan. 'Paying greater attention to our well-being, for whatever reason, connects us with parts of ourselves that now lie dormant and makes it more likely that there will no longer be any split between being successful at work and thriving in life', Huffington writes.[90]

Coinciding with her best-selling sales of *Thrive*,

Huffington's long-time friend and sometime spiritual guru, John-Roger, died of pneumonia in Los Angeles in October 2014. In an emailed statement to the *Los Angeles Times*, Huffington said, 'John-Roger was an important teacher and a dear friend, and I'm very grateful both for his teachings and for our friendship.'[91] Shortly after his death, another statement was posted by John-Roger's Movement of Spiritual Inner Awareness followers, saying, 'While we are, of course, greatly saddened by this loss, we are also aware that this is a particularly sensitive and sacred time to use what we have learned to go within and connect with John-Roger, and the Christ, in Spirit . . . J-R's loving spiritual presence is with us, perhaps more than ever, and will comfort and guide us as we allow it.' Huffington's sister, Agapi, also followed John-Roger's teachings, according to the *Telegraph* of London, earning a psychology degree from the University of Santa Monica in California set up by John-Roger.[92] In an article on the death of John-Roger, the *Daily Mail* noted Huffington was John-Roger's most prominent follower.[93] The story featured a photo of Huffington at her 2004 book launch for *Fanatics and Fools*, her expression contemplative, her right arm thrown protectively around John-Roger's shoulders.[94]

In her writings, Huffington increasingly referred to her own personal wellness and spiritual journey, as well as her lifelong exploration examining how to live the best life. Throughout her many incarnations, this fixation never seemed to be very far from her mind. She considered it, in many ways, to be an inherently Greek journey. 'To the

Stoics, the most secure kind of happiness could be found in the only thing that we are in sole control of: our inner world', she writes.[95] This reflected the teachings of John-Roger, who urged his followers that the answers were not to be found in the external world, but from within (hence, the name of his group, the 'Movement of Spiritual Inner Awareness'). Even a cursory reading of Huffington's spiritual musings can be seen to directly echo John-Roger's teachings and do so to this day. 'Everything outside us can be taken away, as too many in Greece know full well, so how can we entrust our future happiness and well-being to it? Once we realize that, we can bring about a sense of imperturbability – or *ataraxia*, as the Greeks called it – and from that place, we can much more effectively and power-fully bring about change in our lives and the world around us', Huffington wrote in a *HuffPost* blog post in November 2014, days after John-Roger's death.[96]

By now, Huffington had authored fourteen books, in-cluding five best-sellers translated into sixteen languages. She was consistently named on the annual *Forbes* list of the 'World's 100 Most Powerful Women in Media' and *Time*'s '100 Most Influential People' lists. Citing her global influ-ence, *Athens Insider* magazine asked her in December 2014 whether she planned on going back into politics. 'No,' she said, 'not politics. It is a combination of *The Huffington Post* and getting the word out for *Thrive*. I feel very strongly about speaking and writing about the message of *Thrive*.' If she could relive her life, the magazine asked, what would she have done differently? 'I would have done lots of things differently,' she said. 'Slept more, worried less, judged myself less critically . . .'[97]

From the outset of 2015, competitors of *The Huffington Post* in the online news arena – *BuzzFeed*, *Vice*, *Business Insider*, *Vox*, among others – were rapidly gaining on Huffington's site, stealing its traffic and millions of its readers. *HuffPost*'s traffic in the US fell to 86 million unique visitors by September 2015 from 126 million in November 2014.[98] In a statement to the *International Business Times* (yet another *HuffPost* rival), *HuffPost* said its primary focus was not the US, but overseas growth in video and distributed content. *The Huffington Post* also revealed that more than 50 per cent of its traffic was now coming from outside the US.[99] Huffington herself, when pressed, shrugged off the comparisons to the other news sites, remarking to *Forbes*'s Jeff Bercovici in 2014:

> The media loves to perpetuate a narrative of competition . . . For many years, they tried to do it with *The Daily Beast* and Tina Brown and *HuffPost* and me. Now it's *BuzzFeed* and *HuffPost*. The truth is that there are going to be more and more great digital media players, and I personally love Jonah [Peretti] and Ben [Smith, editor-in-chief of *BuzzFeed*] and what they're doing with *BuzzFeed*. I just wish the media would abandon the competitive narrative and instead present the facts with accurate and consistent numbers.[100]

At this point, Huffington could afford to be fairly circumspect. Her years of hard work had reaped her and AOL frothy dividends. While many of her *HuffPost* co-founders had completely cashed out around the time of the AOL merger, she took half cash, half stock – a decision she did not regret.[101] From 2013 to 2015, AOL's stock price rose, albeit haltingly, to the $30s and $40s. Then, in 2015, it hit a four-year high above $50 a share. While Huffington's true net worth is not public information, the climbing stock price of AOL meant that she may have made much more on the merger of her company than has been previously published. In June 2015 AOL's stock leap came as Verizon, the telecommunications giant, agreed to buy AOL, along with *The Huffington Post*, for $4.4 billion. Huffington, who initially agreed to stay on with the newly merged company as editor-in-chief of *The Huffington Post*, quickly changed her mind when, a year later, Verizon announced that it would also acquire Yahoo's core internet business in another multibillion-dollar mega-deal. If she remained at *HuffPost* she would inevitably be swallowed up by one of the largest companies in the US, with a market capitalization of around $200 billion.[102]

Huffington's ability to be her own master, as well as to direct *The Huffington Post* as she saw fit, was becoming more tenuous. In August 2016 she announced plans to leave *HuffPost*. She had presided over the site as its top editor for eleven years and was widely seen as the 'queen of digital media'. Her image and influence in the world

– instrumental to her identity and success – was, at this point, indisputable. She didn't need to be subverted by the largesse of a Fortune 500 company.

Notably, it was just before the announcement of AOL's merger with Verizon that Huffington received the extra encouragement she needed to leave *HuffPost*. It was at the Alibaba Global Conference on Women and Entrepreneurship at the upscale Dragon Hotel in Hangzhou where, at a dinner in May 2015, Alibaba's founder, Jack Ma, told her she should start a company based on her book *Thrive*. In an interview with *Inc.* magazine, Huffington says Ma had asked her to speak at the conference. 'I assumed he wanted me to speak on media, because at that time everybody wanted me to speak on media. And he said "no, I want you to speak on the themes of *Thrive*." The book had just come out in China, actually. He said, "Because in China, at the moment, stress is one of our biggest problems and we're having over 100 million people suffering from mental-health issues that are stress-related."' After her presentation, Ma leaned in over dinner and made Huffington an offer. As she recounts it:

> That night after my speech, he said to me, 'You know, this is a business and, if I were you, I would leave *The Huffington Post* and launch a new company around it, because there's no market leader and I will invest in it.' And at the time I literally thought, 'This guy's crazy and I'm never leaving *The Huffington Post*, it's like my third child. I built it, I run it, I'm never leaving

it. I don't know what he's talking about.' Politely though, I said, 'Thank you so much, you know, I have no plans to leave *The Huffington Post*.' Fast forward, to my getting more and more engaged in these issues, speaking around the world about these issues, and realizing that I wanted to do something more than speak and write about them, I wanted to help people implement the changes in their lives. So, when the time came to re-up for another four years at AOL, which owned *The Huffington Post*, which by then was owned by Verizon, I said in order for me to re-up, I need a carve-out to launch Thrive . . . They were not happy with it, but it was the only way for me to stay on.[103]

In spring 2016, Huffington released her fifteenth book, *The Sleep Revolution: Transforming Your Life, One Night at a Time*, which became an international best-seller. Years earlier, when Huffington had coyly confided to Jon Stewart of *The Daily Show* that her 'secret passion' was sleep, she was, in fact, getting very little sleep. This was still true in 2015, according to *The New York Times* magazine's David Segal. 'Her oft-repeated claim to sleep eight hours a night notwithstanding, she rarely seems to be idle,' he wrote. 'Emails from her cease, several ex-employees told me, only between 1 a.m. and 5 a.m.'[104] Her book on sleep, Huffington said, was inspired by her 2007 accident when she collapsed from overwork and exhaustion. During a TED talk two years after the event, Huffington told the audience, 'I studied, I met with medical doctors, scientists, and I'm here to tell you that the way to a more productive, more inspired, more joyful life is getting enough sleep.'[105] Like her last book, *The Sleep Revolution* was copyrighted under the Christabella name and once again received glowing reviews by many of her A-list friends, including Facebook's Sheryl Sandberg, who also reviewed *Thrive*. The book, around 400 pages of sleep science and the consequences of not getting enough sleep, was included on JP Morgan's annual summer reading list for high-net-worth individuals. 'If we don't continue to chip away at our collective delusion that burnout is the price we must pay for success, we'll never be able to restore sleep to its rightful place in our lives', Huffington writes.[106] In 2016, Huffington was once again on the *Forbes* 'World's 100 Most Powerful Women in Media' list, as well as Oprah Winfrey's 'SuperSoul 100' list of leaders and visionaries.

Leaving *The Huffington Post*, Huffington told *The New York Times* in an August 2016 interview, had been on her mind for 'a while'. Yet her decision was abrupt enough that no successor was immediately named. 'It was my decision,' she explained. Following the announcement, which stunned many of her staff, AOL CEO Armstrong issued a brief statement calling Huffington a 'visionary who built *The Huffington Post* into a truly transformative news platform'.[107] As Huffington made plans to go, one person who spoke with *Vanity Fair* in 2016 acknowledged that while Huffington's close celebrity relationships, corporate ties and constant self-promotion undoubtedly made *The*

Huffington Post a success, the practice had reached its limit of usefulness. 'The main directive of *The Huffington Post,* at its core, is not about producing great journalism, but it is about maintaining Arianna Huffington's position in the world,' the person said.[108] Even as Huffington continued to promote her site and personal brand, *HuffPost* had become an entity all its own – one that could stand on its merits. Huffington, in announcing her departure, was the first to agree with this notion. 'Great companies always succeed beyond their founder,' she said in a staff meeting at *HuffPost*'s New York headquarters. 'Even though *HuffPost* bears my name, it is absolutely about all of you and about this amazing team we've been for over 11 years.'[109]

While Huffington's decision to move on came as a shock to some, it followed a series of bumpy years inside *HuffPost*, as she took steps to carve her own path. Throughout Huffington's tenure, reporters and editors regularly expressed concerns about Huffington's frequent absences from the newsroom, in some cases jetting off to give paid speeches at corporate events, even as *HuffPost* covered some of those same companies. Because the speeches at times paid Huffington tens of thousands of dollars, this was considered to be a conflict of interest and a breach of journalistic ethics. 'She didn't give a shit and didn't think there was a conflict there,' a departed executive told *Vanity Fair*'s Cohan in 2016.[110] There were also fears that Huffington sometimes put her famous chums ahead of the interests of *HuffPost*'s readers. In 2014, when her friend, CNN television host Fareed Zakaria, came under fire for allegedly plagiarizing

other writers' work (this, after having been suspended
in 2012 by CNN and *Time* for an earlier infraction), he
made clear he was unhappy about *The Huffington Post*'s
coverage of the story, according to *Vanity Fair*. Rather than
defend her newsroom, Huffington sought to punish some
of the staff members who published the story, according
to the magazine.[111] 'Huffington's friendships became an
increasing source of concern and potential conflicts in
the newsroom' wrote *Vanity Fair*'s Cohan. 'According to
numerous sources, Huffington protected her allies ag-
gressively, even intemperately. The Zakaria incident was a
perfect example. "That made her extremely angry," recalls
a former editor who was in the newsroom that day'. In
response to queries from *Vanity Fair* about the incident,
Huffington said she strongly disagreed that her site ever
treated her friends with favour. 'There has never been a
different dynamic about how my friends were written
about on *HuffPost*. And of course, countless articles have
appeared critical of friends of mine,' she said.[112]

When Huffington joined the board of the ride-sharing
company Uber in April 2016, there also was consternation
in the newsroom. Huffington, by this time, had served
on a number of boards – including the Center for Public
Integrity, a non-profit investigative news organization in
Washington, and the Berggruen Institute, a Los Angeles
non-profit think tank – but many of her colleagues felt it
wasn't appropriate for her to serve on the board of a cor-
poration so long as she was *HuffPost*'s editor-in-chief. In an
effort to allay their worries, Huffington promised to recuse

herself from any decisions involved in the news coverage of Uber. As she joined the board, Uber's then-CEO Travis Kalanick praised her, saying he had personally benefited from her guidance 'over the years'. He said, 'She's built one of the most successful, innovative media companies in the world . . . from scratch. And on top of that, she's a best-selling author.' Kalanick went on to say that Huffington's 'emotional intelligence' would be an asset to the Uber board, as it was sometimes too preoccupied with data. 'I'm confident she will bring some ethos and pathos to our Uber logos,' he said.[113]

Years before, Huffington's friend Laurie David, one of the early funders of *HuffPost* and an environmental activist, had convinced Huffington to ditch her gas-guzzling vehicle for a hybrid Prius, and Huffington was known to use Ubers herself. Though she'd married into an oil fortune, she enthusiastically backed David's goal of lowering American dependence on fossil fuels.[114] Much later, when Huffington met Kalanick at a conference in Munich, they'd 'bonded over Uber's potential to solve big, urban problems', according to *The New York Times* in 2017.[115] As she took her seat on Uber's board, Huffington said, 'What I love about Uber is that [it] is clearly transforming not just transportation, but cities and that, to me, means a lot.'[116] Her decision to join the board was a calculated one, not only allowing her to remain relevant in Silicon Valley and on the front lines of a growing international company, but also affording her fresh insights into how to build her next global business.

In her final year at *HuffPost*, Huffington made one of the

most polarizing decisions of her reign as editor-in-chief. Witnessing the stunning rise of Donald J. Trump as a Republican presidential contender, she decided to post all articles about him in the 'entertainment' section of *HuffPost*, rather than the 'politics' section. In addition, *HuffPost* began appending an editor's note to the articles it published about Trump, notifying its readers that he was a 'serial liar' and 'racist'. This, according to *The New York Times*, 'raised questions about whether Ms. Huffington was unduly influencing coverage to suit her political agenda'. Many believed it was appropriate, however. And once it became clear that Trump would be participating in presidential debates and running in the election, Huffington, reversing her earlier decision, published a blog in December 2015 headlined 'We Are Not Entertained'. In it, she said that following stories of Trump's insistence on a 'total and complete shutdown of Muslims entering the United States' she now regarded him as 'an ugly and dangerous force in American politics', who posed a threat to America's democracy and national security. As a result, she moved coverage of Trump to *HuffPost*'s politics section, making the promise: 'If Trump's words and actions are racist, we'll call them racist. If they're sexist, we'll call them sexist. We won't shrink from the truth or be distracted by the showmanship.'[117]

While juggling the travails of Trump's election to president of the United States and her company's serial mergers, Huffington also quietly began to build Thrive Global – the enterprise that would catapult her into her dream role of

CEO, spiritual teacher and self-styled wellness evangelist. During an interview after the publication of her book *Thrive*, she said:

I have always been passionate about what is a good life, a meaningful life, a life that makes a difference. And that involves leadership in the role of women in history and today ... We simply cannot wait any longer for the third revolution to begin ... Having it all has to include a sense of peace, and well-being, and the ability to make a difference beyond our own lives. Women are leading the way in reimagining the workplace, reimagining success and the world at large. This is the time when we have to say, 'Hey guys, you know, this hasn't really worked, we need to change it!' And if we change it, it's going to be better for women and better for men as well. You're going to be very grateful to us ... [118]

In June 2016, when Huffington announced the founding of Thrive Global, she did not initially plan to leave *The Huffington Post*. Six weeks after the company went live, however, Thrive brought in twice the revenue Huffington had expected[119] and, in August, when it attracted roughly $7 million of early funding, Huffington decided she would have to choose between *HuffPost*, what she had once called her 'third child', and her new company.[120] 'The original idea was that I could do both,' she told *The New York Times*. 'But it very quickly turned out to be an illusion.'[121]

PART 7

CREATING THRIVE

'We are no longer acknowledging that technology is exclusively virtuous.'

Not long before Huffington's mother died, she caught Arianna reading her email while talking to her children. 'My mother got angry with me,' Huffington recalls. 'I abhor multitasking,' her mother said with a grimace. It was a frequent admonition from Elli to her children, Huffington says, reflecting her mother's strong belief that 'being connected in a shallow way to the entire world can prevent us from being deeply connected to those closest to us, including ourselves, and that is where wisdom is found.'[1]

For most of her life, Huffington had made an undeclared pastime of doling out homespun wisdom in the various traditions of her mother and a phalanx of spiritual advisors. Two weeks after her mother's death, Huffington felt reflective. 'Now that she's gone', she wrote, 'I know that however difficult, however inconvenient, even unnatural it may be for a while, there is only one way to honor her – by living differently, living more like she lived.'[2] It would be a pledge that, during *The Huffington Post* years, she would repeatedly, if reluctantly, abandon. With Thrive Global, she would at last follow her mother's wishes. Huffington would not only seek to lead what she calculated to be a $4 trillion global wellness industry as its self-appointed evangelist and sage, she would begin the process of empirically testing prevailing wisdom, backing it up with studies, science and data.[3]

Offering seminars, a range of consumer products and web courses designed to help companies, individuals and communities 'improve their well-being and performance', she billed Thrive as a 'behavior change and technology company'. For those closely watching the trajectory of Huffington's life and career, these programmes, in ways both obvious and nuanced, could be seen as redolent of her 1970s spiritual enlightenment days, placing a strong emphasis on meditation, health, happiness, productivity and personal performance. 'I would say that the great thing today is we have so much scientific evidence,' Huffington told the *Guardian* in 2013, acknowledging that her book *Thrive* was the result of years of her own spiritual searching. She added:

'New Age' – it's flakey, it feels speculative. [*Thrive*] is based on hardcore science. A lot of the ideas are the same, you're absolutely right. Ever since I was a little girl it's taken many forms, but it's part of the same search for transcendence, for meaning. And this has been a big part of my life as a quest, if you like. But people are really open to these ideas in a way that they weren't. There's a very different interest now. And part of it is all these new scientific findings that have made such a difference in how all these ideas are presented. I love reading all the latest scientific findings.[4]

With Thrive Global, Huffington would attract powerful allies in the technology, health and science fields, creating regimens based on data and working with partners from Stanford University, the University of Southern California, Harvard University, the University of Wisconsin-Madison, the Wharton School at the University of Pennsylvania, the Rockefeller Neuroscience Institute at West Virginia University and Oxford University. Within a few months, Huffington announced Thrive's business was taking off and she was expanding its SoHo headquarters.[5] By March 2018, she publicized on social media that Thrive had outgrown its New York offices and would be moving to a bigger space, noting this was 'a good problem to have'. As of 2019, she had opened branches in San Francisco, Mumbai, Athens and Melbourne and planned to expand further globally, particularly deeper into Asia, with a focus on China and India.

Thrive's SoHo offices are compact but airy, with an open floor plan and a central seating area flowing into a small kitchen. There are glass walls and a floor-to-ceiling bookshelf at the front entryway, stuffed with books by Arianna and a multitude of wellness titles. Launching in November 2016, Thrive began with twenty employees, but that number more than quadrupled by the end of 2019, with Huffington working to create a global online media platform highlighting wellness and health in much the same way she built *HuffPost* as a destination for news and politics.

From the outset, Thrive attracted many of the same investors who put their money behind *The Huffington Post*: Huffington's long-time friend and former business partner Ken Lerer of Lerer Hippeau Ventures; Fred Harman of Oak Investment Partners; Greycroft Partners; and also her ex-husband, Michael Huffington. She also brought in venture capital firms such as Silicon Valley's IVP, Jack Ma's Blue Pool Capital in Hong Kong, and Female Founders Fund in New York.[6] Over the next few years, Huffington would raise funds for the new venture that would outstrip *The Huffington Post*'s pace of growth by nearly 50 per cent. In fact, Thrive Global reported an estimated valuation of more than $120 million by May 2018.[7] Huffington also landed a deep-pocketed stable of clients and multinationals interested in her wellness programmes, including JPMorgan, Alibaba, Bank of America, Accenture, Nestlé, SAP, Hilton, and Goldman Sachs.[8]

Starting a new venture at the age of sixty-six, Huffington says, was not easier than doing it the first time. But for her, founding Thrive Global felt like more of a calling than any venture she had yet undertaken. In her updated preface to *The Sleep Revolution*, she offered more insight into her decision to launch another new business:

I've been asked a lot why I left *The Huffington Post*, a very successful business, to found a start-up. Wasn't it hard, people have wondered, leaving an established business with my name on the front door to start all over again? It's always hard to leave something you built and love, but given how big this epidemic of stress and burnout is around the world, and how hungry people are for change, I realized I could no longer just write about the problem – I had to do something about it. It was a call to action I couldn't ignore. And sleep, of course, is at the heart of this culture shift.[9]

The venture also gave Huffington a chance to work more closely with her sister, Agapi, who narrated Huffington's audio book for *The Sleep Revolution*, and soon joined her at Thrive, helping teach busy executives and corporate clients how to tap into the benefits of meditation. (As one Thrive employee notes, 'Agapi always says, "If you can breathe, you can meditate."') Since her mother's death, Huffington says, 'it became much clearer to my sister and me that if our life's journey is to evolve as human beings, there's no faster way to do it than through giving and service.' The expression Arianna and Agapi's mother had frequently used – 'Take care of your capital' – now became the mantra they shared with others.[10] 'To her, capital was the value that she placed on our own lives, taking care of ourselves and our well-being, the basics, such as eating well, sleeping well, doing things that you enjoy and being discerning about the people you spend time with,' says Agapi. 'It was all about how you nurture things, inside and out, not getting caught up in the triviality of life or, as she used to say, toxic people. By example, she encouraged us to value the precious gift of life, always creating a sacred environment.'[11]

In the years ahead, Huffington's departure from *The Huffington Post* would seem extremely well-timed, especially amid the write-downs, bloodletting and mass layoffs razing the media industry – including at *The Huffington Post*. Huffington did not speak very much about this. Instead, she subsumed the act of stepping away from *Huff-Post* within her own well-crafted, personal storytelling paradigm. As she launched Thrive in the final quarter of 2016, she and Agapi did rounds of interviews, recalling Huffington's decades of work burnout, her rush to the hospital in 2007 and Agapi's sustained efforts to nurse her sister back to health. 'She and I have always supported each other,' Agapi told the *Telegraph* in December 2016. 'So I was her cheerleader in helping her get more sleep, meditate, take walks and ease her schedule.' To this day, Huffington calls Agapi her 'spiritual mentor'. The sisters take holidays together and share Huffington's loft in New York, as well as the mansion that Huffington continues to keep in Brentwood, California. Agapi told the *Telegraph* she does all the cooking, because Arianna can 'barely do an egg'.[12] Perhaps it is ironic that Huffington, who created a digital media empire, would now seek to build a new empire around curing digital burnout. But by invoking the stories of her sister, her mother and herself, she presented a seamless narrative linking her journey from *The Huffington Post* to Thrive, anchored by her family and spiritual inclinations.

Greek storytelling has a long history of persuasion, says historian Robin Waterfield. Over the centuries, the Greeks created the iconic imagery of Athens, where Arianna walked the streets to and from school as a child with the myths of countless ages coursing in her blood. 'Athens is always present in the heart and mind of anyone educated in the West who aspires to greatness,' he writes, adding:

> It was not just for the romantics that Athens was an ideal; it was for Pericles and his peers, too. Greece has this ability to combine dream and reality, humor and poverty, metaphysics and cunning. The ancient Greeks were not as autonomous as Byron and his peers would have us believe, but they were in love with freedom . . . Athens never was what it made itself out to be. It is not now, and it was not then. Yes, the place had more than its fair share of geniuses and wonderful buildings, but there was plenty that was unsound about it, and the myth of Athenian perfection was a creation of orators, starting as early as the fifth century itself.[13]

Huffington, keenly aware of this, has always had a natural and innate ability to tell stories, persuade others and get them to join her in her enterprises. This is, perhaps, the biggest single secret to her success.

Huffington's new venture, though still in its infancy, has already made headlines, as she once again uses her expertise in handling the media to promote Thrive with the same vigour she once did *The Huffington Post*. She travels the world to talk about wellness across cultures, interviews celebrities from Katy Perry to Gisele Bündchen for her Thrive podcasts, and appears regularly on television news programmes and the talk-show circuit, tying the mission of Thrive to her own books, spiritual teachings and amalgamated wisdom of her Greek heritage. 'Thrive is very much based on our Greek philosophy,' she says. 'At the heart of Thrive is the question that philosophers addressed, "What is a good life?" which today has been reduced to success – and success has been further reduced down to two metrics: money and power. That is like trying to sit on a two-legged stool. Sooner or later you topple over . . . Greeks have never felt limited by their circumstances. We've always been a small country and yet, we always did things way beyond our size.'[14]

Those close to Arianna say one of her favourite books, which she keeps by her bed, is *Meditations* by Marcus Aurelius, the Roman emperor and Stoic philosopher who lived from AD 121 to 180. He presided over the Pax Romana, a period of relative tranquillity during the Roman Empire, but also faced devastating plague, religious clashes and military conflict, and many personal trials and betrayals. His internal state of calm amid life's chaos, for Huffington, has made him a personal hero and guide throughout her own life. Thrive Global's homepage in 2019 prominently featured one of his quotes: 'People look for retreats for themselves in the country, or in the hills . . . There is nowhere that a person can find a more peaceful and trouble-free retreat than in his own mind . . . So constantly give yourself this retreat, and renew yourself.'

Since leaving *HuffPost*, Huffington also has not hesitated to continue injecting herself into public debates or parley with other famed entrepreneurs. In 2018 she chided Tesla co-founder and CEO Elon Musk for not getting enough sleep after he gave an interview with *The New York Times*, bemoaning the state of his health due to working 120-hour weeks. Huffington, who remains active on social media, sent Musk an open letter on Twitter with an exhortation that could have come from her mother: 'Dear Elon, please change the way you work to be more in line with the science around how humans are most effective. You need it, Tesla needs it and the world needs it.'[15] An excerpt:

> You're demonstrating a wildly outdated, anti-scientific and horribly inefficient way of using human energy . . . You're a science and data-driven person. You're obsessed with physics, engineering, with figuring out how things work. So, apply that same passion for science not just to your products but to yourself. People

are not machines. For machines – whether of the First or Fourth Industrial Revolution variety – downtime is a bug; for humans, downtime is a feature. The science is clear.[16]

At 5.32 in the morning, two days later, Musk responded, via Twitter: 'Ford and Tesla are the only two American car companies to avoid bankruptcy. I just got home from the factory. You think this is an option. It is not.'[17]

The year before, Huffington drew media attention for taking a lead role in smoothing over a series of scandals that forced a major shake-up in the top ranks at Uber, where she remained director and her friend, Uber founder and CEO Travis Kalanick, was compelled to step down from his position. Damaged by a series of gender-bias, sexual harassment and discrimination scandals, Uber's management relied heavily on Huffington's leadership and media savvy to navigate the worst of the fallout. She led a public campaign to resuscitate the company's tarnished image, proclaiming at an Uber all-staff meeting that the company would henceforth eschew its toxic culture and embrace a new era of 'no more brilliant jerks'.[18]

Huffington's rise at Uber may have surprised many, but not those who truly knew her. Fred Harman, the former *HuffPost* board member and investor who was now investing in Thrive through his firm, Oak Investment Partners, told *The New York Times*, 'She sows the seeds of trust and makes you feel her interests are aligned with yours. When you get down to making decisions, you can focus on how persuasive she is.' Her ascent at Uber, the *Times* said, was just 'the latest chapter in a life marked by dramatic career shifts that included political pundit, media mogul and corporate fixer'.[19] In many ways, she was still all of these things.

Huffington, who understood too well the difficulties of overseeing a fast-growing company, told *Vox*'s Kara Swisher that she felt that her experience at Uber had been a 'teachable moment', remarking, 'When you sacrifice it all on hyper growth, it has a price on human capital.'[20] Huffington benefited enormously from her relationship with Uber, winning the company over as a client of Thrive and, when Uber went public in 2019, raking in an estimated $100 million on the 22,000 shares she reportedly owned in the company.[21] She stepped down from the board of Uber in 2019, saying she wanted to focus on growing her own company.

While Huffington's central focus remained on wellness, she couldn't help but still weigh in on US politics from time to time, making a crucial connection between the stress that many Americans felt in the aftermath of the 2008–9 financial crisis and their burnout over the scandals of the incoming Trump administration. Publishing a piece in February 2017 in the 'Thrive Journal', Huffington's new online portal for speaking directly to her followers, she urged people to 'step out of the storm' and channel their energy into taking action – such as participating in marches or protests – rather than living in a constant state of fear and anxiety: 'Trump has brought many new things to our lives. And one of them is this state of perpetual outrage (Trumprage? Trumpdignation?) provoked in reaction to the state of perpetual chaos his administration seems to generate on a daily, even hourly, basis. This is no way to live. Literally. We're only 17 days in and people are literally exhausted by it.'[22]

That same year, she also saw *The Huffington Post* go through a major rebranding under its new editor-in-chief, Lydia Polgreen, formerly a *New York Times* associate masthead editor and the editorial director of NYT Global. Officially changing the name of the website from *The Huffington Post* to a more abbreviated *HuffPost*, Polgreen, looking to increase the site's readership amid heightened competition and political changes, shifted *HuffPost*'s focus in 2017 to attract more moderate and even conservative readers. In the future, she said, *HuffPost* would try to appeal to a 'much broader audience', as the site had turned into 'fundamentally, a populist brand rather than an ideological brand'.[23] In keeping with this ethos, Polgreen ended *HuffPost*'s tradition of using unpaid bloggers as of 2018 – a welcome change to many who felt that *HuffPost* had exploited writers for too long.[24] Although the site changed its name to its much shorter moniker, the move in no way sought to distance *HuffPost* from its founder, Polgreen said. 'Everything that *HuffPost* is today stands on the shoulders of what Arianna Huffington has built.'[25] Huffington, responding to the site's makeover on Twitter, wrote: 'Love *HuffPost*'s new look. As it turns 12, great to see it growing up, continuing to evolve, but staying playful.'[26]

If Huffington had not proven it already, the year 2018 would make patently clear that her instincts and timing in leaving *HuffPost* to start her own business were impeccable. That year, *Forbes* would again name her one of the 'World's 100 Most Powerful Women'.[27] At the same time, Verizon would write down nearly the entire value of the media properties that it had purchased from AOL and Yahoo – which included *HuffPost* – to the tune of $4.6 billion. Verizon's grand experiment to attract web-based advertising through popular sites like *HuffPost* had been eviscerated by competitors Google and Facebook, which, as of 2018, controlled more than 50 per cent of the US digital ad market, estimated to be worth more than $100 billion, and far more globally. These were the same powerful headwinds that were destroying newspapers and digital media properties reliant on advertising for revenue around the world.[28]

Huffington's wellness company, by contrast, was taking off, with the venture raising an estimated $65 million of funding by mid-2019, led by neurosurgeon and Silicon Valley venture capitalist Andrew Firlik of JAZZ Venture Partners. This round put Thrive Global's total estimated valuation at $150 million. In addition to expanding offices around the world, Thrive was signing more corporate clients and partners for its wellness training courses and workshops, creating habit-changing apps for smart phones, and offering a slate of retail products following many of Huffington's lifestyle recommendations about how to recharge and unplug to improve personal and professional performance. 'Arianna Huffington's Phone Bed Charging Station', designed for tablets and smart phones, became one of Thrive Global's better-known offerings. The product – a miniature bed with headboard, mattress and blanket – allows users to tuck their devices in at bedtime as 'a regular part of your nightly ritual', according to the company literature. The charger bed, priced at around $65, is available on Amazon. Huffington, who uses the bed charging station for her own smart phone at night, leaves it in an adjacent room while she sleeps, so she won't be tempted to check for messages, she says. 'We take better care of our smart phones than we take care of ourselves,' she told *People*. 'You know exactly how much battery remains in your smart phone; you get alerts and you rush around anxious to find a charger.'

Huffington was also taking a page from the *HuffPost* business model at Thrive by offering corporations a way to advertise their wellness products through 'editorial sponsorship' packages that allowed them to pay to place custom-branded media and content on Thrive's website, alongside its original articles, blogs and columns by wellness experts, celebrities and academics. Once again, Huffington was creating an online global media platform and web community to promote clients, as well as those writing for her site, for a profit. Huffington also began contributing her own content, including the Thrive podcasts where she talks about health, wellness and spirituality with celebrities, and a 'Weekly Thoughts' column where she continues to write about politics and current events, often linking her messages to themes of wellness and health.

Corporate clients from Proctor & Gamble to Sleep Number have signed on to advertise through Thrive's media and marketing business model, which also provides custom-built branded events and podcast partnerships. 'That's where Arianna is working her magic,' says Harman. 'Where there's a wellness proposition with a product, she can provide a platform and a message.'

Huffington's contracts with corporate clients have been lucrative, reportedly reaching as high as six and seven figures. Thrive tailors its wellness programmes and custom-branded content to fit each company, its culture, its employees and products. While it remains unclear whether Huffington will be able to generate the kind of consistent profits at her new venture that eluded *HuffPost*, her mastery at building a company, attracting a well-capitalized clientele and gaining a public following through her use of the press and social media is beyond question. 'We are no longer acknowledging that technology is exclusively virtuous,' Huffington told Bloomberg recently in a televised interview. 'We have a lot of data about what it's done to our lives and a lot of it has been incredibly positive. But we have more and more data about what [else] it's doing . . . horrific data about mental health problem increases among young kids and teenagers, depression, anxiety, suicides. And the connection between how much time you spend on your devices and mental health problems is very clear . . . So, something amazing is happening in our culture . . . to address this growing concern.'[29] The World Health

Organization bolstered her case in 2019 by officially declaring burnout to be a syndrome of 'chronic workplace stress', adding it to its handbook of 'International Classification of Diseases and Related Health Problems'.[30] Huffington immediately highlighted the findings in a blog post for Thrive when the report came out in May of that year. 'There's something almost cathartic about legitimizing burnout', she writes, 'as the medical world catches up with a ubiquitous condition that has long-shaped our lives.'[31]

Shortly after having a hip replacement, Huffington also found a new way to fight burnout. Extending her company's search for ways to predict, influence and even transcend human behaviour, she announced the acquisition of Boundless Mind, a Los Angeles neuroscience-based artificial intelligence company, in late 2019. As part of the merger, Thrive received exclusive access to Boundless's AI technology, allowing it to gather consumer data that can predict and drive positive behaviour changes for its clients. 'I have been obsessed with Boundless since I first came across them', Huffington wrote in a blog post. 'I loved the fact that they were using the same technology designed to hook people to social media and gaming to instead unhook us, and help drive us to more healthy habits.'[32] Appearing on CNBC, she noted that one of the greatest challenges of the global healthcare industry is inspiring people to change their habits. 'What's happening right now is that 90 per cent of healthcare costs and healthcare problems are stress-related, lifestyle-related, and preventable,' she said, adding, 'This product is going to make everything else that we do sustainable and scalable around the world.'[33]

An unspoken, if obvious, goal for Huffington, those close to her say, has long been to touch as many lives as possible. 'She's focused on how do we make our limited life on this planet better,' says Harman. After years of carving out a place for herself in politics and within the global political conversation, Huffington has learned that, when it comes to improving lives, politics is not the answer. 'In politics, you represent 40 per cent of the people at best,' he says. 'She's always had the goal. She doesn't just want to make a narrow group of people better off. She wants to make the world better off.' As Huffington writes in *The Fourth Instinct*:

'It matters, it matters very much what each of us chooses to do. The journey toward self-discovery and self-knowledge is not only life's highest adventure, but also the only way to transform society from one based on self-centredness and compulsory compassion to one based on service and mutual responsibility.'[34]

Facing the prospect of turning seventy in 2020, Huffington has continued to put in ten-hour work days. She recently released her daily schedule to show how she optimizes her own performance, waking up at 7 a.m. to meditate, do yoga, exercise on her stationary bike and watch the news. She arrives at work at 9 a.m., her Manhattan condo a short stroll from her SoHo offices (she usually wears white sneakers, colleagues say, even when dressed up or conducting celebrity interviews). Huffington's work day typically ends around 7 p.m., and she tries to be home for dinner with her family most nights.

Still, even for a media queen, there are sacrifices. 'I haven't seen *Game of Thrones*,' she laments, referencing the popular television series. 'I haven't seen *House of Cards*. I have a long list of shows I haven't seen.'[35] Rather, at 9:30 p.m., she has a hot bath with Epsom salts, reads a book and heads to bed by 11 p.m. – without electronics. She spends her evenings with her sister, Agapi, and her daughters, whenever possible.[36] 'It's kind of amusing when the Americans complain that their children have to go back home after college because of tougher times,' she says. 'You know people in the US always ask, "Are you supporting your family?" Nobody ever asks that in Greece. You just know that if you have any money, you will support your family.'[37]

Asked if her busy day will one day include writing an autobiography, Huffington demurs. 'Don't you think that's a sign that you are done?'[38] She may, in fact, never write any account of her life, one person close to her says, because, 'Arianna does not believe in looking back.'

She also has no plans to retire. 'I really thought I would die running *The Huffington Post*,' Huffington says. 'The reason I changed my mind was because I realized there was something more important I could do.'[39]

BOOKS BY
ARIANNA HUFFINGTON

By Arianna Stassinopoulos:

The Female Woman (London: Davis-Poynter, 1973)

By Arianna Huffington:

After Reason (Briarcliff Manor, NY: Stein and Day, 1978)

Maria Callas: The Woman Behind the Legend (New York: Simon & Schuster, 1981)

The Gods of Greece (New York: Atlantic Monthly Press, 1984); revised edn with illustrations by Françoise Gilot (1993)

The Fourth Instinct: The Call of the Soul (New York: Simon & Schuster, 1994)

Greetings from the Lincoln Bedroom (New York: Crown Publishers, 1998)

How to Overthrow the Government (New York: Harper-Collins, 2000)

Pigs at the Trough: How Corporate Greed and Political Corruption are Undermining America (New York: Crown Publishers, 2003)

Fanatics & Fools: The Game Plan for Winning Back America (New York: Miramax Books, 2004)

On Becoming Fearless . . . In Love, Work, and Life (New York: Little, Brown, 2006)

Right Is Wrong: How the Lunatic Fringe Hijacked America, Shredded the Constitution, and Made Us All Less Safe (New York: Alfred A. Knopf, 2008)

Third World America: How Our Politicians Are Abandoning the Middle Class and Betraying the American Dream (New York: Crown Publishing, 2010)

Thrive: The Third Metric to Redefining Success and Creating a Life of Well-Being, Wisdom, and Wonder (New York: Harmony Books, 2014)

The Sleep Revolution: Transforming Your Life, One Night at a Time (New York: Harmony Books, 2016)

By Arianna Stassinopoulos Huffington:

Picasso: Creator and Destroyer (New York: Simon & Schuster, 1988)

REFERENCES

Part 1: Greece

1 Robin Waterfield, *Athens: From Ancient Ideal to Modern City* (New York: Basic Books, 2004).

2 Ibid.

3 Ibid.

4 Arianna Huffington, *On Becoming Fearless . . . In Love, Work, and Life* (New York: Little, Brown, 2006).

5 https://www.pbs.org/video/at-the-paley-center-arianna-huffington/

6 Ibid.

7 Ibid.

8 Jeri Freedman, *Arianna Huffington: Media Mogul and Internet News Pioneer* (New York, Cavendish Square, 2018).

9   Ibid.

10   Waterfield, *Athens.*

11   Ibid.

12   Ibid.

13   Arianna Stassinopoulos, *The Female Woman* (London: Davis-Poynter, 1973); Huffington, *On Becoming Fearless;* https://www.inc.com/magazine/20100201/how-i-did-it-arianna-huffington.html

14   https://www.newyorker.com/magazine/2008/10/13/the-oracle-lauren-collins?reload=true

15   Ibid.

16   https://www.inc.com/magazine/20100201/how-i-did-it-arianna-huffington.html

17   Arianna Huffington, *The Fourth Instinct: The Call of the Soul* (New York: Simon & Schuster, 2003).

18   Freedman, *Huffington: Media Mogul.*

19   https://www.telegraph.co.uk/family/relationships/found-sister-arianna-huffington-lying-pool-blood-knew-had-help/

20   Huffington, *Fourth Instinct.*

21   Waterfield, *Athens.*

22   'The Rise and Rise of Arianna Stassinopoulos,' (*New York Magazine*, July 1983).

23   https://www.nytimes.com/2012/05/13/opinion/sunday/greek-tragedy.html

24   Huffington, *On Becoming Fearless.*

25   https://www.nytimes.com/2012/05/13/opinion/sunday/greek-tragedy.html

26   'The Rise and Rise of Arianna Stassinopoulos'.

27 Huffington, *Fourth Instinct.*

28 https://www.telegraph.co.uk/family/relationships/found-sister-arianna-huffington-lying-pool-blood-knew-had-help/

29 https://www.nytimes.com/2012/05/13/opinion/sunday/greek-tragedy.html

30 https://www.huffpost.com/entry/yassou-from-athens-introducing-huffpost-greece_b_6180208

31 https://www.inc.com/magazine/20100201/how-i-did-it-arianna-huffington.html

32 https://www.nytimes.com/2012/05/13/opinion/sunday/greek-tragedy.html

33 https://www.pbs.org/video/at-the-paley-center-arianna-huffington/

34 Ibid.

35 https://www.nytimes.com/2012/05/13/opinion/sunday/greek-tragedy.html

36 Huffington, *On Becoming Fearless.*

37 https://www.pbs.org/video/at-the-paley-center-arianna-huffington/

38 https://www.telegraph.co.uk/family/relationships/found-sister-arianna-huffington-lying-pool-blood-knew-had-help/

39 https://www.nytimes.com/2012/05/13/opinion/sunday/greek-tragedy.html

40 'The Rise and Rise of Arianna Stassinopoulos'.

41 https://www.telegraph.co.uk/family/relationships/found-sister-arianna-huffington-lying-pool-blood-knew-had-help/

42 Huffington, *Fourth Instinct*.

43 https://www.huffpost.com/entry/yassou-from-athens-introducing-huffpost-greece_b_6180208

44 Ibid.

45 https://www.nytimes.com/2012/05/13/opinion/sunday/greek-tragedy.html

46 https://www.makers.com/blog/7-things-you-never-knew-about-arianna-huffington

47 https://www.nytimes.com/1986/04/13/style/arianna-stassinopoulos-author-wed-to-r-michael-huffington-executive.html

48 'The Rise and Rise of Arianna Stassinopoulos'.

49 https://www.newyorker.com/magazine/2008/10/13/the-oracle-lauren-collins?reload=true

50 'The Rise and Rise of Arianna Stassinopoulos'.

51 https://www.newyorker.com/magazine/2008/10/13/the-oracle-lauren-collins?reload=true

52 Huffington, *On Becoming Fearless*.

53 https://www.huffingtonpost.com/arianna-huffington/third-world-america-why-i_b_706673.html

54 https://thriveglobal.com/stories/arianna-huffington-overcome-self-doubt-advice/

55 https://www.pbs.org/video/at-the-paley-center-arianna-huffington/

56 https://www.inc.com/magazine/20100201/how-i-did-it-arianna-huffington.html

57 https://www.pbs.org/video/at-the-paley-center-arianna-huffington/

58 Ibid.

59 https://www.washingtonpost.com/archive/life-style/1987/02/17/in-the-jet-stream-with-arianna/a66952a2-4541-4bef-aa5f-a9b9c9a2c89a/?utm_term=.a5b99b1603de

60 https://www.questia.com/magazine/1G1-237929457/gaining-courage-from-failure-arianna-huffington-pushes

61 https://medium.com/thrive-global/to-my-mother-elli-11dfa39e956f

62 https://www.telegraph.co.uk/family/relationships/found-sister-arianna-huffington-lying-pool-blood-knew-had-help/

63 https://www.inc.com/hitendra-wadhwa/steve-jobs-self-realization-yogananda.html

64 https://www.newyorker.com/magazine/2008/10/13/the-oracle-lauren-collins?reload=true

65 https://www.lifeposts.com/p/milestone/206/elli-stassinopoulos-memorial/lifestory/

66 https://thriveglobal.com/stories/arianna-huffington-overcome-self-doubt-advice/

67 https://www.pbs.org/video/at-the-paley-center-arianna-huffington/

68 Huffington, *Fourth Instinct*.

Part 2: London and Cambridge

1 https://www.pbs.org/video/at-the-paley-center-arianna-huffington/

2 https://www.telegraph.co.uk/culture/10770377/Arianna-Huffington-recalls-being-elected-President-of-the-Cambridge-Union-1971.html

3 https://www.pbs.org/video/
   at-the-paley-center-arianna-huffington/
4 Huffington, *On Becoming Fearless.*
5 https://www.newyorker.com/magazine/2008/10/13/
   the-oracle-lauren-collins?reload=true
6 https://www.telegraph.co.uk/culture/10770377/
   Arianna-Huffington-recalls-being-elected-Presi-
   dent-of-the-Cambridge-Union-1971.html
7 https://www.newyorker.com/magazine/2018/03/12/
   christopher-steele-the-man-behind-the-trump-dossier
8 https://www.telegraph.co.uk/culture/10770377/
   Arianna-Huffington-recalls-being-elected-Presi-
   dent-of-the-Cambridge-Union-1971.html
9 https://www.pbs.org/video/
   at-the-paley-center-arianna-huffington/
10 Huffington, *On Becoming Fearless.*
11 https://www.pbs.org/video/
   at-the-paley-center-arianna-huffington/
12 'The Rise and Rise of Arianna Stassinopoulos'.
13 Huffington, *On Becoming Fearless.*
14 Ibid.
15 https://www.newyorker.com/magazine/2008/10/13/
   the-oracle-lauren-collins?reload=true
16 https://www.telegraph.co.uk/culture/10770377/
   Arianna-Huffington-recalls-being-elected-Presi-
   dent-of-the-Cambridge-Union-1971.html
17 https://people.com/archive/an-unflattering-portrait-of-
   picasso-leaves-art-critics-in-a-hanging-frame-of-mind-
   vol-30-no-4/

18 https://www.success.com/
arianna-huffington-pushing-the-limits/.

19 https://www.telegraph.co.uk/culture/10770377/
Arianna-Huffington-recalls-being-elected-Presi-
dent-of-the-Cambridge-Union-1971.html

20 https://www.washingtonpost.com/archive/life-
style/1987/02/17/in-the-jet-stream-with-arianna/
a66952a2-4541-4bef-aa5f-a9b9c9a2c89a/?utm_term=.
a5b99b1603de

21 https://www.pbs.org/video/
at-the-paley-center-arianna-huffington/

22 https://www.telegraph.co.uk/technology/inter-
net/8309732/Arianna-Huffington-mover-and-shaper.html

23 https://www.huffpost.com/entry/
bernard-levin_b_9114200

24 'The Rise and Rise of Arianna Stassinopoulos'.

25 Huffington, *On Becoming Fearless*.

26 https://www.theguardian.com/media/2016/may/01/
arianna-huffington-uber-directors-huffington-post

27 https://www.pbs.org/video/
at-the-paley-center-arianna-huffington/

28 https://www.newyorker.com/magazine/2008/10/13/
the-oracle-lauren-collins?reload=true

29 https://www.huffpost.com/entry/
bernard-levin_b_9114200

30 https://www.pbs.org/video/
at-the-paley-center-arianna-huffington/

31 https://www.huffpost.com/entry/
bernard-levin_b_9114200

32 Ibid.

33 https://www.thetimes.co.uk/article/
times-obituary-bernard-levin-2x2pbfwg93s

34 https://www.washingtonpost.com/archive/life-
style/1987/02/17/in-the-jet-stream-with-arianna/
a66952a2-4541-4bef-aa5f-a9b9c9a2c89a/?utm_term=.
a5b99b1603de

35 https://www.pbs.org/video/
at-the-paley-center-arianna-huffington/

36 https://www.huffpost.com/entry/
bernard-levin_b_9114200

37 Ibid.

38 https://www.thetimes.co.uk/article/
times-obituary-bernard-levin-2x2pbfwg93s

39 https://www.theguardian.com/theobserver/2012/jul/15/
arianna-huffington-post-journalism-interview

40 https://www.huffpost.com/entry/
bernard-levin_b_9114200

41 Ibid.

42 Ibid.

43 https://www.theguardian.com/theobserver/2012/jul/15/
arianna-huffington-post-journalism-interview

44 Freedman, *Huffington: Media Mogul*; Arianna Stassinopoulos, *The Female Woman* (London: Davis-Poynter,
1973).

45 https://www.pbs.org/video/
at-the-paley-center-arianna-huffington/

46 Ibid.

47 Ibid.

48 Ibid.

49 Huffington, *On Becoming Fearless.*

50 Huffington, *Fourth Instinct.*

51 Michael Llewellyn Smith, *Athens: A Cultural and Literary History.* (Northampton, MA: Interlink Books, 2004).

52 https://www.pbs.org/video/
at-the-paley-center-arianna-huffington/

53 Stassinopoulos, *The Female Woman.*

54 Huffington, *On Becoming Fearless.*

55 https://www.pbs.org/video/
at-the-paley-center-arianna-huffington/

56 https://www.theguardian.com/media/2014/mar/30/
arianna-huffington-interview-find-stories-every-
where-huffington-post-news

57 https://www.pbs.org/video/
at-the-paley-center-arianna-huffington/

58 Ibid.

59 Huffington, *Fourth Instinct.*

60 https://www.pbs.org/video/
at-the-paley-center-arianna-huffington/

61 Ibid.

62 Arianna Huffington, *After Reason* (Briarcliff Manor, NY: Stein and Day, 1978).

63 Ibid.

64 https://www.pbs.org/video/
at-the-paley-center-arianna-huffington/

65 Huffington, *On Becoming Fearless.*

66 Ibid.

67 Ibid.

68   Ibid.

69   https://www.pbs.org/video/
      at-the-paley-center-arianna-huffington/

70   https://www.newyorker.com/magazine/2008/10/13/
      the-oracle-lauren-collins?reload=true

71   https://www.vanityfair.com/news/2005/12/
      huffington200512

72   https://www.pbs.org/video/
      at-the-paley-center-arianna-huffington/

73   Huffington, *On Becoming Fearless*.

74   Huffington, *After Reason*.

75   Huffington, *On Becoming Fearless*.

76   https://www.vanityfair.com/news/2005/12/
      huffington200512

77   https://www.independent.co.uk/voices/rear-window-ari-
      anna-stassinopoulos-the-siren-of-the-seventies-1443305.
      html

78   https://www.vanityfair.com/news/2005/12/
      huffington200512

79   'The Rise and Rise of Arianna Stassinopoulos'.

80   https://www.pbs.org/video/
      at-the-paley-center-arianna-huffington/

81   https://medium.com/insight-seminars/arianna-huffing-
      ton-on-her-insight-seminars-experience-f2e0552e87b4

82   https://www.washingtonpost.com/archive/life-
      style/1987/02/17/in-the-jet-stream-with-arianna/
      a66952a2-4541-4bef-aa5f-a9b9c9a2c89a/?utm_term=.
      a5b99b1603de

83   https://medium.com/insight-seminars/

arianna-huffington-on-her-insight-seminars-experi-
ence-f2e0552e87b4

84   Ibid.
85   Ibid.
86   https://www.huffpost.com/entry/
     bernard-levin_b_9114200
87   Quoted in ibid.
88   https://www.vanityfair.com/news/2005/12/
     huffington200512
89   Quoted in ibid.
90   Freedman, *Huffington: Media Mogul*; https://www.
     vanityfair.com/news/2005/12/huffington200512
91   https://medium.com/insight-seminars/arianna-huffing-
     ton-on-her-insight-seminars-experience-f2e0552e87b4
92   https://www.theatlantic.com/politics/
     archive/2014/06/a-strange-but-true-tale-of-voter-fraud-
     and-bioterrorism/372445/
93   https://news.google.co.uk/newspapers?id=k4AiAAAAI-
     BAJ&sjid=wakFAAAAIBAJ&pg=2100,3636170&dq=ra-
     jneesh+heart-failure&hl=en
94   https://www.facebook.com/AriannaHuffington/pho-
     tos/a.158003868278/10152428994938279/?type=1&the-
     ater; https://www.thedailybeast.com/
     arianna-huffington-denies-involvement-in-sex-cult-de-
     picted-in-netflixs-wild-wild-country
95   https://www.huffingtonpost.in/author/oshotimes/
96   https://www.washingtonpost.com/archive/life-
     style/1987/02/17/in-the-jet-stream-with-arianna/
     a66952a2-4541-4bef-aa5f-a9b9c9a2c89a/?utm_term=.

a5b99b1603de

97 https://medium.com/insight-seminars/arianna-huffing-ton-on-her-insight-seminars-experience-f2e0552e87b4

98 https://www.newyorker.com/magazine/2008/10/13/the-oracle-lauren-collins?reload=true

99 https://www.theguardian.com/media/2004/aug/10/press-andpublishing.guardianobituaries

100 https://www.thetimes.co.uk/article/times-obituary-bernard-levin-2x2pbfwg93s

101 https://www.theguardian.com/media/2004/aug/10/press-andpublishing.guardianobituaries

102 https://www.nobelprize.org/prizes/literature/1913/tagore/article/

103 https://www.latimes.com/archives/la-xpm-1994-11-01-mn-57257-story.html

104 https://www.vanityfair.com/culture/1994/11/huffington-199411

105 Ibid.

106 https://www.newyorker.com/magazine/2008/10/13/the-oracle-lauren-collins?reload=true; https://www.dailymail.co.uk/news/article-2803264/MSIA-founder-Roger-Dela-no-Hinkins-dies-age-80.html

107 https://www.pbs.org/video/at-the-paley-center-arianna-huffington/

108 https://www.nytimes.com/1981/07/31/books/publish-ing-callas-book-stirs-dispute.html

109 Ibid.

110 'The Rise and Rise of Arianna Stassinopoulos'.

111 https://www.nytimes.com/1981/07/31/books/

publishing-callas-book-stirs-dispute.html

112 https://www.vanityfair.com/news/2016/09/
how-arianna-huffington-lost-her-newsroom

113 https://www.washingtonpost.com/archive/life-
style/1987/02/17/in-the-jet-stream-with-arianna/
a66952a2-4541-4bef-aa5f-a9b9c9a2c89a/?utm_term=.
a5b99b1603de

114 https://www.news24.com/World/News/
Maria-Callas-bore-child-by-Onassis-20000908

115 'The Rise and Rise of Arianna Stassinopoulos'.

116 https://www.pbs.org/video/
at-the-paley-center-arianna-huffington/

117 Quoted in Huffington, *On Becoming Fearless*.

118 Ibid.

119 Ibid.

120 Ibid.

121 https://www.makers.com/
blog/7-things-you-never-knew-about-arianna-huffington

122 https://www.pbs.org/video/
at-the-paley-center-arianna-huffington/

Part 3: New York and Beyond

1 'The Rise and Rise of Arianna Stassinopoulos'.

2 Ibid.

3 https://www.nytimes.com/1989/10/22/magazine/ann-get-
ty-publish-and-perish.html

4 Ibid.

5 https://www.washingtonpost.com/archive/life-
style/1987/02/17/in-the-jet-stream-with-arianna/

a66952a2-4541-4bef-aa5f-a9b9c9a2c89a/?utm_term=.a5b99b1603de

6   https://www.newyorker.com/magazine/2008/10/13/the-oracle-lauren-collins?reload=true; 'The Rise and Rise of Arianna Stassinopoulos'.

7   https://www.washingtonpost.com/archive/lifestyle/1987/02/17/in-the-jet-stream-with-arianna/a66952a2-4541-4bef-aa5f-a9b9c9a2c89a/?utm_term=.a5b99b1603de; https://www.newyorker.com/magazine/2008/10/13/the-oracle-lauren-collins?reload=true

8   https://www.washingtonpost.com/archive/lifestyle/1987/02/17/in-the-jet-stream-with-arianna/a66952a2-4541-4bef-aa5f-a9b9c9a2c89a/?utm_term=.a5b99b1603de

9   https://www.newyorker.com/magazine/2008/10/13/the-oracle-lauren-collins?reload=true

10 https://www.newyorker.com/magazine/2008/10/13/the-oracle-lauren-collins?reload=true; https://www.washingtonpost.com/archive/lifestyle/1987/02/17/in-the-jet-stream-with-arianna/a66952a2-4541-4bef-aa5f-a9b9c9a2c89a/?utm_term=.a5b99b1603de; 'The Rise and Rise of Arianna Stassinopoulos'.

11 https://www.washingtonpost.com/archive/lifestyle/1987/02/17/in-the-jet-stream-with-arianna/a66952a2-4541-4bef-aa5f-a9b9c9a2c89a/?utm_term=.a5b99b1603de

12 'The Rise and Rise of Arianna Stassinopoulos'.

13 https://www.washingtonpost.com/archive/

lifestyle/1987/02/17/in-the-jet-stream-with-arianna/
a66952a2-4541-4bef-aa5f-a9b9c9a2c89a/?utm_term=.
a5b99b1603de

14　Ibid.

15　Ibid.

16　https://www.latimes.com/archives/la-xpm-1988-06-07-
vw-3914-story.html

17　Arianna Stassinopoulos and Françoise Gilot, *The Gods
of Greece* (New York: Atlantic Monthly Press, 1984;
revised edn, 1993).

18　https://www.washingtonpost.com/archive/life-
style/1987/02/17/in-the-jet-stream-with-arianna/
a66952a2-4541-4bef-aa5f-a9b9c9a2c89a/?utm_term=.
a5b99b1603de

19　https://www.huffpost.com/entry/
bernard-levin_b_9114200

20　Ibid.

21　'The Rise and Rise of Arianna Stassinopoulos'.

22　https://www.vanityfair.com/culture/1994/11/
huffington-199411

23　'The Rise and Rise of Arianna Stassinopoulos'.

24　Ibid.

25　https://www.washingtonpost.com/archive/life-
style/1987/02/17/in-the-jet-stream-with-arianna/
a66952a2-4541-4bef-aa5f-a9b9c9a2c89a/?utm_term=.
a5b99b1603de

26　Ibid.

27　https://www.msia.org/newdayherald/
archives/18327-an-interview-with-michael-feder-100-

living-dying-with-john-roger

28 https://www.washingtonpost.com/archive/life-
style/1987/02/17/in-the-jet-stream-with-arianna/
a66952a2-4541-4bef-aa5f-a9b9c9a2c89a/?utm_term=.
a5b99b1603de

29 https://www.vanityfair.com/culture/1994/11/
huffington-199411

30 https://www.vanityfair.com/culture/1994/11/huff-
ington-199411; https://www.latimes.com/archives/
la-xpm-1994-11-01-mn-57257-story.html.

31 https://www.washingtonpost.com/archive/life-
style/1987/02/17/in-the-jet-stream-with-arianna/
a66952a2-4541-4bef-aa5f-a9b9c9a2c89a/?utm_term=.
a5b99b1603de

32 Ibid.

33 https://www.latimes.com/local/obituaries/la-me-john-
roger-20141023-story.html

34 https://www.washingtonpost.com/archive/life-
style/1987/02/17/in-the-jet-stream-with-arianna/
a66952a2-4541-4bef-aa5f-a9b9c9a2c89a/?utm_term=.
a5b99b1603de

35 https://www.msia.org/newdayherald/
archives/18327-an-interview-with-michael-feder-100-
living-dying-with-john-roger

36 https://www.washingtonpost.com/archive/life-
style/1987/02/17/in-the-jet-stream-with-arianna/
a66952a2-4541-4bef-aa5f-a9b9c9a2c89a/?utm_term=.
a5b99b1603de

37 Ibid.

38 https://www.newyorker.com/magazine/2008/10/13/
    the-oracle-lauren-collins?reload=true

39 https://www.theatlantic.com/politics/
    archive/2014/06/a-strange-but-true-tale-of-voter-fraud-
    and-bioterrorism/372445/

40 https://www.facebook.com/AriannaHuffington/pho-
    tos/a.158003868278/10152428994938279/?type=1&the-
    ater; https://www.thedailybeast.com/
    arianna-huffington-denies-involvement-in-sex-cult-de-
    picted-in-netflixs-wild-wild-country; https://www.
    huffingtonpost.in/author/oshotimes/

41 https://www.newyorker.com/magazine/2008/10/13/
    the-oracle-lauren-collins?reload=true

42 https://medium.com/insight-seminars/arianna-huffing-
    ton-on-her-insight-seminars-experience-f2e0552c87b4

43 https://www.washingtonpost.com/archive/lifestyle/1987/
    02/17/in-the-jet-stream-with-arianna/a66952a2-4541-
    4bef-aa5f-a9b9c9a2c89a/?utm_term=.a5b99b1603de

44 https://www.newyorker.com/magazine/2008/10/13/
    the-oracle-lauren-collins?reload=true; https://www.
    washingtonpost.com/archive/lifestyle/1987/02/17/
    in-the-jet-stream-with-arianna/a66952a2-4541-4bef-aa5f-
    a9b9c9a2c89a/?utm_term=.a5b99b1603de

45 https://classic.esquire.com/article/1999/1/1/
    the-strange-odyssey-of-michael-huffington

46 https://www.washingtonpost.com/archive/life-
    style/1987/02/17/in-the-jet-stream-with-arianna/
    a66952a2-4541-4bef-aa5f-a9b9c9a2c89a/?utm_term=.
    a5b99b1603de

47 https://classic.esquire.com/article/1999/1/1/
the-strange-odyssey-of-michael-huffington

48 Ibid.

49 https://www.washingtonpost.com/archive/life-
style/1987/02/17/in-the-jet-stream-with-arianna/
a66952a2-4541-4bef-aa5f-a9b9c9a2c89a/?utm_term=.
a5b99b1603de

50 https://www.newyorker.com/magazine/2008/10/13/
the-oracle-lauren-collins?reload=true

51 https://www.washingtonpost.com/archive/lifestyle/1987/
02/17/in-the-jet-stream-with-arianna/a66952a2-4541-
4bef-aa5f-a9b9c9a2c89a/?utm_term=.a5b99b1603de

52 Ibid.

53 https://classic.esquire.com/article/1999/1/1/
the-strange-odyssey-of-michael-huffington

54 David Brock, *Blinded by the Right: The Conscience
of an Ex-Conservative* (New York: Crown Publishing,
2002); https://www.vanityfair.com/culture/1994/11/
huffington-199411

55 https://classic.esquire.com/article/1999/1/1/
the-strange-odyssey-of-michael-huffington

56 https://www.nytimes.com/1986/01/19/style/arian-
na-stassinopoulos-to-be-married.html

57 https://www.huffpost.com/entry/
bernard-levin_b_9114200

58 https://www.washingtonpost.com/archive/life-
style/1987/02/17/in-the-jet-stream-with-arianna/
a66952a2-4541-4bef-aa5f-a9b9c9a2c89a/?utm_term=.
a5b99b1603de

59   https://www.newyorker.com/magazine/2008/10/13/
      the-oracle-lauren-collins?reload=true

60   https://www.washingtonpost.com/archive/life-
      style/1987/02/17/in-the-jet-stream-with-arianna/
      a66952a2-4541-4bef-aa5f-a9b9c9a2c89a/?utm_term=.
      a5b99b1603de

61   https://www.washingtonpost.
      com/archive/lifestyle/1987/02/17/
      in-the-jet-stream-with-arianna/a66952a2-4541-4bef-
      aa5f-a9b9c9a2c89a/?utm_term=.a5b99b1603de;
      https://www.newyorker.com/magazine/2008/10/13/
      the-oracle-lauren-collins?reload=true

62   https://www.washingtonpost.com/archive/lifestyle/1987/
      02/17/in-the-jet-stream-with-arianna/a66952a2-4541-
      4bef-aa5f-a9b9c9a2c89a/?utm_term=.a5b99b1603de.

63   https://www.newyorker.com/magazine/2008/10/13/
      the-oracle-lauren-collins?reload=true

64   https://www.washingtonpost.com/archive/life-
      style/1987/02/17/in-the-jet-stream-with-arianna/
      a66952a2-4541-4bef-aa5f-a9b9c9a2c89a/?utm_term=.
      a5b99b1603de

65   Ibid.

66   Ibid.

67   https://www.vanityfair.com/culture/1994/11/
      huffington-199411

68   David Brock, *Blinded by the Right: The Conscience
      of an Ex-Conservative* (New York: Crown Publishing,
      2002); https://www.vanityfair.com/culture/1994/11/
      huffington-199411

69   https://www.newyorker.com/magazine/2008/10/13/
the-oracle-lauren-collins?reload=true

70   https://www.washingtonpost.com/archive/life-
style/1987/02/17/in-the-jet-stream-with-arianna/
a66952a2-4541-4bef-aa5f-a9b9c9a2c89a/?utm_term=.
a5b99b1603de

71   Quoted in ibid.

72   https://classic.esquire.com/article/1999/1/1/
the-strange-odyssey-of-michael-huffington

73   Ibid.

74   https://www.huffpost.com/entry/arianna-christina-huff-
ington-talk-to-me_n_56fd789fe4b0a06d58053be9

75   https://www.huffpost.com/entry/
bernard-levin_b_9114200

76   https://www.newyorker.com/magazine/2008/10/13/
the-oracle-lauren-collins?reload=true

77   https://classic.esquire.com/article/1999/1/1/
the-strange-odyssey-of-michael-huffington; https://www.
nytimes.com/1986/04/13/style/arianna-stassinopoulos-au-
thor-wed-to-r-michael-huffington-executive.html

78   https://classic.esquire.com/article/1999/1/1/
the-strange-odyssey-of-michael-huffington

79   Ibid.

80   https://classic.esquire.com/article/1999/1/1/
the-strange-odyssey-of-michael-huffington; https://www.
vanityfair.com/culture/1994/11/huffington-199411

81   https://www.huffpost.com/entry/
bernard-levin_b_9114200

82   https://www.washingtonpost.com/archive/

lifestyle/1988/06/07/picasso-the-art-of-mudslinging/0df-4ca82-7dc6-48f4-840d-0b5b52f04ca5/?utm_term=.7ac4f-9fece1c

83 https://www.latimes.com/archives/la-xpm-1988-06-07-vw-3914-story.html

84 https://timesmachine.nytimes.com/timesmachine/1988/06/01/813888.html?action=click&-contentCollection=Archives&module=LedeAsset&pageNumber=77

85 https://newrepublic.com/article/105858/hughes-basquiat-new-york-new-wave

86 https://www.washingtonpost.com/archive/lifestyle/1988/06/07/picasso-the-art-of-mudslinging/0df-4ca82-7dc6-48f4-840d-0b5b52f04ca5/?utm_term=.7ac4f-9fece1c

87 Arianna Huffington, *On Becoming Fearless . . . In Love, Work, and Life* (New York: Little, Brown, 2007).

88 https://www.washingtonpost.com/archive/life-style/1987/02/17/in-the-jet-stream-with-arianna/a66952a2-4541-4bef-aa5f-a9b9c9a2c89a/?utm_term=.a5b99b1603de

89 Freedman, *Huffington: Media Mogul.*

90 https://www.latimes.com/archives/la-xpm-1988-06-07-vw-3914-story.html

91 Quoted in https://www.vanityfair.com/culture/1994/11/huffington-199411

92 Ibid.

93 https://www.huffpost.com/entry/happy-birthday-pablo-pica_n_2011263

Part 4: Washington and California

1   Arianna Huffington, *On Becoming Fearless . . . In Love, Work, and Life* (New York: Little, Brown, 2007).
2   https://www.imdb.com/name/nm0400251/bio
3   Arianna Huffington, *The Fourth Instinct: The Call of the Soul* (New York: Simon & Schuster, 2003).
4   https://www.imdb.com/name/nm0400251/bio
5   https://classic.esquire.com/article/1999/1/1/the-strange-odyssey-of-michael-huffington
6   https://www.pbs.org/video/at-the-paley-center-arianna-huffington/
7   https://classic.esquire.com/article/1999/1/1/the-strange-odyssey-of-michael-huffington
8   https://www.vanityfair.com/culture/1994/11/huffington-199411
9   https://people.com/archive/california-dreamin-vol-42-no-15/
10 https://www.huffpost.com/entry/bernard-levin_b_9114200
11 Ibid.
12 https://www.vanityfair.com/culture/1994/11/huffington-199411
13 Quoted in ibid.
14 https://www.latimes.com/archives/la-xpm-1988-06-07-vw-3914-story.html
15 Ed Rollins, *Bare Knuckles and Back Rooms: My Life in American Politics* (New York: Broadway Books, 1996).
16 Quoted in https://www.newyorker.com/

magazine/2008/10/13/the-oracle-lauren-collins?re-
load=true; https://charlierose.com/videos/6655

17 https://www.vanityfair.com/culture/1994/11/
huffington-199411

18 Quoted in https://www.washingtonpost.com/archive/
lifestyle/1987/02/17/in-the-jet-stream-with-arianna/
a66952a2-4541-4bef-aa5f-a9b9c9a2c89a/?utm_term=.
a5b99b1603de.

19 https://www.vanityfair.com/culture/1994/11/
huffington-199411

20 https://www.latimes.com/archives/la-xpm-1994-02-20-
vw-25079-story.html

21 Ibid.

22 https://charlierose.com/videos/6655

23 Ibid.

24 https://classic.esquire.com/article/1999/1/1/
the-strange-odyssey-of-michael-huffington

25 Arianna Huffington, *Fourth Instinct*.

26 https://www.kirkusreviews.com/book-reviews/
arianna-huffington/the-fourth-instinct/

27 https://www.washingtonpost.com/archive/
lifestyle/1994/06/05/her-brains-his-money/022dde4b-
a068-4655-8e30-871dfa83bdb4/

28 https://www.latimes.com/archives/la-xpm-1994-11-01-
mn-57257-story.html

29 https://www.gocomics.com/doonesbury/1994/10/06

30 https://www.latimes.com/archives/la-xpm-1994-11-01-
mn-57257-story.html

31 https://www.newyorker.com/magazine/2008/10/13/

the-oracle-lauren-collins?reload=true

32 https://classic.esquire.com/article/1999/1/1/
the-strange-odyssey-of-michael-huffington

33 David Brock, *Blinded by the Right: The Conscience of an Ex-Conservative.* (New York: Crown Publishing, 2002).

34 https://gawker.com/5018484/
arianna-huffingtons-great-illegal-nanny-search

35 https://www.sun-sentinel.com/news/fl-xpm-1996-08-10-9608120209-story.html

36 https://www.amazon.com/Arianna-Huffing-ton-Playboy-Interview-Singles-ebook/dp/
B009YKRMOY

37 Brock, *Blinded by the Right.*

38 https://classic.esquire.com/article/1999/1/1/
the-strange-odyssey-of-michael-huffington

39 Freedman, *Huffington: Media Mogul.*

40 https://www.newyorker.com/magazine/2008/10/13/
the-oracle-lauren-collins?reload=true

41 Brock, *Blinded by the Right.*

42 https://www.politico.com/story/2011/12/
newt-and-arianna-a-90s-story-070406

43 https://www.vanityfair.com/culture/1994/11/
huffington-199411

44 Ibid.

45 https://www.pbs.org/video/
at-the-paley-center-arianna-huffington/

46 Ibid.

47 https://classic.esquire.com/article/1999/1/1/
the-strange-odyssey-of-michael-huffington

48 https://classic.esquire.com/article/1999/1/1/
the-strange-odyssey-of-michael-huffington; : archived at
https://www.latimes.com/archives/la-xpm-1997-06-27-
mn-7357-story.html

49 https://classic.esquire.com/article/1999/1/1/
the-strange-odyssey-of-michael-huffington.

50 https://www.newyorker.com/magazine/2008/10/13/
the-oracle-lauren-collins?reload=true

51 https://www.latimes.com/archives/la-xpm-1997-06-27-
mn-7357-story.html

52 https://www.huffpost.com/entry/
my-road-to-damascus-led-t_b_38761

53 Ibid.

54 https://www.newyorker.com/magazine/2008/10/13/
the-oracle-lauren-collins?reload=true

55 https://www.inc.com/magazine/20100201/how-i-did-it-ar-
ianna-huffington.html

56 https://www.huffpost.com/entry/
arianna-huffington-divorc_n_5030812/

57 https://www.makers.com/
blog/7-things-you-never-knew-about-arianna-huffington

58 Freedman, *Huffington: Media Mogul.*

59 https://www.bbc.com/news/world-us-canada-12385455

60 https://www.washingtonpost.com/wp-srv/politics/talk/
zforum/huffington121698.htm

61 https://www.digitalriptide.org/person/arianna-huffington/

62 Ibid.

63 http://www.cnn.com/chat/transcripts/2000/7/29/huffing-
ton/index.html

64 Freedman, *Huffington: Media Mogul*.

65 http://www.cnn.com/chat/transcripts/2000/7/29/huffington/index.html

66 https://www.theguardian.com/theobserver/2003/jun/01/features.review17

67 Freedman, *Huffington: Media Mogul*.

68 http://www.cnn.com/chat/transcripts/2000/7/29/huffington/index.html

69 Freedman, *Huffington: Media Mogul*.

70 http://www.cnn.com/chat/transcripts/2000/7/29/huffington/index.html

71 Ibid.

72 'Arianna Huffington: Left, Right and Center' (*Los Angeles* Magazine, October 2004).

73 https://www.theguardian.com/theobserver/2003/jun/01/features.review17

74 https://www.amazon.com/Arianna-Huffington-Playboy-Interview-Singles-ebook/dp/B009YKRMOY

75 https://www.washingtonpost.com/wp-srv/politics/talk/zforum/huffington121698.htm

76 https://www.theguardian.com/theobserver/2003/jun/01/features.review17

77 https://www.huffpost.com/entry/what-we-learned-from-our_b_9611372

78 https://medium.com/thrive-global/the-end-of-a-grand-adventure-dd3026976003

79 https://www.huffpost.com/entry/what-we-learned-from-our_b_9611372; https://medium.com/thrive-global/

the-end-of-a-grand-adventure-dd3026976003

80 https://www.politico.com/story/2011/12/
newt-and-arianna-a-90s-story-070406

81 Ibid.

82 https://www.huffpost.com/entry/
what-we-learned-from-our_b_9611372

83 https://medium.com/thrive-global/
to-my-mother-elli-11dfa39e956f

84 https://www.huffpost.com/entry/
my-mothers-death-one-of-t_b_5303024

85 https://www.huffpost.com/entry/
what-we-learned-from-our_b_9611372

86 https://www.vanityfair.com/news/2005/12/
huffington200512

87 Freedman, *Huffington: Media Mogul.*

88 https://www.motherjones.com/politics/2003/04/
driving-force-arianna-huffington/

89 Freedman, *Huffington: Media Mogul.*

90 https://www.theguardian.com/theobserver/2003/jun/01/
features.review17

91 https://archive.commondreams.org/scriptfiles/head-
lines03/0811-05.htm

92 https://www.nytimes.com/2008/10/27/business/me-
dia/27blogs.html

93 https://www.cbsnews.com/news/
the-return-of-michael-huffington/

94 https://www.glamour.com/story/arianna-huffing-
ton-s-daughter-christina-huffington-opens-up-about-co-
caine-addiction

95   http://www.cnn.com/2003/ALLPOLITICS/08/07/huffing-
     ton.recall/

96   Ibid.

97   Ibid.

98   https://www.latimes.com/archives/la-xpm-2003-sep-03-
     me-arianna3-story.html

99   https://archive.commondreams.org/scriptfiles/head-
     lines03/0811-05.htm

100 Ibid.

101 https://www.latimes.com/archives/la-xpm-2003-sep-03-
     me-arianna3-story.html

102 https://www.latimes.com/archives/la-xpm-2003-aug-14-
     me-ariannatax14-story.html

103 Ibid.

104 https://www.nytimes.com/2003/09/25/
     us/live-the-arnold-and-arianna-show.
     html?module=ArrowsNav&contentCollection=U.S.&ac-
     tion=keypress&region=FixedLeft&pgtype=article

105 Ibid.

106 Ibid.

107 https://www.c-span.org/video/?178005-2/
     california-recall-election-debate

108 https://www.youtube.com/watch?v=91SxLb3ZmkI

109 https://www.nytimes.com/2003/09/11/us/trailing-in-cali-
     fornia-but-hollywood-s-pick.html

110 Arianna Huffington, *On Becoming Fearless*.

111 Freedman, *Huffington: Media Mogul*.

112 https://www.inc.com/magazine/20100201/how-i-did-it-ar-
     ianna-huffington.html

113 http://www.cc.com/video-clips/da9szs/
the-daily-show-with-jon-stewart-arianna-huffington

114 https://www.glamour.com/story/arianna-huffing-
ton-s-daughter-christina-huffington-opens-up-about-co-
caine-addiction

115 Ibid.

116 Ibid.

117 Arianna Huffington, *On Becoming Fearless*.

118 Ibid.

119 https://www.huffpost.com/entry/
bernard-levin_b_9114200

120 Ibid.

Part 5: Building *The Huffington Post*

1 https://www.yahoo.com/lifestylc/arianna-huffington-
founder-huffpost-ceo-201624980.html

2 Ibid.

3 https://tim.blog/2018/02/02/
the-tim-ferriss-show-transcripts-arianna-huffington/

4 https://www.pbs.org/video/
at-the-paley-center-arianna-huffington/

5 Ibid.

6 https://www.nytimes.com/2011/02/08/business/me-
dia/08huffington.html

7 Ibid.

8 https://www.thedailybeast.com/kenneth-lerer-the-stealth-
partner-in-huffington-post-aol-sale

9 https://www.nytimes.com/2005/04/25/technolo-
gy/a-boldface-name-invites-others-to-blog-with-her.

html?searchResultPosition=1

10 https://www.yahoo.com/lifestyle/arianna-huffington-founder-huffpost-ceo-201624980.html

11 https://www.huffpost.com/entry/arthur-schlesinger-jr-his_b_42388

12 https://www.pbs.org/video/at-the-paley-center-arianna-huffington/; https://www.huffpost.com/entry/arthur-schlesinger-jr-his_b_42388

13 https://tim.blog/2018/02/02/the-tim-ferriss-show-transcripts-arianna-huffington/

14 https://www.pbs.org/video/at-the-paley-center-arianna-huffington/

15 https://tim.blog/2018/02/02/the-tim-ferriss-show-transcripts-arianna-huffington/

16 https://www.newyorker.com/magazine/2008/10/13/the-oracle-lauren-collins?reload=true

17 https://www.vanityfair.com/culture/1994/11/huffington-199411

18 https://www.nytimes.com/2011/02/08/business/media/08huffington.html

19 https://www.huffpost.com/entry/arthur-schlesinger-jr-his_b_42388

20 https://www.pbs.org/video/at-the-paley-center-arianna-huffington/

21 https://www.nytimes.com/2005/04/25/technology/a-boldface-name-invites-others-to-blog-with-her.html?searchResultPosition=1

22 Ibid.

23 Arianna Huffington, *Thrive: The Third Metric to*

Redefining Success and Creating a Life of Well-being, Wisdom, and Wonder (New York: Harmony Books, 2014).

24 https://www.theguardian.com/media/2011/feb/07/huffington-post-who-gets-money

25 https://www.vanityfair.com/news/2005/12/huffington200512

26 https://www.nytimes.com/2005/04/25/technology/a-boldface-name-invites-others-to-blog-with-her.html?searchResultPosition=1

27 Ibid.

28 https://www.vanityfair.com/news/2005/12/huffington200512

29 https://www.nytimes.com/2005/04/25/technology/a-boldface-namc-invites-others-to-blog-with-her.html?searchResultPosition=1

30 https://www.nytimes.com/2011/02/08/business/media/08huffington.html

31 https://www.pbs.org/video/at-the-paley-center-arianna-huffington/

32 https://www.vanityfair.com/news/2005/12/huffington200512

33 https://www.pbs.org/video/at-the-paley-center-arianna-huffington/

34 https://tim.blog/2018/02/02/the-tim-ferriss-show-transcripts-arianna-huffington/

35 Ibid.

36 https://www.nytimes.com/2011/02/08/business/media/08huffington.html

37 https://www.nytimes.com/2005/04/25/technology/a-boldface-name-invites-others-to-blog-with-her.html?searchResultPosition=1

38 https://www.huffpost.com/entry/dont-be-a-blogger-manque_b_3310

39 https://www.huffpost.com/entry/arthur-schlesinger-jr-his_b_42388

40 Arianna Huffington, *Pigs at the Trough: How Corporate Greed and Political Corruption are Undermining America* (New York: Crown Publishing, 2003).

41 https://www.newyorker.com/magazine/2008/10/13/the-oracle-lauren-collins?reload=true

42 https://tim.blog/2018/02/02/the-tim-ferriss-show-transcripts-arianna-huffington/

43 Ibid.

44 https://www.pbs.org/video/at-the-paley-center-arianna-huffington/

45 https://archives.cjr.org/behind_the_news/huffington_post_and_the_art_of.php

46 https://www.independent.co.uk/news/business/analysis-and-features/jonah-peretti-the-nerd-genius-is-keeping-his-cool-7837123.html

47 https://www.niemanlab.org/2014/06/inside-jonah-peretti-on-lacanian-psychoanalysis-not-wasting-time-on-the-mediocre-and-the-god-metric/

48 https://techcrunch.com/2010/05/12/buzzfeed-8-million/

49 https://www.nytimes.com/2006/03/20/business/a-guest-blogger-and-an-unwritten-law.html

50 Huffington, *On Becoming Fearless*.

51 https://www.politico.com/blogs/onmedia/0710/HuffPo_
    loses_top_Technorati_slot_to_Hot_Air.html

52 https://www.theguardian.com/media/2011/feb/07/
    huffington-post-who-gets-money

53 https://www.makers.com/
    blog/7-things-you-never-knew-about-arianna-huffington

54 Freedman, *Huffington: Media Mogul.*

55 https://www.amazon.com/Arianna-Huffing-
    ton-Playboy-Interview-Singles-ebook/dp/
    B009YKRMOY

56 https://www.vanityfair.com/news/2005/12/
    huffington200512

57 https://www.theguardian.com/media/2011/feb/07/
    huffington-post-who-gets-money

58 https://www.businesswire.com/news/
    home/20070423005545/en/Yahoo!-Huffington-Post-Slate-
    Host-First-Ever-Online-Only

59 https://charlierose.com/videos/11242

60 Ibid.

61 https://www.telegraph.co.uk/family/relationships/
    found-sister-arianna-huffington-lying-pool-blood-knew-
    had-help/

62 http://ariannahuffington.com/sleep-resources

63 https://www.telegraph.co.uk/family/relationships/
    found-sister-arianna-huffington-lying-pool-blood-knew-
    had-help/

64 http://ariannahuffington.com/sleep-resources

65 https://www.entrepreneur.com/video/278593

66 https://www.thedailybeast.com/

kenneth-lerer-the-stealth-partner-in-huffington-post-aol-sale

67 https://observer.com/2011/02/from-mudslinger-to-maverick-the-transformation-of-kenneth-lerer/

68 https://www.thedailybeast.com/kenneth-lerer-the-stealth-partner-in-huffington-post-aol-sale

69 https://observer.com/2011/02/from-mudslinger-to-maverick-the-transformation-of-kenneth-lerer/

70 https://www.csmonitor.com/Books/Book-Reviews/2008/1123/den-of-thieves-classic-review-from-the-monitor-archives

71 Ibid.

72 https://observer.com/2011/02/from-mudslinger-to-maverick-the-transformation-of-kenneth-lerer/

73 https://www.thedailybeast.com/kenneth-lerer-the-stealth-partner-in-huffington-post-aol-sale

74 https://observer.com/2011/02/from-mudslinger-to-maverick-the-transformation-of-kenneth-lerer/

75 https://www.thedailybeast.com/kenneth-lerer-the-stealth-partner-in-huffington-post-aol-sale

76 Ibid.

77 https://www.businessinsider.com/2007/9/estimating-valu

78 https://www.theguardian.com/media/2011/feb/07/huffington-post-who-gets-money

79 https://www.thedailybeast.com/kenneth-lerer-the-stealth-partner-in-huffington-post-aol-sale

80 Ibid.

81 https://wealthygorilla.com/arianna-huffington-net-worth/#forward

82 https://www.newyorker.com/magazine/2008/10/13/
    the-oracle-lauren-collins?reload=true
83 Ibid.
84 Arianna Huffington, *Right is Wrong: How the Lunatic
    Fringe Hijacked America, Shredded the Constitution,
    and Made Us All Less Safe* (New York: Alfred A. Knopf,
    2008).
85 Ibid.
86 http://www.cc.com/video-clips/tkrgq6/
    the-daily-show-with-jon-stewart-arianna-huffington
87 https://www.poynter.org/reporting-editing/2009/
    huffington-post-investigative-team-a-nonprofit-mod-
    el-in-the-making/
88 https://www.newyorker.com/magazine/2008/10/13/
    the-oracle-lauren-collins?reload=true
89 https://gawker.com/5369520/
    jets-dont-count-for-greed-hater-arianna-huffington
90 https://www.newyorker.com/magazine/2008/10/13/
    the-oracle-lauren-collins?reload=true
91 https://www.vanityfair.com/news/2005/12/
    huffington200512

Part 6: Going Global

1 https://www.huffpost.com/entry/
   huffington-post-aol_b_819373
2 Ibid.
3 https://www.vanityfair.com/news/2016/09/why-arian-
   na-huffington-left-the-huffington-post?verso=true
4 https://www.forbes.com/sites/jeffbercovici/2011/06/07/

aol-after-the-honeymoon/

5 https://www.nytimes.com/2010/11/28/fashion/28Divorce.html

6 https://www.newsday.com/news/new-york/arianna-huffington-the-making-of-a-mogul-1.2683922

7 https://www.vanityfair.com/news/2016/09/why-arianna-huffington-left-the-huffington-post?verso=true

8 https://www.bloomberg.com/news/articles/2010-12-14/huffington-post-nears-first-annual-profit-expects-sales-to-triple-by-2012

9 https://www.pbs.org/video/at-the-paley-center-arianna-huffington/

10 Ibid.

11 https://www.huffpost.com/entry/huffington-post-aol_b_819373

12 https://www.forbes.com/sites/jeffbercovici/2011/06/07/aol-after-the-honeymoon/

13 https://www.huffpost.com/entry/huffington-post-aol_b_819373

14 Ibid.

15 https://www.forbes.com/sites/jeffbercovici/2011/06/07/aol-after-the-honeymoon/

16 Ibid.

17 Ibid.

18 https://www.huffpost.com/entry/huffington-post-aol_b_819373

19 https://nypost.com/2015/05/05/huffington-post-turns-10-but-its-profits-are-still-a-mystery/

20 https://www.nytimes.com/2011/02/07/business/

media/07aol.html?auth=login-email&module=Ar-
rowsNav&contentCollection=Media&action=key-
press&region=FixedLeft&pgtype=article

21 https://www.wired.com/2011/03/aol-cuts-900-jobs/

22 http://www.thesmokinggun.com/documents/
    arianna-huffington-aol-money-756432

23 https://www.vanityfair.com/news/2016/09/why-arian-
    na-huffington-left-the-huffington-post?verso=true

24 http://www.thesmokinggun.com/documents/
    arianna-huffington-aol-money-756432

25 Ibid.

26 https://www.thedailybeast.com/kenneth-lerer-the-stealth-
    partner-in-huffington-post-aol-sale

27 Ibid.

28 Ibid.

29 Ibid.

30 https://www.newyorker.com/magazine/2008/10/13/
    the-oracle-lauren-collins?reload=true

31 https://www.wired.com/2011/04/tasini-sues-arianna/

32 https://www.theguardian.com/media/pda/2010/nov/17/
    huffington-post-founders-sued

33 https://www.forbes.com/sites/jeffbercovici/2014/05/15/
    huffington-post-settles-lawsuit-over-its-founding/#574c-
    42d2e9b0

34 https://www.reuters.com/article/
    us-aol-huffingtonpost-bloggers/unpaid-bloggers-law-
    suit-versus-huffington-post-tossed-idUS-
    BRE82T17L20120330

35 Ibid.

36   https://www.theguardian.com/media/2011/apr/12/
     arianna-huffington-post-sale
37   https://fivethirtyeight.blogs.nytimes.com/2011/02/12/
     the-economics-of-blogging-and-the-huffington-post/
38   https://www.theguardian.com/media/2012/apr/01/
     huffington-post-bloggers-aol-millions
39   https://www.theguardian.com/media/2011/apr/12/
     arianna-huffington-post-sale
40   https://www.forbes.com/sites/jeffbercovici/2011/06/07/
     aol-after-the-honeymoon/
41   https://www.wired.com/2011/03/aol-cuts-900-jobs/
42   https://www.vanityfair.com/news/2016/09/why-arian-
     na-huffington-left-the-huffington-post?verso=true
43   https://www.pbs.org/video/
     at-the-paley-center-arianna-huffington/
44   https://www.forbes.com/sites/jeffbercovici/2011/06/07/
     aol-after-the-honeymoon/
45   https://www.nytimes.com/2015/07/05/magazine/arian-
     na-huffingtons-improbable-insatiable-content-machine.
     html
46   https://chadhensley.net/work/arianna-huffington
47   Ibid.
48   https://digiday.com/uk/
     arianna-huffington-huffington-post-international/
49   Ibid.
50   https://www.huffpost.com/entry/yassou-from-athens-in-
     troducing-huffpost-greece_b_6180208
51   https://www.athensinsider.com/
     arianna-huffington-in-conversation/

52 https://digiday.com/uk/
arianna-huffington-huffington-post-international/

53 https://www.vanityfair.com/news/2016/09/why-arian-
na-huffington-left-the-huffington-post?verso=true

54 https://www.britannica.com/topic/The-Huffington-Post

55 https://www.theatlantic.com/business/archive/2011/06/
huffington-post-passes-new-york-times-traffic/351611/

56 https://www.huffpost.com/entry/
huffington-post-aol-first-year_b_1249497

57 Freedman, *Huffington: Media Mogul*; Arianna Huffington, *Third World America: How Our Politicians Are
Abandoning the Middle Class and Betraying the American Dream* (New York: Crown Publishing, 2010).

58 Arianna Huffington, *Third World America*.

59 Freedman, *Huffington: Media Mogul*; Arianna Huffington, *Third World America*.

60 https://www.huffpost.com/entry/
huffington-post-aol-first-year_b_1249497

61 https://wealthygorilla.com/arianna-huffington-net-worth/

62 https://www.forbes.com/sites/jeffbercovici/2012/04/16/
arianna-huffington-and-tim-obrien-on-huffposts-pulit-
zer-win/#7ff589721631

63 Ibid.

64 https://www.forbes.com/sites/jennagoudreau/2012/08/23/
the-worlds-most-powerful-women-in-media/#45f-
2b846190a

65 https://www.nytimes.com/2015/07/05/magazine/arian-
na-huffingtons-improbable-insatiable-content-machine.
html

66   https://www.gobankingrates.com/net-worth/
     business-people/arianna-huffington-net-worth/

67   https://www.pbs.org/video/
     at-the-paley-center-arianna-huffington/

68   https://www.nytimes.com/2015/07/05/magazine/arian-
     na-huffingtons-improbable-insatiable-content-machine.
     html

69   https://www.pbs.org/video/
     at-the-paley-center-arianna-huffington/

70   https://www.nytimes.com/2015/07/05/magazine/arian-
     na-huffingtons-improbable-insatiable-content-machine.
     html

71   https://www.vanityfair.com/news/2016/09/why-arian-
     na-huffington-left-the-huffington-post?verso=true

72   https://www.huffpost.com/entry/
     huffington-post-aol-first-year_b_1249497

73   https://www.vanityfair.com/news/2016/09/why-arian-
     na-huffington-left-the-huffington-post?verso=true

74   https://nypost.com/2015/05/05/huffington-post-turns-10-
     but-its-profits-are-still-a-mystery/

75   https://www.nytimes.com/2015/07/05/magazine/arian-
     na-huffingtons-improbable-insatiable-content-machine.
     html

76   https://www.imdb.com/name/nm0400251/

77   http://nymag.com/intelligencer/2011/03/arianna_huffing-
     ton_finally_tur.html

78   https://www.nytimes.com/2015/07/05/magazine/
     arianna-huffingtons-improbable-insatiable-con-
     tent-machine.html ; https://www.wsj.com/articles/

is-huffington-post-worth-1-billion-1434101405

79 https://www.bbc.com/news/av/business-23582797/
amazon-boss-jeff-bezos-buys-washington-post-for-250m

80 https://www.forbes.com/sites/greatspeculations/2014/
12/24/huffington-post-can-boost-aols-valuation/
#198df71d3af6

81 https://www.wsj.com/articles/
is-huffington-post-worth-1-billion-1434101405

82 https://nypost.com/2015/05/05/huffington-post-turns-10-
but-its-profits-are-still-a-mystery/

83 https://www.nytimes.com/2015/07/05/magazine/arian-
na-huffingtons-improbable-insatiable-content-machine.
html

84 https://adage.com/article/media/
huffington-post-broke-146-million-revenue/299293

85 https://www.nytimes.com/2015/07/05/magazine/arian-
na-huffingtons-improbable-insatiable-content-machine.
html

86 https://www.huffpost.com/entry/100-million-thank-yous-
to-huffposters-around-the-world_b_5822998

87 https://adage.com/article/media/
huffington-post-broke-146-million-revenue/299293

88 https://digiday.com/uk/
arianna-huffington-huffington-post-international/

89 https://www.pbs.org/video/
at-the-paley-center-arianna-huffington/

90 Arianna Huffington, *Thrive: The Third Metric to Redefining Success and Creating a Life of Well-being, Wisdom
and Wonder* (New York: Harmony Books, 2014).

91 https://www.latimes.com/local/obituaries/la-me-john-roger-20141023-story.html

92 https://www.telegraph.co.uk/family/relationships/found-sister-arianna-huffington-lying-pool-blood-knew-had-help/

93 https://www.dailymail.co.uk/news/article-2803264/MSIA-founder-Roger-Delano-Hinkins-dies-age-80.html

94 Ibid.

95 https://www.huffpost.com/entry/yassou-from-athens-introducing-huffpost-greece_b_6180208

96 Ibid.

97 https://www.athensinsider.com/arianna-huffington-in-conversation/

98 https://www.ibtimes.com/huffington-posts-us-traffic-tanks-2015-buzzfeed-vice-media-grow-2142607

99 Ibid.

100 https://www.forbes.com/sites/jeffbercovici/2014/08/21/heres-how-buzzfeed-and-huffpost-really-stack-up/#1007ee0d6d82

101 https://nypost.com/2015/05/05/huffington-post-turns-10-but-its-profits-are-still-a-mystery/

102 https://www.macrotrends.net/stocks/charts/VZ/verizon/market-cap

103 https://www.inc.com/video/how-jack-ma-gave-arianna-huffington-her-latest-business-idea.html

104 https://www.nytimes.com/2015/07/05/magazine/arianna-huffingtons-improbable-insatiable-content-machine.html

105 http://ariannahuffington.com/sleep-resources

106 Arianna Huffington, *The Sleep Revolution: Transforming*

Your Life, One Night at a Time (New York: Harmony Books, 2016).

107 https://www.nytimes.com/2016/08/12/business/arianna-huffington-post.html

108 https://www.vanityfair.com/news/2016/09/why-arianna-huffington-left-the-huffington-post?verso=true

109 https://www.nytimes.com/2016/08/12/business/arianna-huffington-post.html

110 https://www.vanityfair.com/news/2016/09/why-arianna-huffington-left-the-huffington-post?verso=true

111 https://www.vanityfair.com/news/2016/09/how-arianna-huffington-lost-her-newsroom

112 Ibid.

113 https://www.uber.com/newsroom/ariannahuffington/

114 https://www.vanityfair.com/news/2005/12/huffington200512

115 https://www.nytimes.com/interactive/2017/06/14/technology/uber-travis-kalanick-executives.html

116 https://www.uber.com/newsroom/ariannahuffington/

117 https://www.huffpost.com/entry/a-note-on-trump_b_8744476

118 https://www.makers.com/blog/7-things-you-never-knew-about-arianna-huffington

119 Freedman, *Huffington: Media Mogul.*

120 https://www.inc.com/zoe-henry/thrive-global-arianna-huffington-latest-venture.html

121 https://www.nytimes.com/2016/08/12/business/arianna-huffington-post.html

Part 7: Creating Thrive

1 https://www.lifeposts.com/p/milestone/206/
elli-stassinopoulos-memorial/lifeqs/4187/answer/

2 https://medium.com/thrive-global/
the-end-of-a-grand-adventure-dd3026976003

3 https://www.cnbc.com/video/2019/10/17/arianna-huffing-
ton-thrive-global-micro-steps-habits-squawk-box.html

4 https://www.theguardian.com/media/2013/aug/02/
arianna-huffington-success-mother-love

5 Freedman, *Huffington: Media Mogul.*

6 https://www.businesswire.com/news/home/
20171129005301/en/Thrive-Global-Raises-30-Million-
Series-Funding

7 https://venturebeat.com/2018/05/10/thrive-global-closes-
series-b-extension-with-43-million-raised-to-date-golden-
state-warriors-kevin-durant-san-francisco-49ers-enter-
prises-and-jeffrey-katzenbergs-wndrco-amon/

8 https://www.businesswire.com/news/home/
20171129005301/en/Thrive-Global-Raises-30-Million-
Series-Funding

9 Arianna Huffington, *The Sleep Revolution: Transforming
Your Life, One Night at a Time* (New York: Harmony
Books, 2016).

10 Stassinopoulos and Gilot, *Gods of Greece*; Arianna
Huffington, *Pigs at the Trough: How Corporate Greed
and Political Corruption are Undermining America* (New
York: Crown Publishing, 2003).

11 Stassinopoulos and Gilot, *Gods of Greece*;

https://www.lifeposts.com/p/milestone/206/
elli-stassinopoulos-memorial/lifestory/

12 https://www.telegraph.co.uk/family/relationships/
found-sister-arianna-huffington-lying-pool-blood-knew-
had-help/

13 Waterfield, *Athens*.

14 https://www.athensinsider.com/
arianna-huffington-in-conversation/

15 https://qz.com/work/1363492/arianna-huffington-wrote-
an-open-letter-to-tesla-ceo-elon-musk/

16 Ibid.

17 Ibid.

18 https://www.theguardian.com/technology/2017/jul/30/
uber-ariana-huffington-travis-kalanick-ceo

19 https://www.nytimes.com/interactive/2017/06/14/technol-
ogy/uber-travis-kalanick-executives.html

20 https://www.vox.com/2017/11/29/16714392/arianna-huff-
ington-30-million-thrive-global-120-million-valuation

21 https://www.ibtimes.com/jeff-bezos-net-worth-
uber-ipo-add-400m-more-richest-man-2791077
; https://www.marketwatch.com/story/
uber-ipo-5-things-you-need-to-know-about-potentially-
the-biggest-ipo-in-years-2019-04-12

22 https://medium.com/thrive-global/how-to-get-out-of-the-
cycle-of-outrage-in-a-trump-world-ffc5b2aa1b5f

23 https://www.huffpost.com/entry/
huffington-post-huffpost-lydia-polgreen_n_58f-
ce1cae4b00fa7de1522ee ; https://www.
usatoday.com/story/money/nation-now/2017/04/25/

arianna-huffington-ok-huffpost-name-change-re-brand/100875490/

24 https://www.nytimes.com/2018/01/18/business/media/huffpost-unpaid-contributors.html

25 https://www.huffpost.com/entry/huffington-post-huff-post-lydia-polgreen_n_58fce1cae4b00fa7de1522ee

26 https://www.usatoday.com/story/money/nation-now/2017/04/25/arianna-huffington-ok-huffpost-name-change-rebrand/100875490/

27 https://www.forbes.com/profile/arianna-huffington/#6b0e56f22075

28 https://www.nbcnews.com/tech/tech-news/verizon-signals-its-yahoo-aol-divisions-are-almost-worth-less-n946846

29 https://www.bloomberg.com/news/videos/2018-01-16/huffington-on-social-media-uber-and-me-too-movement-video

30 https://thriveglobal.com/stories/burnout-officially-a-workplace-crisis-world-health-organization-arianna-huff-ington/

31 Ibid.

32 https://thriveglobal.com/stories/arianna-huffington-boundless-mind-acquisition-neuroscience-artificial-intel-ligence/

33 https://www.cnbc.com/video/2019/10/17/arianna-huffing-ton-thrive-global-micro-steps-habits-squawk-box.html

34 Arianna Huffington, *The Fourth Instinct*.

35 https://www.tmc.edu/news/2018/10/arianna-huffington-offers-wisdom-for-huffington-center-

on-agings-30th-anniversary/

36 https://thriveglobal.com/stories/day-in-the-life/

37 https://www.athensinsider.com/
arianna-huffington-in-conversation/

38 https://www.newyorker.com/magazine/2008/10/13/
the-oracle-lauren-collins?reload=true

39 https://www.tmc.edu/news/2018/10/
arianna-huffington-offers-wisdom-for-huffington-center-
on-agings-30th-anniversary/

INDEX